The Father, Son, and Holy Shuttle

Growing Up an Astronaut's Kid in the Glorious 80s

Patrick Mullane

Copyright © 2020 Patrick J. Mullane

All rights reserved.

ISBN: 9798638708986

To Dad and Mom
No kid had a better childhood …

CONTENTS

	Prologue	1
1	The Shit Tank	5
2	Men and Their Marvelous Flying Machines	26
3	My Imaginary Mob Boss	39
4	Getting "Lucky"	57
5	Bullies, Basketballs, and Bowels	71
6	Flying the Friendly Skies	94
7	Dad's Turn	115
8	Launch?	140
9	Wages and Women	159
10	Astronaut	171
11	Cheerleader	191
12	College Bound	210
13	Cold Day	226
14	Moving On	240
	About the Author	255
	Acknowledgements	256
	To Contact Me …	257

A NOTE …

All of this really happened. However, the names of some of those who unwittingly played a part in my story have been changed.

THE SPACE TRANSPORTATION SYSTEM (STS)

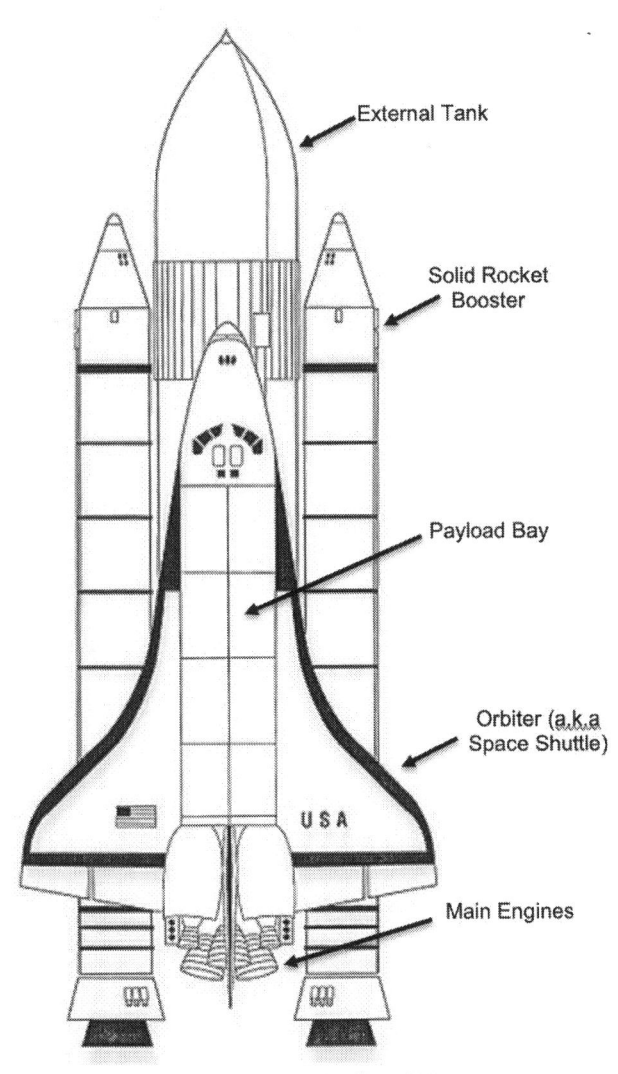

Credit: NASA

Mullane Family Homes 1968-1990

Location	Base	From	To
Sacramento, CA	Mather AFB	Jul 1967	May 1968
Mt. Home, ID	Mt. Home AFB	Jun 1968	Dec 1968
Albuquerque, NM	Kirtland AFB	Jan 1969	Oct 1969
Brampton, UK	RAF Alconbury	Jan 1970	Dec 1973
Dayton, OH	Wright Patterson AFB	Jan 1974	Jun 1975
Edwards, CA	Edwards AFB	Aug 1975	Jul 1976
Ft. Walton, FL	Eglin AFB	Aug 1976	Jun 1978
Houston, TX	Johnson Space Center	Jun 1978	Jun 1990

LIST OF ACRONYMS AND OTHER TERMS

AFB	Air Force Base
CDR	Commander
DoD	Department of Defense
Doff	"take off"
Don	"put on"
ET	External Tank
EVA	Extravehicular Activity
JSC	Johnson Space Center (Houston, Texas)
KSC	Kennedy Space Center (Cape Canaveral, Florida)
Lake	Shorthand for "Clear Lake High School"
LCC	Launch Control Center (Kennedy Space Center)
LCVG	Liquid Cooling Ventilation Garment
MS	Mission Specialist
NASA	National Aeronautics and Space Administration
Orbiter	Alternate name for space shuttle
PAO	Public Affairs Officer
PLT	Pilot
SRB	Solid Rocket Booster
Stack	The space shuttle, external tank, and solid rocket boosters together as a single unit
STS	Space Transportation System – name of the entire shuttle system including the orbiter, external tank, and SRBs
T-38	Twin engine NASA jet flown by Astronauts
TFNG	"Thirty-Five New Guys" – nickname of astronaut group 8
USMA	United States Military Academy (West Point)
WETF	Weightless Environment Training Facility

PROLOGUE

I heard an explosion roll across the swampland, a low rumble that came to a peak and then faded with a groan like a dying monster. *I just witnessed my father's death,* I thought.

I looked to my mother for reassurance, but she was sobbing after letting her body fall limply into a government-issue folding metal chair. Panic set in and my breathing came in shallow gulps. My heart raced even faster than it had just twenty seconds earlier. My sisters were equally distraught. The explosion had reached through three miles of fog and slapped the color from their faces with a tactile thud. I raised my hand to my brow to try to shield the glare of the sun rising behind the space shuttle *Discovery* and felt my sodden shirt tug at my skin. But my attempt to see the launch pad was thwarted by a wet haze that the sun seemed unable to burn away, as if the vapor were complicit in the unfolding terror. I had been to Cape Canaveral many times before and had seen morning fog burn off quickly in the heat of a summer sunrise. But that had not happened today as if, on this day, of all days, the laws of physics did not hold. Was it an omen?

I tried to will myself to be strong, to be the man my father would want me to be at a time like this. But it was hard to find the reserves to steel myself for the moment at hand or the ones likely to come.

My father…

There was the launch pad! Or was it? Ghosts appeared in the glare and my watering eyes made the feinting shadows seem mystical. I dropped my head, rubbed the moisture from beneath my closed lids, and then looked up to assess the situation around me on the roof of the Launch Control Center (LCC). Given the explosion, I expected to see a scene of frenetic activity – men in short-sleeved dress shirts on radios calling important people in Washington or running back into the guts of the LCC, taking up contingency positions. But instead, there was a quiet stillness.

It was a stillness I noted when we emerged onto the roof just fifteen minutes earlier. I remembered thinking as I stepped onto the expanse: *Where is everybody?* After all, didn't something as important as the twelfth space shuttle launch deserve more of an audience? But the nearly one-and-a-half-acre roof was thinly populated. Some high-ranking officials and a photographer or two were there. And, of course, the other astronaut families were as well. The only others present were the family escorts – astronauts who acted as tour guides throughout the day, helping the crew's families understand the cryptic radio calls that came too loudly from speakers nearby. Dad had filled me in on the other, unspoken duty of these escorts – to be there in case something went wrong.

And something had gone terribly wrong.

But even in the face of the obvious "anomaly," the escorts were maddeningly quiet. I wanted scream at them. *Why aren't you telling us what's happening? Why won't you* do *something?* But my tongue was thick in my mouth and no words came. I had idolized the *Right Stuff* composure of these men and longed to be just like them. A panicked outburst now would show I was nothing like them, that I was exactly what I appeared to be – a frightened, pimple-faced, beanpole of a teenager. So I remained quiet and instead watched our escorts listen with furrowed brows to the calls coming from the speakers on nearby stanchions. There wasn't much to listen to. The commentary from the NASA public affairs official was infrequent and confused; the dying echoes of each of his sentences were swallowed quickly by the silence between them, adding further tension to a day that had started like a dream.

My father ...

As we arrived at the LCC hours before, I found myself wondering: was Dad really out there on that rocket ready to do what only 144 people before him had done? Even after listening to the crew do their communication checks with the launch control team once they were strapped into *Discovery* – and hearing my father's voice chime in with,

"M-S-one, loud and clear" – it didn't seem real. It didn't seem real when we saw him hours earlier on television, leaving the crew quarters in a light blue flight suit with his crewmates, waving to gathered reporters and NASA workers. It didn't seem real as he stepped into the iconic "Astrovan" that would take him to the launch pad. It didn't seem real as we watched him stand in the white room at the end of the access arm ten stories above the launch pad shaking the hands of the team that would help him into the shuttle before closing the hatch. And it didn't seem real when our astronaut escorts told us, "It's time to head to the roof," as the countdown clock reached T-9 minutes.

But now it seemed real. The relatively benign was a dream. The terror was real.

My father ...

In the milliseconds after hearing the explosion roll across Florida's alligator-infested marshes, my mind behaved in an unexpected way. It was as if *I* were the one in mortal danger, but instead of seeing my own life flash before my eyes in that stereotypical way, I saw my father's life at the intersection of mine. I saw myself at a very young age latching on to *his* dream, wanting just as badly for him what he wanted for himself: to ride a rocket into space after years of being shackled inside the earth's atmosphere, cheating death in high-performance aircraft. I saw him shaping my life with his boundless wonder about the unknown beyond the next mountain, around the next bend, or above us in the heavens. And I saw how I had let his curiosity and goofy imagination about all things seep into my pores like the moisture in Houston's summer air.

It would have been natural to conclude that the connection between who he was and who I was becoming would mean that pieces of him would live on in me. But as the swamps around us became eerily quiet, the bonds that tied me to him felt less like treasures to be cherished than chains pulling me into the past by way of the explosion I had heard to the east. Three miles distant wasn't just a launch pad, it was the termination point of a thousand threads, a thousand stories, and a thousand moments that defined my father's life – and mine.

"Break, break! Break, break!" The controller's voice exploded from the speakers with a panicked urgency, shocking me back to the moment. The concern on the faces of our escorts deepened as the controller's amplified words hit us like tiny darts. The chatter on the radios increased in frequency and momentum pushing an unsettling realization into my core: we were wrong about what had happened out on that launch pad. But a part of me wished we had been right.

There were worse things than a cataclysmic explosion that takes your father in a painless instant.

In the moments that followed, we watched as a licking fire grew slowly at the base of *Discovery*, feet away from nearly four million pounds of fuel. And as the flames grew in intensity, so too did a nauseous fear that I'd have a front row seat to Dad being burned alive as he and his crewmates pleaded for help that would never come.

CHAPTER 1: THE SHIT TANK

My earliest memories are dominated by the smell of water in the air, of ever-present rain and fog. As the son of an Air Force officer and aviator, we moved a lot. And while I was born in California, I lived in Idaho and New Mexico before I reached my third birthday. The rain and fog were courtesy of East Anglia, England where my father was stationed shortly after his tour in Vietnam and where the recorded scenes of my own life started to take root in my consciousness.

My dad, Richard "Mike" Mullane, was a West Point graduate who grew up in Albuquerque, New Mexico, a hometown my mother, Donna Sei, shared. My sisters and I often heard the story of how they reconnected at a party (having been introduced to each other earlier by Mom's cousin) while my father was on break from West Point. According to my father, my mother kissed him at the soiree after the plane that was going to whisk him back to hell – his euphemism for West Point – was delayed and, if not for that kiss, my twin sister, younger sister, and I would never have existed. Like a lot of humans, I'm ultimately the result of hormones mixed liberally with alcohol.

Dad was a handsome guy with a quick wit and ready smile – a smile that showed a distinctive gap between his two front teeth displayed under an angular nose and hazel eyes. The gap always seemed to make his smile more meaningful, as if his joyous spirit escaped from between his separated incisors every time his lips parted. Dad was slight relative to other men, not so much because of his 5'9" height but because of his sinewy limbs and washboard stomach, both borne of a life of activity. Even today, into his seventies, Dad is the picture of fitness many Americans would expect of a retired astronaut.*

My mother was a homemaker who raised my sisters and me as if she was a 1930s Italian village matron, broom in hand, shooing us out of the house if we crossed the threshold with even a micron of dust on our shoes. She ruled whatever house we occupied with order, process, cleanliness, and – when necessary – discipline. Every object had its place, every happening had its time, and every child had his or her tasks. It was as if Mom was trying to force order into an unmoored, nomadic military life that, absent her efforts, would descend into chaos. My sisters and I sensed this and, fearing what might happen without that order, jumped at Mom's commands knowing that we were all better off doing so.

There was a comfort in this. From our two-story, very small brick apartment in England, to our ranch home in Florida, to our bungalow in California, a consistent sense of place permeated. The walls and floors may have changed every few years, but the same pictures hung on those walls and the same furniture sat on those floors, their positions and prominence relative to each other consistent from floorplan to floorplan. Mom's design sense was good at duping us into believing that nothing had changed. I was happy for that.

Mom had a beauty about her that in a different age might have been discovered by a photographer from Vogue looking for a young woman that readers could relate to. She was a tan-skinned, girl-next-door with no single feature that defined her beauty but a collection of pedestrian ones that, in combination, made her striking without making her seem impossible to exist. Her full lips and brown, expressive eyes were surrounded by dark, full hair that was often shorter than the styles of the time dictated, giving her a sort of Mary Tyler Moore air.

Nine months after Mom and Dad were married – in March of 1968 – my twin, Amy, and I were born.

---

* In 2010, my father, at the age of 65, summited Mt. Kilimanjaro with my cousin and me. On our five-day trek to 19,341 feet, my father never showed a sign of fatigue or altitude sickness. Something I (as a fit 42-year-old) could not say about myself.

The year was arguably one of the most tumultuous in U.S. history since the end of World War II. A month before we were born, the North Vietnamese launched the Tet Offensive, a brazen attack on the U.S. and its allies in the south, belying claims by the Johnson administration that all was well in hand, changing the trajectory of public sentiment regarding the war. On March 5th, the day Amy and I entered the world, the "Prague Spring" saw the Czechoslovakian government abolish censorship, challenging Soviet influence and ultimately leading to the invasion of the country by the Soviet Union in August. Just a month after our birth, Martin Luther King was assassinated in Memphis while there to support sanitation workers who had gone on strike. On June 4th, Robert F. Kennedy was assassinated at the Ambassador Hotel in Los Angeles, less than five years after his brother was killed in Dallas. Riots broke out at the Democratic National Convention in Chicago.

Amy and I couldn't know it at the time but that year would set the country on a path of despair and doubt that would culminate more than ten years later in the election of Ronald Reagan and the onset of a new era of optimism that would underlie the decade we would spend our formative years in, the glorious eighties.

Amy was about as different from me as somebody could be. This isn't that surprising. After all, we were fraternal twins, no different than a boy and girl born years apart to the same parents. But most people don't seem to understand this. I've been asked frequently if we are identical and I am always tempted to say, "Except for the penis, we're exactly alike."

Amy and I might be proof that nature is much more powerful than nurture. I was the bookworm who loved school and excelled at academics. An extrovert, I could walk into a room of people I didn't know and start a conversation with virtually anybody. I loved the challenge of a good math problem and would plug away at it until the solution was found. From a very young age, I enjoyed watching the news with my father each evening after he returned home from work. Amy's interests didn't overlap at all. She relished family time together without intrusions from the outside world, whether those intrusions came from strangers, a television, or homework. She was braver than me in so many ways; unlike me, she could step out of her comfort zone and be a different person for short bursts. This was particularly true if she believed somebody she loved had been wronged. Asking me, on the other hand, to be something I naturally wasn't was like asking the tides not to rise and fall.

If Amy and I were as far apart as alpha and omega, our younger sister, Laura, wasn't even a Greek letter. She wasn't any letter. She was whatever the furthest thing from a letter could be. Maybe a bungee cord or a smoke detector. Three years younger than Amy and me, Laura was artistic and from a young age loved to be on a stage. Plays, interpretive dance programs, and concerts were often performed for anybody who would watch. This inclination to be a star came with the baggage that many in the arts carry: a need to fight demons real and imagined, a belief that she was not understood and never could be, and a propensity to rebel – all by the age of ten.

***

Despite the fact that my father went to West Point, the army's military academy, the rules of the time allowed him to take his commission as a second lieutenant in the U.S. Air Force. He wanted to fly and that's what he did. While he wasn't a pilot because of bad eyesight, he served as a "back-seater" in two-crew fighter/bombers. Like the "Goose" character in Top Gun, my father worked with the pilot to accomplish the mission at hand. But while my dad was a military man, he did not fit the stereotype of a buzz-cut authoritarian. He was a particularly patient man, more *Father Knows Best* than *Great Santini*; my mother was the one who was quick to frustration. Of course, it was easier for Dad to be patient, he wasn't the one who was home with two fussy infants.

By the time I was out of diapers, I had already embraced a starry-eyed wonder when it came to my father. Dad had grown up with a passion for flight borne of his own status as the son of an aviator and he made his passion mine. That's not to say that Dad forced his interests on me. Rather, he simply shared the beauty he perceived in aviation and the nobility he saw in its use in the defense of freedom. It was an idealistic and simple perspective, one that an idealistic and simple boy could easily absorb. But it was a firm anchor in an early life that had few anchors. I was in a new school and new home every few years as Dad was assigned and then re-assigned to various squadrons.

Our moves gave Mom an opportunity to further demonstrate her dominion over anarchy. I grew up thinking that all mothers had her uncanny skills in planning and executing a relocation. She'd stage boxes in the house we were leaving and label them neatly with a black marker so she would know, once at our destination, where to instruct movers to stack them. At our new home, she'd stand in the yard and point at the containers stacked two-high in movers' arms, barking instructions like a sergeant in the quartermaster corps.

"That one, kitchen! That one, bedroom number one!"

Mom's penchant for organization, order, and predictability made her more military than any top graduate from West Point. The movers sensed this in her and followed her commands without deviation. As a young boy, I viewed Mom much like those movers did. She was all business all the time.

With each move, friends were made, then lost, then made again, none from my early years becoming close enough to remember by the time I graduated from high school. But aviation was always there. It was there even when Dad wasn't. In the evening I'd lay in bed in our base housing and hear night missions begin in the distance, aircraft lighting their afterburners as they accelerated into the blackness, knowing at times that Dad was on one of those planes roaring down the runway. I'd hear fighters throttle down as they passed over our roof on their way to a landing a short distance away. I'd go to the commissary with Mom and see men walking the aisles in their flight suits, grabbing milk and eggs after landing an hour earlier from a mission where they probed Soviet air defenses over Scandinavia. Around every base we called home, static displays of aircraft, always with their noses up and in a slight turn, reminded me of the airborne history of the facility where we lived. Aviation became my ever-present friend.

That friend was one that I could engage with even though I couldn't fly myself. I drew airplanes. I built models of airplanes. I hung airplanes from my bedroom ceiling using nearly invisible fishing line. I was such an aviation nerd that those airplanes hanging above my bed weren't just static displays, but they told stories: an American World War II fighter was lined up behind a Japanese or German aircraft, guns blazing. I glued together cotton balls and painted them a fiery red and an oily brown to mimic a billowing plume from the engine compartment of the doomed enemy plane, which had fallen victim to the injection-molded plastic pilot in the cockpit of the American aircraft. I had those models hanging in my bedroom until I was well into my high school career. Suffice it to say, girls were not lining up to see that bedroom.

I became closer to my aviation friend with each move. After living in California, Idaho, and New Mexico we moved back to the states from England so that Dad could go to graduate school at the Air Force's Institute of Technology in Dayton, Ohio. From there it was off to Edwards Air Force Base (AFB) in California where Dad attended the Air Force Test Pilot School engineering program. Then, back across the country to Florida and Eglin AFB. While at Eglin, when I was ten years old, my father was selected by NASA to join the very first group of space shuttle astronauts. For a boy enamored with his father, with aviation, and with space travel, I might have been more excited than he was. Not surprisingly, I channeled that excitement into building a space shuttle model and then drawing it in my portfolio of crayon and pencil aviation drawings.

While Dad's interest in aviation seeped into me indirectly by virtue of my proximity to him and the culture of flight that permeated life on military bases, he actively cultivated in my sisters and me a wonder about the world and the universe it occupied. He had an immense love of the outdoors and imbued in us the curiosity to crane our necks around the next bend and peek over the next mountaintop to discover what lay beyond, to seek adventure. This push to understand the natural world and the universe found a welcome repository in me. I devoured books on everything from dinosaurs to the solar system to the space travel of the future, letting my mind wander to imaginings that blended things I'd read from each source. One evening I'd dream of flying a rocket ship over a land of dinosaurs, sightseeing like a tourist at an ancient zoo, before rocketing into space to destroy the asteroid that threatened their demise. The next night I'd be an archeologist sent to an uncharted planet to investigate clues to a culture that had mysteriously disappeared. Already, the universe was seeming unfathomably big to me and I felt daunted by the need to do something unfathomably big in it.

***

During the time we lived at Edwards AFB while Dad was attending the Air Force Test Pilot School and I was a seven-year-old kid, we had a second-hand motorhome we used on numerous family excursions throughout the western half of the country. I loved that vehicle. I'd crawl into the loft above the front cabin and look through the long window that gave an elevated view out the front of the RV. If I put my face right up against that window, immersing my field of vision completely in the view outside, I had the sensation I was flying above the road like a World War II pilot strafing a convoy of troop transport trucks. When not in the loft, I'd retire to bench seats that ringed a table in the back of the RV and play UNO with Amy and Laura or stick my head out the side window, letting the warm air run through my hair, the smell of piñon and sage making the endless desert seem intimate in some way. Those moments made me feel fully American, a much-delayed participant in Manifest Destiny.

That sense of being a part of the American experience was enhanced by the songs Dad played on an eight-track player in the center console of the RV. He would serve up an assortment of cowboy songs by Marty Robbins. "El Paso," a tune about a cowboy who dies while trying to defend his claim on Felina, his Mexican lover, was a favorite. So too was Robbins's song, "Big Iron," the tale of how an Arizona ranger went looking for the outlaw Texas Red and, when he found him, killed him in a duel (using the "big iron" on his hip).

As the songs played and we sped along, I would look out the window and imagine what it would have been like to be a ranger doggedly hunting villains throughout the land that now whizzed by me in a blur, the silhouetted mountains on the horizon becoming an imaginary sanctuary for Texas Red. My frequent viewing of reruns of *Gunsmoke* and *The Lone Ranger* only made the stories that played out in my mind more real. Oh, to have been one of those brave men whom scofflaws feared, men admired, and women swooned for!

The RV in some ways felt like a covered wagon traversing the untamed, dramatic lands of the west – and not just because of our forays into long-forgotten swaths of empty land demarcated by lonely, untraveled roads. Some creative maintenance on our motor home by Dad made him seem like an improvising trail hand – a guy who, like the 1985 TV character MacGyver, could fashion a new axle using a rudimentary lathe, a dry piece of wood, and an old bridle. Dad got tired of pressing on the gas pedal on long trips in the RV since it had no cruise control so he cut a broom handle to just the right length and wedged it between the pedal and the underside of the instrument panel to hold the RV at 60 miles per hour. When we lost the gas cap for our RV, Dad, rather than pay a king's ransom to order an original equipment part, whittled a new cap out of redwood, as if his name was Zeke or Cody. Even as a child, I thought this was a bad idea. I had seen how wood could absorb gasoline and worried that in the heat of the southern California desert, the redwood would sop up the moist vapors rising from the tank and spontaneously ignite, trapping all of us as we slept. And while it never happened, I've never seen another vehicle with a redwood component as part of its fuel systems, so I'm guessing it's not considered a preferred fix.

One reason I knew of the gasoline absorption properties of wood was my father's propensity to use gasoline to ignite everything. I had seen him douse logs in a fire pit to start a campfire. More disturbingly, he used it to get the grill going at home. After assembling the Kingsford charcoal, he'd pour a half-gallon's worth of gasoline over the matte-black bricks until they glimmered.

Then came the fun part.

He'd hold a match against the strike area on a matchbook and in one fluid motion swipe the match along the friction strip and toss it onto the pyre, all the while retreating a safe distance from the conflagration that ensued.

Whoosh!

I always loved the sound, flash of heat, and orange fireball that let me know I was minutes away from enjoying a well-done burger infused with a flavor you might get if you licked the engine block of a burned-out NASCAR motor dipped in animal fat. Oh, and this was in the days of leaded gasoline. When I hear the EPA talking about how only a flake or two of old lead paint can poison a child, it's hard for me not to say "bullshit" under my breath. While I assume there is no FDA guideline regarding the safe number of lead-encrusted burgers somebody can eat in a given year, if they had one, I would have exceeded it many times over. And I seem to have turned out just fine…

Along with the camper, we had a 1972 VW station wagon. With two bucket seats in the front, a bench seat in the middle and an enclosed cargo compartment in the rear, it was a multipurpose vehicle if you didn't care about a lot of room, a quiet ride, or air conditioning. I had always been fascinated by the car because of the backwards nature of it: the trunk was in the front where most cars had an engine and the motor was in the rear under the cargo area.

One year, when I was eleven, Dad and I were out running errands on a hot Houston summer day when the throttle cable in the car broke; pressing on the accelerator was like stepping on a fake pedal in a Boy Scout's engineless soapbox derby car. The motor was stuck at idle. My father resorted to his go-to swear (he'd grunt "goddamnit" from behind clenched teeth, a guttural emphasis on the "damn" syllable) as he removed the thin board in the floor of the back compartment to reveal the engine. He showed me where the cable that ran from the accelerator pedal was supposed to attach to the engine but had torn off. Then, he grabbed the metal arm to which the cable had been affixed and showed me how it was intended to work.

"Watch what happens when I move this!" he shouted over the engine noise.

He moved the metal arm just as it would move if it had been connected to the accelerator pedal with an intact cable and, as he did, more fuel was delivered to the engine and it revved loudly. When he eased the metal arm back, the engine quieted back to idle.

"See?" he shouted.

I nodded, mouth gaping in wonder at the machinery and my father's knowledge of it.

He moved the arm back and forth a few more times as I watched. I was on the back seat, knees on the cushions, my body leaning over the backrest to see into the engine compartment. It was like being in my own shop class. But I soon learned that Dad wasn't showing me this just for educational purposes.

"You try!" he said.

I looked up, surprised. He nodded at the metal arm, encouraging me. I grabbed it cautiously and flinched for a moment. It was hot. But not too hot to touch. I revved the engine by pushing on the lever and then let it return to idle.

"Good," Dad shouted. "I'm gonna get back in the driver seat and we're gonna drive home."

Come again?

"Don't worry," he said, sensing my concern. "Just push on that piece when I tell you, okay?" I nodded.

He got into the driver's seat, took off the emergency brake, shifted the manual transmission into first gear, and shouted, "Power!"

I pushed on the arm but probably too much; as my father let out the clutch, the car lurched forward with a jolt.

"Easy!" Dad shouted.

I was sweating profusely and becoming light-headed. The combination of ninety-plus degree temperatures outside, ninety percent humidity, and the heat from the engine made me feel like I was in the bowels of a steam ship shoveling coal into the burners as it navigated the Caribbean. The engine exhaust fumes were coming into the car and I coughed and wheezed.

"I'll roll down the window!" Dad said. I looked over my shoulder and saw his left shoulder dip as he furiously turned the crank handle in the side of the driver's door.

Oh, good. Yeah, that'll work.

"Idle!" I let up on the lever and the engine quieted as Dad pushed in the clutch and shifted to second gear. Then, "Power!"

This time I applied pressure more evenly and the shift was executed smoothly. I was proud of myself. It really *was* like I was in the engine control room of a ship. I imagined the captain, my father, at the helm shouting commands into a bell-mouthed pipe to the loud, hot, noisy engine room. On the "bridge," Dad would see the machine change its state as if by magic – my magic!

I continued to get light-headed. I was likely adding carbon monoxide poisoning to the lead poisoning of my father's cooking. My childhood body was a Superfund site.

As we drove, I had the opportunity to catch a glimpse of other cars as they passed us, their drivers looking at the scene next to them with mouths open and eyebrows raised. We must have made quite a sight: a man driving a car, his window down, intermittently raising his head to the ceiling to shout at the top of his lungs a seemingly random string of commands.

"Power!"

"Idle!"

"Easy now!"

"Accelerate!"

"I'm passing somebody – gas!"

Behind him, a boy, ass in the air, bent over the back seat, face blue from carbon monoxide poisoning made worse by constant coughing. Today, the scene would prompt a call to 911 and an Amber alert would promptly be issued. The APB would detail a light blue VW station wagon driven by a man with a psychotic dementia yelling at a boy, shirt drenched in sweat, and suffering from symptoms of asphyxiation.

***

My father's luck (or lack thereof) with vehicles apparently carried over from his father. Hugh Mullane, whom my sisters and I called "Pop Pop," was a World War II veteran who had contracted polio at the end of the war in the Pacific. After a stint on crutches, he was eventually confined to a wheelchair, the only way I ever knew him. My grandmother, Marjorie Mullane, was his doting care-giver, her efforts augmented by her children.

I loved Pop Pop but was afraid of him too. He had a brashness borne of his Irish, New York upbringing that was foreign to a kid growing up in southeast Texas with parents who enforced politeness and deference to others above all else. His forearms were like Popeye's, thick and hard from years of wheeling himself around in a wheelchair, lifting himself onto toilets, and exercising, which he did regularly into his later years using uneven metal bars and a swimming pool in his backyard. His arms were complemented by a barrel of a chest, but the strength of his upper body contrasted sharply with his legs, which were nothing more than skin on bone. He could move his legs only with his hands. To cross them, he would put both palms under the thighbone of his right leg and lift that leg over the other. It was hard to see him do this and not think of the legs of a marionette, slack with uselessness until animated by the strength of working hands.

In early 1981, when I was thirteen and three years after Dad was selected as an astronaut, Pop Pop and Grandma were planning to drive to Edwards AFB in California by way of El Paso, Texas to watch the return to earth of the very first space shuttle mission. They invited me to join them and I said yes with an excited scream.

The anticipation of the trip led to many sleepless nights as I imagined what it would be like to see the space shuttle *Columbia* gliding to a landing at the same base where Chuck Yeager had broken the sound barrier and where I had lived earlier in my short life. My excitement was amplified by the fact that Dad would be supporting *Columbia's* mission. In the year before the launch, he had been assigned to serve as part of a NASA chase plane crew that would be waiting in El Paso during *Columbia's* launch. This was part of a contingency plan; should the shuttle not successfully get all the way into orbit, it would have the ability to abort and land at White Sands, New Mexico, just north of El Paso, after only one revolution of the earth.

If *Columbia* did end up aborting to White Sands, Dad and his team would fly to intercept the shuttle in their chase planes (small, sleek NASA T-38 jets) and fly formation with it as it descended to the runway. As they flew alongside *Columbia*, they would survey the heat tiles and take pictures of them for later analysis. They would also let the crew of *Columbia* know if there was anything to be concerned about based on their quick inspection of the outside of the vehicle. Assuming all went well and an abort to White Sands was not necessary, the chase team would fly their jets to Edwards AFB in California following the launch to await the landing of the shuttle there, two-and-a-half days later. I would follow them westward in the RV Grandma and Pop Pop owned.

On the morning of *Columbia's* launch, Grandma, Pop Pop and I were in the El Paso airport flight operations center with Dad and his fellow astronauts. I loved "flight ops" buildings. Dad had taken me into many of them at the bases where we'd been stationed, and they invariably looked the same. Walls and bulletin boards were festooned with hundreds of squadron patches left behind by the crews who had passed through. The patches were the graffiti of the aviation world, an alpha-male way to piss on the same hydrant those before you had, to show that your squadron would not be upstaged by another. I could look at those patches for hours. Cartoon characters, predatory birds, scorpions, skeletons, wasps, bees, and other animals were centerpieces of many of the squadron emblems. I loved deciphering what each patch said about the mission of the unit that had left it.

We all huddled around a television in the flight ops building to tune into the countdown of *Columbia*. As we watched, I considered that while the trademark NASA-blue flight suits Dad and his colleagues wore made them look like astronauts and they were called "astronauts," nobody wearing one of those flight suits felt like an astronaut. A person didn't officially earn that distinction until he or she had made it to at least fifty miles up, an arbitrary altitude determined early in the history of space travel as the point at which a person entered space.* The "astronauts" watching that day knew that if *Columbia* failed spectacularly, they'd all likely lose their opportunities to fly in space. They'd return to their roles as captains, majors, and lieutenants in their respective military branches, no closer to space than the nerdy kid clinging to them like a sycophantic political aid at the foot of a presidential candidate.

There were good reasons to worry about a successful launch. For the first time ever, astronauts would be traveling into space on a spacecraft that had never actually launched.+ In the past, rockets that would eventually carry people had been blasted into space without humans on board to make sure they would work as expected. The shuttle, by contrast, had never gotten off a launch pad. Instead, the shuttle stack's engine thrust and associated stresses had been modeled in a world of digital ones and zeroes passing information from algorithm to algorithm in an endlessly complicated chain of computer code. Launches and landings had only occurred in the ether.

On the morning of April 12th, 1981, those of us in that flight operations office knew that *Columbia's* crew, John Young and Bob

---

* The fifty-mile marker is a distinctly American one. The Fédération Aéronautique Internationale (the World Air Sports Federation) sets the altitude at 100 km or 62 miles. If you are European, it's twelve miles harder to get your astronaut wings.

+ While the entire space shuttle stack had never been launched, a test version of the shuttle, the *Enterprise*, had been dropped from the back of a 747 five times beginning in 1977 to test the gliding properties of the shuttle.

Crippen, were embarking on one of the riskiest test flights ever. Their survival depended on the skills and knowledge of thousands of computer scientists, engineers, and physicists. Dad's dreams – and mine – rested on blind faith in a whole lot of really smart people getting the math right.

We watched CBS's broadcast of the countdown which featured Dan Rather hosting from Kennedy Space Center (KSC). He remained silent, as did we, while the clock approached zero. The only noise was the NASA public affairs officer (PAO) narrating the events in short bursts, each sentence a milestone passed. The main engines came to life at T minus six seconds and shortly thereafter the solid rocket boosters (SRBs) ignited. The commentary of the PAO on the TV was overwhelmed by the engines' roaring crackle. The inability to hear the narration of the events unnerved me. Since a launch had never occurred, it was hard to know what "normal" would look like and so I had planned to rely on the PAO to tell me that things were going smoothly … or not. I gasped when I saw the violence with which the SRBs lit. There was a flash of light beneath the launch pad that leapt back up around the bottom of the boosters and for a moment I thought that an abnormal, uncontrolled explosion had occurred. But any worries I had were supplanted by the next surprise: the entire stack, weighing more than four million pounds, jumped emphatically from the launch pad. It was not the slow, dramatic crawl up the gantry that I had seen in old footage of Apollo launches. The shuttle looked like it had power to spare.

The energy being released 1,500 miles away in Florida was mirrored in the room we occupied. Cheers erupted as the video feed cut to a wide shot of the shuttle while it rose above its own plume, cleared the tower, and began to tilt toward the horizon and streak to orbit. Eight-and-a-half minutes later, the main engines cut off. Young and Crippen were in orbit. Dad's smile stretched wide, the gap in his front teeth looking like parted barn doors. He and the other astronauts who, moments before, worried that they had left their careers to chase a fool's dream at NASA now congratulated each other with an assured bravado. I broke in and hugged dad.

"Wasn't that awesome?!" he said.

"So awesome!" I replied. And I meant it.

It was time to go to California.

***

Grandma and Pop Pop's motorhome was very much like the camper Dad owned when we lived at Edwards, sans the redwood gas cap. Because of my grandfather's use of a wheelchair, it was his only mode of transportation. The vehicle had a ramp that folded into the side of the living compartment while driving but extended when the door was opened to allow him to lower himself safely to the ground. I loved playing with that electric ramp as a child. The fun of the access ramp often made me forget about the reason it was there: to help a crippled man live as normal a life as possible in a time when accommodations for the handicapped were virtually nonexistent.

The driver's position of the RV had been modified with hand controls since my grandfather's atrophied legs were useless. While Pop Pop was adept with those controls, he confirmed a stereotype that has held true for me in the decades since that trip: if you are issued a handicapped placard for your car, it genetically modifies your DNA in a way that does not allow you to drive anywhere close to the speed limit. If we got above eighty percent of the posted limits at any point during our trip between El Paso and Edwards, I'd be surprised. In fact, I had very real concerns that we would miss the landing in California. The shuttle was only slated to be in orbit for fifty-four hours. It's about 830 miles from El Paso to Edwards. At forty miles per hour, that's twenty-one hours of travel. And forty wasn't too unreasonable an average; in 1981 the highest speed limit posted on the straightest, safest freeway was fifty-five. Of course, that math doesn't account for stops to allow Pop Pop to urinate, which could be a thirty-minute operation given his physical disability if he tried to use a toilet. Fortunately, he often didn't use a commode. He instead urinated into empty two-liter soft drink bottles. For reasons that were never clear to me, we often kept those bottles in the RV half filled with urine rather than empty them right away, making the inside of the motor home look like an ante room in a mansion owned by Howard Hughes.

In addition to my concerns about how fast Pop Pop drove, our trip would be lengthened by the fact that we'd also have to spend a night on the road. Pop Pop couldn't sit in the driver's seat for long stretches; a half-lifetime of sitting had made his ass sore. Much of the fifty-four hours we had to make it to Edwards were now eaten up. But there was some contingency time. I prayed we wouldn't have to use it.

While Pop Pop didn't need a bathroom to urinate, he did if he had to have a bowel movement. Fortunately, we had a toilet in the RV, so it wasn't necessary to find a gas station or restaurant if any of us needed to relieve ourselves. And thank God for that because I needed to drop a load frequently. My grandmother brought her homemade chocolate pudding on the trip, which was concocted with the liberal use of milk and butter. While I didn't make the connection until I was much older, I suffered from lactose intolerance that made my body an incredibly efficient converter of milk and milk-based products into hot, odiferous farts and soft, dark turds. That chocolate pudding came out looking much like it did going in. The RV toilet got a good workout.

As we were driving along an isolated road in southern Arizona, Pop Pop decided it was time to empty the toilet holding tank given its frequent use by me. The lack of appropriate facilities to purge the tank seemed of little concern to him. The highway we were on cleaved a desert landscape that was as flat as it was barren. Looking out the back window of the RV, the asphalt disappeared at a singular point on the horizon through the distorting waves of the heat that created mirages of water on the pavement. The view out the front window was no different. Seeing no cars for miles behind us and none in front, Pop Pop identified an intersecting dirt road, dutifully put on his blinker, turned off the pavement, drove over a cattle guard flanked by barbed wire fences, and motored off at walking speed into the desert.

Once he'd put a mile between us and the road, he put the RV in park, struggled into his wheelchair, and rolled back to the ramp. He pushed down on one toggle switch that opened the side door and then on another to lower the ramp until it was even with the floor of the RV. I loved to watch the process. As a super-fan of *Star Wars*, it reminded me of the ramp on the *Millennium Falcon* spaceship and I imagined myself as Han Solo preparing to step onto the sands of the planet Tatooine. (It turns out that my imagination wasn't far from reality. For the last film in the original *Star Wars* trilogy, *The Return of* *the Jedi*, some scenes of Tatooine were filmed nearby in Yuma, Arizona.) *

When the ramp was partially down, Pop Pop asked me to hop down to the desert floor and then wheeled out onto the metal platform into the baking sunlight. He had a pipe in his mouth that he had packed with tobacco and lit before rolling onto the ramp. Now, in his position above me, with smoke billowing around his head, he looked like a grizzled sea captain barking orders from the bridge.

"Pat, I'm gonna tell you what to do to empty the tank," he said. Grandma was in the galley preparing lunch.

"What tank?" I asked, not certain of his plan.

"The shit tank!" he barked back, clearly taking pleasure in the shock that registered on my face.

"Here?" I asked. Even in the days before concerns about climate change, the depleting ozone layer, and the dangers of not properly disposing of fluorescent light tubes, I had a sense that depositing your fecal matter and the associated blue fluid of an RV waste system on the desert floor wasn't kosher.

"Pay attention now," he shouted. Then, he paused, and sensing my concern, he added, "What's the matter? It's fine! Animals shit out here!"

Hmmm, I thought, *that is true*.

He directed me to open a small door in the side of the RV and then told me to remove the cap on a tube protruding from inside the body of the vehicle. Then he warned me to stand back as I turned a knob that opened a valve and let the tank drain. Onto the sand flowed the blue liquid and the remnants of Grandma's chocolate pudding. Getting a whiff of the toxic brew, I burped up a little bile and

---

* According to the online resource "Wookieepedia: The *Star Wars* Wiki," Tatooine "was a sparsely inhabited circumbinary desert planet located in the galaxy's Outer Rim Territories. It would serve as the home world to the influential Anakin and Luke Skywalker, who would go on to shape galactic history. Part of a binary star system, the planet was oppressed by scorching suns, resulting in the world lacking the necessary surface water to sustain a large population." An imaginary world from a movie of my youth has a more detailed history than the desert I visited with my grandparents. I may be a nerd, but some people have *way* too much time on their hands.

swallowed it back down. As the tank drained, it occurred to me that I had never seen Han Solo dump his shit tank when he landed the *Millennium Falcon* on a distant world. I had to believe that Chewbacca's turds filled his tank pretty quickly. Alas, this is a matter that Wookieepedia is silent about.

When the operation was complete, I emptied some of Pop Pop's piss bottles into the desert, the three of us ate a lunch of turkey sandwiches in the back of the RV, and then we battened down the hatches. Pop Pop started the engine, put the motorhome into drive, and released the emergency break to head back to the highway and further west.

Except we didn't move. He pushed down a second time on the hand lever that worked the accelerator pedal, but the RV didn't budge. I could hear a wheel in the back spinning impotently.

"Balls!" Pop Pop said, using his favorite swear.

"I think she's stuck in the sand!" he shouted. When he called a machine "she," it was hard not to imagine him in the belly of a B-17 in flight over the Pacific. "She's leaking oil godDAMNit! Keep her in the air, lieutenant!" I could tell he relished the adversity that had come our way.

He put the RV into park and sighed.

"Pat, go look at how bad she's stuck."

I made my way to the back of the motor home and found one of the tires buried nearly to the rim in the sand. I reported the finding back to my grandfather. "She's got a wheel sunk in the sand. She ain't moving," I said, adopting Pop Pop's feminine pronoun for the RV.

I put my hands on my hips trying to show my lack of concern despite the very real threat we might be indefinitely stranded. If I had chewed tobacco at my tender age, I would have spat a dark, phlegmy globule to the ground. But my hidden concern was short-lived. I was to learn from Pop Pop what I was also learning from Dad: that men of our ilk solved problems. We stayed calm. We persevered. We didn't panic. I was getting a chance to practice being the man I one day hoped I'd be. A man who did great things when others lost their nerve.

After some failed attempts to gain traction by wedging rocks in front of the tire, we were left with the prospect of finding help in an age before cell phones and GPS, miles from anything or anybody.

"I think I should go for help," Grandma said.

"Why don't you and Pat go," Pop Pop said to her after contemplating our situation while chewing his pipe. "Walk back to the main road and hitchhike to the nearest town." It's funny, I don't remember being concerned at all about this plan. It was another adventure. So, after gathering some water to take with us, Grandma and I started tracing the tracks from the RV back to the main road.

Marjorie Pettigrew was a hell of a woman. She met Hugh (Pop Pop) at eighteen and married shortly thereafter as the United States was already a year into World War II. Even in her later years, she was an attractive lady and a photo in her home, somewhat hidden in a back room, confirmed that she was also a hottie as a young woman. In that picture, she is an eighteen- or nineteen-year-old sitting on a beach in a swimsuit that, while appropriate for the time, still seemed elegant and sexy many years later. It's easy to see what Pop Pop saw in her.

All in the family agreed that she was born a generation or two too soon. Fiercely independent and constantly moving, she likely would have been a Nobel prize recipient or astronaut herself had she been born in an era where women had value beyond their ability to bear and raise offspring. Not that she wasn't capable of that—in addition to my father she had five other children. She was a renaissance woman whom I never saw cry, unless from tears of laughter. You could always count on a few of those tears when, many years later, she watched *Something about Mary*, her favorite movie. I'm sure when it was being made, grandmas were not assumed to be in the target demographic. Scenes of a man masturbating only to lose track of his semen, which his date ultimately finds on his earlobe and mistakes for hair gel—well, scenes like that were likely meant for frat boys. But it made no difference; my grandmother laughed her ass off every time she watched that snippet. And when she laughed her large breasts would rhythmically bounce up and down making all of those around her laugh along with her.

Grandma shared Pop Pop's love of the outdoors. I never saw her turn down a camping trip. She would lace up her sneakers and walk miles every day, hiking at altitudes most Americans had never been to. She had no compunction about standing in a swarm of mosquitos at a campfire or squatting behind a tree to relieve herself. She was no delicate flower. Her drive to explore was so rooted in her that she was hiking nearly until she died. Many years after Pop Pop passed away, she drove with a girlfriend—both of them well into their seventies—from Albuquerque to Anchorage, Alaska, a distance of over 7,000 miles round trip, to see the American west and the untamed lands of the 49th state. So, volunteering to walk through the desert to a road in the middle of nowhere and hitchhike into a town to get help was something that seemed completely expected to me.

Grandma and I were about fifty yards from the RV when I heard Pop Pop summon me back to the motor home. "Stay there Marge!" he yelled to my grandmother when she started to make her way back with me.

"What's up Pop Pop?" I asked, breathless after sprinting back. He was still sitting on the ramp, slightly elevated, smoking his pipe. He reached to his left and grabbed something.

"Pat, take this," he said, handing me a crowbar that he had retrieved from the tire-changing kit. He took his pipe out of his mouth and leaned down to talk to me, as if concerned that Grandma might hear.

"If anybody tries to give you or your grandma any funny business, let 'em have it," he said, sounding like a 1940s Brooklyn gangster giving final instructions to an underling on his way to make a hit.

I took the bar from him slowly and looked at it as I let it settle into my palms, surprised by its weight. Wow, Pop Pop wanted me to protect Grandma. I felt like a man. A man who built model airplanes and dreamed of stepping off the *Millennium Falcon*. A man who had yet to shave. A man who weighed about eleven pounds more than the crowbar he was holding. But a man, nonetheless.

As I reveled in my elevated status, something occurred to me.

"Pop Pop," I said tentatively, "um, if I'm standing with Grandma on the side of the road with this in my hand, won't it make somebody scared to stop?"

I had fast-forwarded to the moment Grandma and I made it back to the paved highway. She would be standing on the side of the road, her thumb out, her dress (she almost always wore dresses) pulled up over her knee, her toe flexed to display her calf and attract the attention of a weak-willed passer-by. Next to her, a boy in an airplane t-shirt, short shorts, and tube socks holding a tire iron in his hands waiting to bludgeon to death any good Samaritan who might stop. It didn't add up.

"Don't you worry about that," Pop Pop said. "Just be ready."

Well, that cleared things up. I felt less confident in my ability to help Grandma should anybody try and give her "the funny business."

Grandma and I made it back to the road in about half an hour. Once there, we started walking in the direction we thought the nearest town laid, both of us holding out our thumbs. It didn't take too long for a stranger to stop in a pickup truck.

"Need help?" he shouted through the open passenger side window. I evaluated him quickly, unsure if I needed to bring the tire iron to the ready. He did look a little like he might be a "funny business" guy. Grandma seemed un-phased.

"My husband, grandson, and I are stuck in the sand about a mile or two that way," she pointed off into the desert. "We need a tow truck."

"Hop in," the stranger said. I got in first and slid over next to the driver. Grandma took the passenger seat, bookending me between the two adults. I laid the crowbar across my lap.

"Where's your husband?" the stranger asked. I gripped the warm metal in my hands a bit tighter.

"He's with the RV," Grandma replied.

I realized that it must have seemed strange to this man that the husband had sent his wife and grandson to get help rather than get it himself. I wanted to blurt out, "He's in a wheelchair!" But I stopped myself, worried this guy would find it easier to give us the funny business if he knew the other member of our threesome was disabled. In the end, it didn't seem to matter; Grandma's answer didn't evoke a hint of a reaction in the driver.

My lack of faith in humanity ultimately proved too cynical. The stranger delivered us to a remote service station with a dust-covered tow truck parked outside. An hour later, it was pulling the motor home out of the sand and we were on our way to Edwards.

CHAPTER 2: MEN AND THEIR MARVELOUS FLYING MACHINES

As an air force aviator and pilot, my father had all things aeronautical running like corpuscles through his veins. And as his son, I had the same affliction. This love of flight was something that we shared in my youth and still share today. Some of the first stories he told me and my sisters revolved around his time as a child making homemade rockets out of vacuum cleaner tubes filled with fuel he baked (dangerously) in Grandma's kitchen oven. He has said many times since those reckless days that he was really making pipe bombs with fins and calling them rockets. Fortunately, by the time he had a second cut at launching model rockets with me, the Estes Corporation had begun making much safer alternatives than his flying/exploding vacuum cleaner tubes.

Vern Estes founded Estes Industries in 1958 after designing a machine that allowed him to mass produce solid fuel model rocket engines. Pre-packaged solid fuel motors were immensely safer than doing what my father and others of his generation had done. In the 1960 book *Rocket Manual for Amateurs*, the forward notes, almost in passing, that "there have been accidents, even fatal ones" in the amateur rocket building community. But building rockets was serious business and was even promoted by the military. The author of the book, Captain Bertrand Brinley, is identified as "Project Officer: U.S. Army Amateur Rocket Program." Educating the populace in the principles of rocket building and ballistic flight, even at the risk of death or dismemberment, was worth it given the Soviet menace. Goddamn commies.

Estes rockets could be bought in small kits at hobby shops and were comprised of a cardboard tube, balsa wood fins, a plastic nose cone, and a tiny parachute. *The Sizzler. Rocket Red. Bandito. Black Hole.* Just the names of the rockets got the adrenaline of an eleven-year-old boy flowing. But reading them now, the names seem more appropriate for a lineup of dildos and vibrators at a local adult novelty store. The engines used to launch the rockets were essentially small firecrackers with a clay nozzle. The engine was put into a holder at the ass end of the cardboard tube – the rocket body. To light the engine, a small wire coated with trace amounts of flammable material was inserted into the nozzle of the motor and taped in place. Small clips were then affixed to the two ends of the igniter. These clips were themselves attached to wires that, if instructions were followed anyway, were supposed to terminate at a small plastic switch with a couple of AA batteries. When the button was pressed on the switch, a small current would flow through the wires to the igniter which would get hot, set aflame the coating deep in the nozzle, and then … "liftoff!" as the motor lit with a bright, brief *hiss*.

For reasons that are still not known to me, my father and I never used the plastic switch with its attendant safety features. A man who poured gasoline on campfires and charcoal grills wouldn't settle for such a candy-ass approach to launch systems. Instead, Dad showed me how to use what were, in effect, jumper cables to ignite the engine. He would pop open the hood of the motor home or car and show me how to touch the ends of the cables to each terminal on the car battery, telling me to be unafraid of the sparks that invariably jumped off the terminals. And because the nose of the car faced the launch pad, the operation was doubly perilous—my body faced the vehicle and the launch pad was behind me, so I had to blindly manipulate the wires while I looked over my shoulder to watch my rocket liftoff. It's amazing I didn't take an arm-numbing jolt every now and then. On the positive side, the current coming from the battery didn't just ignite the flammable substance on the igniter wire, it melted the entire wire. We rarely had unsuccessful ignition with such a robust (and unsafe) launch configuration.

While I loved the out-of-the-box rockets that Estes made, I loved to modify them as well. One idea Dad and I came up with involved an Estes rocket that had a clear compartment just under the nose cone where you could put a "payload." Advertisements for that particular rocket fired the imagination of boys and girls everywhere with ideas about what constituted a likely payload. Half the ideas had to do with insects and other life forms. You could put ants in it! Spiders! Even lizards! I can only imagine the uproar that would ensue at such suggestions today. Scientists would be seen in the press commenting on the trauma inflicted on these tiny creatures by model rocket g-forces which, truth be told, were quite dramatic.

Launching insects didn't give me a second of pause back then – and wouldn't today, come to think of it. I thought a ride on a rocket with an ant-tronaut inside was a far better fate than the alternative – either the ant rode as a payload, or my friends and I would use a magnifying glass to focus the sun's light into a scorching beam which we directed onto the unsuspecting insect until it vaporized in a tiny poof of smoke.

But alas, even in these more modern, enlightened times, the launching of insects still has a hold on the imagination of some Americans. A quick search on Amazon.com quickly brought me to the product page of the very rocket I used to launch. Called the *1960 Nova Payloader*, the item is 17.5 inches long, weighs less than three ounces, and looks identical to the craft I once built.

One 2009 review of the product caught my eye: "The plugs [at each end of the payload compartment] have holes in them where the hooks are cast. This means the bug you stick in there isn't going to die for lack of air. It also means you can't use ants, they'll get out. Medium ladybug is as small as you want to try." A ladybug might work I suppose, but in the universe of insects available doesn't it seem to be the least likely choice? They look so un-athletic and lethargic – the sloths of the bug world. I think a bad-ass praying mantis would make more sense. And praying is something that the insect rocket passenger would want to be capable of; the writer of the review goes on to note matter-of-factly that, "You could always seal the holes though." Apparently in this configuration, the insect-onaut is like one of those adventurous souls that volunteers to take a one-way mission to mars:

the ride will be a kick in the pants, but it will end in death. Oh well, progress cannot be made without sacrifice.

One idea my father and I had was to modify the rocket in a way that allowed us to put a flashlight bulb in the clear cargo compartment and then conduct night launches, something that (for reasons I still don't understand) was advised against in the code of safety for Estes rocket launches. We fashioned a balsa wood holder for the bulb, Dad soldered wires to the bottom of it, and then I ran those wires to a toggle switch on the nose cone that allowed us to turn the light on and off.

We went to a field behind the high school for our first launch. Rocket motors that seemed tame in the daylight became sparkle-trailing welding torches in the night. Watching the rocket streak skyward and then seeing the lightbulb bobbing in the night sky as it swung beneath the parachute brought a huge sense of satisfaction to me. You could see that bulb for miles. And there were times my rockets might have gone miles ... I frequently put engines in them that exceeded Estes safety recommendations. This may explain why, when I entered my design into a contest that Estes hosted, I never heard back from the company.

Today's *Model Rocket Safety Code* as detailed at the website of the National Association of Rocketry might as well be a list of items that my father and I did the opposite of when I was a kid. Rule number three says "Ignition system: I will launch my rockets with an electrical launch system ... [which] will have a safety interlock in series with the launch switch and will return to the 'off' position when released." No mention as to whether a little boy using jumper cables and bare hands to touch two wires to terminals on a car battery is a secondarily acceptable alternative.

Rule number six reads: "I will launch my rocket from a launch rod, tower, or rail ... and I will use a blast deflector to prevent the motor's exhaust from hitting the ground." All Estes rockets had a small soda straw glued to the side of the rocket body that the launch rod would slide through to guide the craft's initial four feet of flight and to ensure the rocket didn't blow over on the launch pad. The Estes version of a launch pad had three large plastic feet to stabilize it, the launch rod, and a metal disk that acted as the aforementioned blast deflector to keep the flame of launch from hitting the ground and starting a grass fire.

Of course, my father and I never used the launcher that Estes sold. Keeping with his fixation on the use of wood to solve all problems, our launcher was a block of pine with a rod pushed through a hole drilled into its center. When my rockets launched, the flame wasn't hitting a metal disk but was scorching a piece of flammable wood. Sometimes the turf around the launch pad would be smoldering post-liftoff and I'd rush to stamp out the burgeoning embers. It's a wonder we didn't burn down half of Houston; only the relentless humidity likely saved the nation's fourth largest city.

If my father wrote the Association of Model Rocketry rules they would have read very differently:

Launch – be sure jumper cables are long enough to reach your car battery. Ignore sparks as wires are applied to battery terminals. To avoid risk of electrical shock, DO NOT ATTEMPT TO EXECUTE LAUNCH BY TOUCHING WIRES TO BATTERY. Instead, have son touch wires to battery.

Launch Pad – ensure block of wood that serves as your blast deflector is large enough to a) catch fire, and/or b) deflect rocket flame and associated sparks across a larger radius of launch area terrain. DO NOT ATTEMPT TO STAMP OUT BRUSH FIRES ALONE. Instead, have son attack the flames with sneakers, pointing out glowing, hot areas from a safe distance.

Engine Use – when using rocket engines larger than manufacturer's recommended size, DO NOT STAND WITHIN FIFTEEN FEET OF LAUNCH PAD. Instead, have son conduct all hazardous operations inside the zone of death.

**

One thing about having an astronaut-aviator as a father is that he's likely to think that all things aviation-related are second nature to him. No need to read instructions or take lessons. "If I can fly a real airplane and a space shuttle, how hard can it be to fly a model airplane?" Hard to argue with that.

When I was in my teens, I bought a control-line airplane. These planes actually flew; they had small gas motors that turned a propeller to get them airborne. Two long wires about thirty or forty feet in length were attached to the plane and the opposite end of those wires were attached to what looked like the handle of a kitchen cabinet. The wires were the "control lines" that gave this type of toy its name and, when manipulated by the operator holding the handle, made the plane rise or descend. To "fly" the airplane the operator strung out the control line in a parking lot or field and had an accomplice start the engine. Then, holding the handle with the wires attached, the "pilot" started turning in place as the airplane became airborne and made circles around him, the control lines defining the radius of the circle. If you think watching racecars go around a track over and over again sounds boring, then this might be its airplane hobby equivalent. As with all my chosen hobbies, girls were not likely driving by and saying, "Who is that pimple-faced boy pirouetting in place as that super cool airplane goes around and around his head? I have to meet him!"

In 1982, when I was a freshman in high school, Dad joined me in my school's empty parking lot for my plane's inaugural flight. It was nearing sunset on a hot, breezy day. I bought the aircraft at the hobby store where I worked and where I spent every dime I made on inventory I was in charge of selling to others. I had had my eye on this plane for quite a while. (I should note for those born in the modern era that a "hobby store" in those times wasn't a phrase used to describe a place to buy bows, dried flowers, and oil paints. Back then, it referred to the sort of establishment where I worked: a small shop with plastic model airplanes and cars, remote control aircraft, model trains, and the like.)

I had many reservations about Dad and me going it alone when it came to the first flight of my plane. I was confident that I needed help to fly the model, but my father didn't share the same insecurity.

"I'm an astronaut for Christ's sake!" he said when I voiced my concern and suggested to him that he was no more knowledgeable than me and that maybe we should seek out some instruction.

"I don't need any instruction," he said with a bravado that made me believe him. I conceded; he would take the first turn flying the plane.

THE FATHER, SON, AND HOLY SHUTTLE

The late afternoon was still brutally hot and humid and a wind whipping across the parking lot brought no relief. I was sweating profusely. The sun was already turning into a visible disk on the western horizon, the thick air filtering the light to make it viewable with unprotected eyes. The air was so thick, in fact, that I thought the plane might levitate by itself as if supported by the moisture alone. Houston in the summertime – and it was summer nine months out of the year – was not hospitable.

Dad stood about thirty feet away from me, the control lines taut as I started the motor. I looked to him once the engine was running and he nodded at me like a pilot on an aircraft carrier giving the "ready to go" signal to the catapult operator. I liked that. It was cool. I released the plane and Dad started to turn in a circle to follow the aircraft as it began to pull itself forward. About a quarter of the way into its first rotation, I ran to join Dad at the center of the circle being traced by the plane. I was to learn at the foot of the master.

He kept the plane on the ground until I got to him so that he could build up some airspeed and I could see what he was doing. He had to speak with a shout; the motor was a very loud, high-pitched annoyance of a noise.

"Okay!" he shouted. "We're going to give it a little elevator!"

He was referring to the control surface on the airplane that made it go up or down. I watched his hand holding the handle attached to the control lines. He rotated the top of the handle up slowly which moved the elevator on the plane up.

"Steady!" he said to no one in particular. He was standing in place, turning himself in a circle as if he was trying to screw himself into the ground. I was behind him, hand on his shoulder, rotating with him. We must have looked like two strange figurines in a music box twirling as the music played.

At first the plane didn't respond, so Dad gave it a bit more elevator by rotating his hand further.

"C'mon goddamnit!" he said when it still didn't get airborne, sounding like one of the Doolittle raiders of *Thirty Seconds Over Tokyo* fame trying to coax a heavy bomber off an aircraft carrier in the Pacific.

For a moment, the model still didn't respond. Then, as it began its second rotation, while its nose was pointed into the brisk wind, it climbed with purpose into the air. Dad had adhered to a fundamental rule of aviation: always take off into the wind if you can; the extra airflow over the wing gives the plane lift at a lower ground speed so it can use a shorter runway. He *is* the master, I thought.

But the problem with a control line plane, we'd soon learn, is that it has to fly in a circle. The operator can't keep the nose pointed into the breeze to take advantage of that extra lift.

Dad continued to guide the plane higher and all looked well. But then, as the model turned in its prescribed arc, the wind that had a moment before been coming straight at its nose was now perpendicular to it, pushing up on the outer wing and forcing the plane to drift upward and toward us. At first, I thought Dad was still in command, that he was beginning an acrobatic maneuver to impress his son, illustrating to me his deftness when at the controls of any flying machine, large or small.

My wonder quickly turned to horror though. In an instant, I realized that things were not as they seemed.

The scene unfolded in slow motion as Dad and I watched the plane continue the momentum of its initial climb until it ran out of steam and rotated around its dipped wing, the wind still pushing the craft toward us. We were looking almost straight up now as the rotation of the plane stopped, its nose pointed squarely at us as the potential energy accumulated during its climb turned into the kinetic energy of a screaming dive. The control lines went slack as if the aircraft was breaking free of bondage and I suddenly felt like one of the toy soldiers I used to place on my bedroom floor to be strafed by an American fighter plane – we needed cover, and none was available. Despite the situation, I had confidence Dad could regain dominion over the renegade craft. He was an astronaut. He had flown more than a 130 combat missions in Vietnam. He had bailed out of an airplane as it crashed on a runway. Certainly, he had a plan to bring my beloved airplane back to the ground safely? Didn't he?

Apparently, I'm a glass-half-full kind of guy.

"Run!" he said as he dropped the handle and darted toward the high school.

That's your fucking plan? I thought.

He didn't grab my arm or throw his body on me. No effort was made to protect me, his progeny, responsible for propagating his genes into the next generation. I guess I shouldn't have been surprised. After all, this was the man who exposed me to the gas chamber that was the back of our VW when the throttle cable broke. This was a man who once had me lie on my back, unrestrained, to work some broken windshield wipers cables under the dash of a '57 Chevy while driving through a snowstorm. It was every man for himself.

I ran in the same direction as him, all the while thinking of the narrative of Herbert Morrison, a radio reporter who witnessed the explosion of the *Hindenburg* as it approached Lakehurst, NJ in 1937.

"Oh the humanity!" Morrison had exclaimed as people (the fortunate ones anyway) escaped the compartment under the burning dirigible and ran from the impact point. Thirty-five people on the Hindenburg died along with one person on the ground. My father and I were like those desperate passengers making an escape. Only our crashing vehicle was not a product of an ascending Nazi regime, it was likely made in China.

I heard behind me a sound like an incoming artillery shell, the Doppler effect causing the noise to get louder and higher pitched as the plane-turned-missile hurled to the ground behind us. At impact, the noise of the motor abruptly stopped and all I could hear was the shrapnel from the crash shoot past me as I ran, making discernable *whiffs* like bullets flying past.

When the noise and fury ended, my father and I stopped running and, chests heaving and hearts racing from a burst of adrenaline, turned to survey the damage. We both didn't speak for a few moments, soaking it all in, wondering how it all ended so fast. There wasn't a single piece of the plane that was identifiable.

I looked to my father who was staring at the impact point and then turned his gaze to the horizon, the soft glow of the setting sun making him look more like a rancher surveying his herd after a hard day of work than a man who had crushed his son's lame dream to fly a control line airplane.

He let out a long breath and we stood there in silence for a heartbeat.

"Should have gotten lessons," he said without a hint of remorse or irony.

If that dream girl of mine had been watching from a distance, I doubt she would have used the lofty words of Morrison as she watched me run, terrified, in my 1980s go-to outfit of short shorts, white sneakers, and knee-high tube socks. Instead, she would have said as I pushed my large, heavy glasses up my sweaty nose, "What a couple of nerdy assholes."

***

The hobby store I worked in and where I bought my control line airplane was owned by two men who worked in mission control at NASA. The shop was located in one of the ubiquitous strip malls all too common in the concrete jungle that Houston and its suburbs are. Whoever is in charge of zoning in Houston has a sick sense of humor; on one stretch of I-45 south of downtown on the way to Clear Lake City, the suburb I grew up in, it was possible to see an Evangelical Church flanked by a strip club and a liquor store. You could find Jesus, a lap dance, and a nip of whiskey all while parked in the same parking lot.

I loved working in the hobby shop. My days were filled with inventory management and helping customers who came through the door at a steady rate on the weekends. But when the store was empty, I'd browse the catalogs shipped from wholesalers and pick through the inventory on the shelves, making a mental list of what I'd buy next when I had saved enough money.

I could pick out the hobby a patron was into as soon as he (and they were always men or boys) pushed open the door with a small bell on it. Remote control (RC) airplane people often had pieces of a finger missing. The propellers on RC planes were just as dangerous as real ones and the nearly unbreakable nylon (vs. wood) props were particularly wicked; the material came to a knife-edge on the leading edge of the prop that was so sharp it would cut you deeply even if it wasn't spinning. When I asked a customer what I could help him with behind the counter, I never got used to seeing him point to a particular sized propeller with a nub.

Model car guys looked much more rugged than those into airplanes. They often wore Harley or NASCAR t-shirts and baseball caps and talked like the guy who ass-raped Ned Beatty in *Deliverance*. Where model airplane customers were likely business owners, oil execs, and lawyers, model car guys were mechanics, oilrig workers, and clients of lawyers. I liked them ... less pretentious than the plane guys, even though I considered myself an aircraft aficionado.

Train guys were introverts with glasses who obsessed over every detail of their setup. They looked down on other hobbyists as hacks who didn't understand, much less appreciate, the history of the miniature, fake machines they built. Train guys took forever to make a decision; they obsessed over which faux grass to use or which building to buy to top off their train set diorama in their basement or garage. Interestingly, given their penchant for authenticity, the model companies didn't sell buildings that looked like low-income housing or pieces of derelict chemical plants to place near the tiny tracks. Realism was carried only so far.

One day, a history teacher from my middle school came into the store. He was an odd fellow with black-rimmed glasses of the sort you saw in black and white photos of engineers who worked for IBM in the 1950s. He wore short sleeved button-down shirts with a tie and had a boyish face. I had seen him in the store every now and then and when he did come in, he gravitated to the books in a rack toward the back of the store where you could find nicely illustrated histories of all sorts of military equipment from planes to guns to tanks. He would take one of the books from the rack and lay it on the glass display in front of our balsa wood collection, put an elbow on the glass and prop up his chin on one hand while he leafed through the large-form paperback.

I had never seen him buy anything, but one day he arrived in the store and asked me to help him special order a book about tanks in Vietnam. Despite the fact that he knew me from the middle school and came in regularly, it was the first time he had ever said a word to me in the shop. I wondered if he was married and his wife shared his passion for multi-ton killing machines and jungle warfare, or if he just returned to a small apartment and watched documentaries on VHS tape while he drank a Pabst Blue Ribbon and polished his gun. He didn't wear a ring, so I suspected the latter.

Despite my own passion for military history and hobbies that revolved around it, I was perplexed by his curiosity about tanks from

Vietnam. It was one thing to be interested in that war – many were and it had ended only about fifteen years earlier – but it was a real niche interest (dare I call it a fetish?) to focus on the history of the use of tanks in that war. Given the terrain of the country, tanks were not that widely used in combat engagements. But who was I to judge? I wouldn't hang *Star Wars* X-Wing Fighters from the same part of my bedroom ceiling as my World War II airplanes because they came from historically different periods. Glasshouses and all that.

A few weeks after placing the order, I called him and told him his book had arrived. He was at the store almost immediately and I removed it from the packaging and handed it to him across the glass case. He opened the book gingerly to the first page and propped his chin on his hand, elbow on the glass, assuming the position he always did. I walked away to stock some shelves. Nobody else was in the store; my co-worker had gone to lunch.

I thought I heard him say something to me and moved toward him to see what he needed but then realized he was talking to himself. I went back behind the glass to take on another task and at first could only hear whispers. Then the words became clearer. I stole glances at him as he spoke, but he was unaware of my espionage. He seemed to be in a sort of trance.

"Oh *yeah*," he said as he flipped the page to a picture of a tank with four large turrets protruding from behind a protective steel plate.

"Look at the *tits* on that thing ..." his voice trailed off.

Then, like a child, he puffed out his cheeks slightly, pursed his lips partially, clenched his teeth, and started making sounds mimicking what he imagined the gun might have sounded like.

Chung...chung...chung. Spit sprayed the glass counter.

I started to move away. He turned the page again. Another picture, this one of a larger tank. Its single large turret was captured at the moment it fired, showing a flash of flame escaping the muzzle. Another rush of testosterone hit his system.

"*Fuck yeah* ..."

If he didn't have both hands visible, I would have worried he was playing with *his* gun. I moved further away.

He leafed through every page of that book over about forty minutes, never changing his position. When he was done, he put the book gently back into the plastic sleeve, placed that back in the packaging, and left the store, holding the box like a baby to his chest.

CHAPTER 3: MY IMAGINARY MOB BOSS

Mom's dad, Joseph Sei (whom we called "Joe Joe"), was a mountain of a man to me – in both the literal and figurative sense. He was a good six feet tall, much bigger than my father, with a firm but not-too-large belly. He had a full head of silver hair well into his seventies and warm, dark eyes that often flashed a twinkle that hinted at a mischievous soul. Of northern Italian descent, he wasn't as dark skinned as those from Sicily were, but he retained enough of the Mediterranean tanning gene to soak up the high-altitude sun of Albuquerque. He was perpetually brown. He spoke and understood Italian and the gold chain around his wrist made him look like a sensitive mob boss when he drove around town in his yellow Lincoln Towncar, the yellow leather interior reflecting the sun from all angles making him look even more brown than he otherwise would.

He never wore a seatbelt and also never used a turn signal. Changing lanes without use of a blinker wouldn't have been so bad if he made even a weak attempt to look to his left or right before changing lanes. But he didn't even do that. I sat terrified on the front bench seat as he drifted across the dashed white lines, the car swaying as if dancing a waltz to the elevator music he always played on the radio … *and one two three, one two three* ….

The drivers around us didn't appreciate his vehicular choreography. Invariably, angry honks were part of every outing with Joe Joe. As the honking horns and livid shouts of other drivers assaulted us, I held on to the door handle for dear life. Joe Joe kept the yellow leather so slick with Amor All, I was like a fried egg on a non-stick pan; a turn to the right would send me sliding across the bench seat into Joe Joe if I wasn't securely strapped in.

When somebody did dare to critique Joe Joe's driving skills by jamming the heel of their palm into the center of their wheel, he'd shout in the direction of the horn noise.

"*Pendejo!*" he would yell, convinced that the other party was at fault for not having yielded to the king of the road. The Spanish insult translates literally to "pubic hair" but I always thought it just meant "asshole." In any case, it wasn't nice, and in a town where Spanish was spoken as often as English, those he shouted at almost certainly knew what he was saying.

I was always perplexed by the fact that when he did hurl the epithet, he *did* have the time and energy to turn his head in the direction of the offended driver, which left me wondering, why not just turn your head *before* changing lanes to ensure the coast is clear and avoid all the trouble? Logic was not Joe Joe's strong suit. In today's world of road rage, particularly in central New Mexico where everybody seems to be high on meth and toting a revolver (*Breaking Bad* was set there for a reason), Joe Joe would have needed his imaginary mob minions to protect him.

My grandmother, Amy Sei, we called Nonnie, a bastardization of the word "nonna," Italian for grandmother. Like Joe Joe, Nonnie was 100% Italian and, also like him, she was out of central casting. It was easy to imagine her in a De Niro movie, the wife of a mob boss pretending to be oblivious to the secret life of her husband, the smoke from her cigarettes carrying away the anxiety that came with being so close to danger. It was easy to imagine because Nonnie *was* a chain smoker, killing two packs of cigarettes a day while she read dime store mystery novels at her kitchen table while wearing horn-rimmed glasses connected to a chain that wrapped around the back of her neck.

My mother was a woman who liked convenience above all else when it came to preparing meals, significantly limiting her culinary repertoire. The same was not true of Joe Joe. He loved to make and eat food. As a boy growing up in the 70s and 80s, this was always confusing to me. It was rare to see a man with a pot handle in one hand, a wooden spoon in another, and dishtowel over his shoulder, stirring up a dinner dish while his wife sat at a table not three feet from him smoking, drinking, snacking, and reading. My confusion didn't keep me from eating what he made though. He knew what he was doing.

One thing my mother did inherit from Joe Joe was his OCD. He had a place for everything. His garage looked like a retail shop: rakes and other yard implements hung on hooks organized left to right by descending lengths of their handles, tools in drawers laid out like surgical instruments, and a freezer packed with foods categorized by type. If the zombie apocalypse ever came, I always thought that being trapped in Joe Joe's garage would have been fortuitous. He even had a BB gun that could be used to scare off the flesh-eating half-humans.

I loved to visit both sets of my grandparents who lived about thirty minutes from each other in Albuquerque. My mom's parents lived in a Spanish-styled white adobe home with arched doors and a slanted red-tile roof. It had a decidedly old-world, Mediterranean style and even included a walled courtyard with a redbrick floor. In contrast, my dad's parents lived in a flat-roofed mid-century modern home with a stylized two-sided fireplace and a lot of windows. Full of open spaces, it was ideal for a man in a wheelchair.

The homes matched the personalities of their occupants: Joe Joe and Nonnie the throwbacks to a different era, Grandma and Pop Pop the modern progressives. This difference was abundantly obvious in areas related to race. I never once heard Pop Pop or Grandma say a derogatory word about a class of people based on their skin color – in fact, if anything, I heard them denounce those who harbored racism in any form. Dad said that his childhood was conspicuously devoid of any racial slurs or other commentary that might have been common among a white couple born in the twenties and living in the mid-sixties. My own mother and father never noted race. Joe Joe, on the other hand ...

The first time I heard racial slurs they were on television – Alex Haley's *Roots* came out in 1977 and Dad made us watch it. But the first time I ever heard a slur "live," it was from Joe Joe. He would use all manner of slurs; even the n-word was pulled out every now and then. It's always been surprising to me that I should have been introduced to such language by my own grandfather and in a place like Albuquerque, where Joe Joe was likely a minority himself given the large Hispanic population. Interestingly, I hadn't been broadly exposed to these things in south Texas – at least not with regularity. In Houston, one of my best friends was Jewish and so I heard others call him names. I also heard the terms "fag" and "homo," but they were general taunts not necessarily directed at somebody who was gay. While these epithets were horrible in their own right, the use of the more common racial slurs I had first come to know through TV was relatively rare.

Joe Joe always laughed nervously when he used a slur in front of me, like a child secretly getting away with something he knew he shouldn't. I don't know if it's because he was subconsciously uncomfortable given my age or if he knew my father would confront him if he heard. I had reasons to suspect the latter theory played a part. Joe Joe once called me a "pecker-head" in front of my friends, causing them all to laugh as my shoulders slumped and my head dropped in shame. Dad had overheard Joe Joe's insult and immediately pulled him aside. As the laughter of my friends died, I glanced toward Dad and Joe Joe in a huddle a short distance away. I could tell that Dad was reprimanding my grandfather. I could also tell from the body language and some lip-reading that while Joe Joe didn't apologize, he was nonetheless cowed. That episode made it obvious to me that Joe Joe was uninterested in being called out by Dad and, in fact, it was one of the only times I'd seen Joe Joe even a bit intimidated.

Joe Joe didn't reserve his brand of racism to the African American community. This was demonstrated time and again by the simplicity of a wrong number dialed. In an age before cell phones and speed dial, it was relatively common for somebody to misdial a phone number. Like any random citizen at the end of a phone line, Joe Joe received his share of mistakenly dialed digits. Several times while on visits to Albuquerque as youngsters, my sisters and I would be relaxing in Nonnie and Joe Joe's T.V. room when the phone rang. Joe Joe would pull himself out of his Lay-z-boy with a grunt and walk to the wall-mounted phone, his breath coming heavy and annoyed.

"Hello?" I'd hear him answer.

"Hello?" he said again when nobody spoke at the other end of the line.

"Hello?" This time he was louder and more agitated.

At this point the line went dead as the dialer realized he'd reached the wrong home. Joe Joe, though, was clearly not a student of the principle known as Occam's Razor. That principle is this: among competing hypothesis, the one with the fewest assumptions should be selected. Said another way, the simplest explanation is likely the right one. But Joe Joe refused to believe that the dialer at the other end of the line had made an innocent mistake. The call had been an intentional attempt to force Joe Joe from his chair as he watched *M*A*S*H* or *Cheers*, his two favorite shows. More interestingly, the call was a conspiracy among a whole culture of people.

"Goddamn Mexicans!" he yelled as he slammed down the receiver.

I remember being confused by this and asking, "Joe Joe, how do you know it's the Mexicans?" The question was an innocent one from an innocent child. A question from somebody who was a believer in Occam's Razor, even though I didn't have a clue that my logic had a name for it.

He didn't answer directly. He looked at me briefly through his wire-rimmed bifocals, angered at my question, and then plopped back down in his Lay-z-boy. "Damn Mexicans," he said as his ass hit the seat.

I remained confused as to how he could possibly know the ethnicity of the caller. It seemed to me a wrong number was a much more likely explanation than an insanely more complicated conspiracy theory. Did Mexicans around the greater Southwest coordinate with each other, taking turns to call Joe Joe every other day or so? If so, why? Maybe it was because he had cut one too many of them off while driving his boat of a car? And maybe when that happened, they had finally gotten fed up with being called "pubic hairs" in Spanish, nearly losing control of their vehicles as they rushed to cover the ears of their children? I suppose we can never be sure, but I'm going with the simplest explanation.

***

At around the same time I was learning about Mexicans targeting Joe Joe, my father and his brother, Mark, invited Amy, Laura, and me on an exciting canoe trip down the Rio Grande River, which travels north to south down the center of New Mexico. The plan was to have Joe Joe drive Uncle Mark's truck, transporting all of us and Uncle

Mark's canoe to Cochiti Dam, an earthen fill dam about sixteen miles due south of Los Alamos. There, we would put into the water and drift twenty-five miles further south on one of America's most famous rivers until we reached Bernalillo just north of Albuquerque, where Joe Joe would pick us up.

On a morning in September, we loaded ourselves into the truck and headed north, paralleling the Rio Grande River. So much of my interest in the world and the wonders of it were stoked in the Rio Grande valley and the stories Dad told me about it. During the Paleozoic period, virtually everything I saw that early fall morning was under a warm sea teeming with life. During the Jurassic period, it was home to dinosaurs right out of the picture books I read when not drawing airplanes. Stegosaurus, Tyrannosaurus, and Allosaurus roamed the land I now visited as a child. With the coming of the Ice Age, Mastodons lumbered about the valley in the shadow of the Sandia Mountains.

As we made our way further north, I looked to the west of Albuquerque over the Rio Grande – its location given away by a green ribbon of Cottonwood trees cutting through the tan desert – and could see the cones of dormant volcanoes that were evidence of significant geological activity. That activity was related to one of the few still-active geological rifts in the world: the Rio Grande rift. A geological feature created by tectonic plates moving apart in areas where the earth's crust is thinning, the rift cutting through New Mexico caused a depression in the land that encouraged water runoff from the surrounding higher elevations to gather into a single water way, the Rio Grande.

Deserts where an ocean used to be! Exploding volcanoes! Dinosaurs and Mastodons! The earth's crust thinning! Dad told me of all these things in my visits to the wondrous land where he and my mother grew up. Drives with him on our many adventures when visiting New Mexico would unwittingly become the seeds that grew into an intense curiosity about how the world worked and my own place in it. But more than feeding the typical childhood curiosities of a boy my age, the stories my dad told me and his prompts asking me to use my mind to picture the area tens of thousands to millions of years ago (*Pat, imagine being chased by a T-Rex along the Rio Grande!*), drove home to me at a very early age how small I was, how large the universe was, and how the two were connected together.

When we finally arrived at Cochiti Dam and got out of the car, I ran to the edge of a steep hill that looked over the spillway, excitement building in me as I looked down upon swiftly moving water cleaving the land. Amy and Laura appeared as enthusiastic as me. The water below us hinted at a trip that would be the equivalent of a twenty-five-mile version of Splash Mountain, the ride at Disneyland which whisked tourists along rapidly moving waterways, culminating in an acceleration down a steep hill into a "splash zone."

Uncle Mark had sought and received permission from a local official for us to cross through Indian reservations during our journey. On the stretch of river we'd be navigating, we'd pass through the Sandia and the San Felipe reservations and through numerous native American pueblos. With that permission in hand, we took the canoe from the truck, said good-bye to Joe Joe, made our way down to just beneath the spillway of the dam, and put into the water. Dad, paddle in hand, took point and Uncle Mark would manage the rear. Amy, Laura, and I sat between them.*

We pushed away and waved to Joe Joe who slowly walked back to the truck parked above us on the side of the road. It was early but dead calm and the sun was already warming us as we rounded a bend in the river, Dad and Mark only having to steer the boat with their paddles as the current's speed whisked us along. Amy, Laura and I were enjoying the ride, talking excitedly as people do when beginning an adventure into the relative unknown. It wasn't quite Splash Mountain, but our journey was shaping up to be a different kind of thrill – how many of our friends got to do something as cool as this? How many got to ride along a geological rift through wilderness punctuated by Indian reservations? We settled into the well of the canoe relaxed and happy,

---

* Later in life while reminiscing about the trip, I asked Dad how five of us fit in a standard aluminum canoe. Dad responded, "Well, you kids were small." Note to self: if your three children are so small that they don't overburden a canoe with two adults on board, then maybe the kids are a bit too small to be on the water for a twenty-five-mile voyage through wilderness in the first place.

hoping that this adventure would be much less traumatic than another one we had been on earlier in our very short lives...

***

On a visit to the Grand Tetons in Wyoming one year when Amy and I were around eight and Laura five, Dad made camp near a beautiful, meandering, and shallow stream. The land around it was flat and sparsely wooded with young pines. Dad got it into his head that it would be fun and relaxing to float down the stream in the brilliant sunshine that was shooting through the branches of the trees in warm, bright slices. Since the land along the shore was flat and easy to walk through, the thinking went, we could float for a while and then paddle to shore and walk back to our camp. The only problem? We had no raft or canoe. Problem solved: Dad decided we could simply use the thin, inflatable mattresses we put between the hard ground and our sleeping bags as our flotation devices.

When Dad suggested this, I had a slight jolt of reservation. Aren't sleeping pads for padding your sleep? But any worry I had passed quickly. Already in my very short life, I had come to see that Dad was not a guy to let perfect be the enemy of "good enough." Lost your gas cap to your RV? A redwood facsimile wasn't ideal, but it worked. Throttle cable on your VW broken? Sure, you could call a tow truck, but why do that when you've got a perfectly capable child to act as a throttle? In any case, the water was like a swimming pool given the benign nature of the current. And more importantly, as Mullanes, we had to know what was around the bend in the river about fifty yards downstream. How could we sleep that evening in our inexpensive tents not knowing what wonders lay beyond? So, it was decided.

After getting on our bathing suits, Amy and I waded into the stream dragging our pads behind us, cautiously walking over the smooth rocks beneath the surface, shivering slightly as the sting of the cold water bit our ankles. Once near the center of the stream where the water was deep enough to ensure we wouldn't bottom-out, we slid onto our pads belly-first and began to drift. Dad had put Laura, much smaller than Amy and me, on his pad and was holding onto the edge of it as he walked toward the center of the stream and in the direction of the current, pulling her along, trying to keep us in sight. As we began to put distance between our little armada and the camp, Mom waved to us from the shore with her usual — and always necessary — "Be careful!"

Things were progressing just fine as Amy and I approached a bridge built over the clear mountain water. But I noticed that the current had accelerated considerably, and I began to use my hands to position my ersatz watercraft so that it would glide between the stanchions supporting the span. Amy did the same. As we approached the shadow of the bridge and glided beneath it, the water around the stanchions confirmed what I had sensed a moment before — the current was much swifter and water much deeper than it had been when we had put in near our campsite. Water piled into a little ridge at the front of the piers and then swiftly streaked away on either side. As I passed under the bridge, I felt my tiny craft accelerate into a stretch of water that looked suddenly more menacing. Like a theme park attraction meant to lull its riders into complacency before springing a spine-tingling surprise on them, the placid stream suddenly became, to my mind anyway, a raging river with Class-V rapids.*

As Amy and I accelerated, we heard Dad shouting just as we were about to be carried around the bend in the river, the river that two minutes before was an ambling stream. I looked back and saw that he was standing in the water under the bridge, leaning into the current as he held Laura with one arm. My little sister was shrieking in terror, her limbs flailing about as if she were trying to find terra firma in the air around her. It was clear what had happened, even from a distance; they had hit one of the piers and she had fallen from the raft. Dad had grabbed her before she was swept away and was now fighting the current and slimy rocks under foot to make it back to the shore.

---

* The International Scale of River Difficulty classifies whitewater rapids into one of six categories. Class-I rapids are defined as "fast moving water with riffles and small waves" containing "few obstructions" all of which are "easily missed with little training" with low risk to swimmers and where "self-rescue is easy." Class-V rapids, on the other hand, are "extremely long, obstructed, and/or very violent rapids which expose a paddler to added risk where "scouting is recommended but may be difficult" and "swims are dangerous" making rescue difficult "even for an expert." Class-VI rapids are essentially waterfalls.

Walking was clearly a struggle though since Laura was not an inert mass, her weight shifting and sliding down his body as she continued her terrified struggle. Dad was yelling over Laura's screams but the sound of water rushing over nearby rocks now filled my ears making it hard to hear him. But it didn't matter. He looked panicked. I could tell what he was saying without hearing a word of it. He was screaming for Amy and me to get to shore, *NOW!!!*

We didn't need to be told twice. We put both arms into the water and wheeled them around like the paddles on a Mississippi paddle boat at a frothy "full speed ahead." I stole a glance back as I paddled and saw that Dad was now running along the shore, trying to keep up with us. But giving chase proved to be very difficult. The change in the land along the banks, not surprisingly, mimicked the change in the water. Where once there were flat, pine needle-laden expanses between widely separated tree trunks, there were now large rocks sprinkled about between more closely spaced trees, the ground between them filled with tangles of exposed roots. Dad looked like he was navigating an obstacle course back at West Point. I notice in my quick look that Laura was not with him. I wondered in a flash where she was and had a sudden pang of terror at the thought that she might have ultimately been swept away. Was Dad asking Amy and me to save ourselves so he could race down river and retrieve Laura from the water? I began to regret all the times I'd made fun of my little sister. She would drown in Wyoming before I got a chance to really *know* her.

After several anus-puckering moments, Amy made it to the same side of the river as Dad. I had been closer to the right bank and so had pulled myself and my "raft" onto a large rock opposite the water from Amy, feeling both amped and exhausted. As I looked across the white water, I saw Dad hugging Amy and then holding her apart from him at the shoulders so as to give her a good inspection, ensuring she was okay. They began walking upstream and I followed them from the opposite shore. Laura was waiting on the shore near the bridge where she had fallen into the water. After several minutes of trekking, I was back at our camp and Mom smiled at me as I approached. Quickly though her smile fell off her face, worry chasing it away.

"Where's Dad and your sisters?" she asked, probably seeing the remnants of my own fear on my face. I just pointed across the river.

Dad, Amy and Laura were coming abreast of the camp and began to walk across the stream back to our outpost. As they got closer, Mom could see in Laura and Amy the look of children that had just had the life scared out of them, like wagon train travelers who had just passed through the gates of a fort after running a gauntlet of arrows.

Mom gave an exasperated sigh. "Michael! What did you do now?" she shouted at Dad.

"It gets a bit rougher around the bend," he said matter-of-factly, as if he were a military cartographer reporting back to a superior.

Mom just shook her head. But at least we knew what was around the bend.

***

Back on the Rio Grande, my mind was shocked alert by the honking of a car horn. At first, I – along with Dad, Uncle Mark, and my sisters – was confused. Once we had floated away from the dam and made a lazy turn, we were in the boonies. There was no evidence of any road nearby. There was no evidence of anything nearby. Then, we saw a pickup truck speeding along the desert floor paralleling the Rio Grande, dodging piñon trees as it threw up dust and bounced violently over scrub brush and small rocks. Leaning out the side of the passenger window was an old, silver-haired man.

Joe Joe?

"You stupes! You stupes!" Joe Joe was shouting a made-up insult – he had turned the adjective stupid into a noun, stupe. I had been called a "stupe" a million times. What was confusing wasn't the silly word though. It was this: why in the world was Joe Joe in the passenger seat of a pickup truck driven by a stranger following us down a river just to hurl insults our way?

"You took the keys! You stupes! You took the goddamn keys!" *Ohhhhh...* We had sailed away with the keys to Mark's truck. And since Mark's truck was Joe Joe's only mode of transportation back to Albuquerque and to our collection point in Bernalillo twenty-five miles downriver – that was a major problem.

"I left them in the car!" Mark shouted back. Even as he said it, he doubted himself and I could see him patting his shirt and pants pockets. "Damn," he said as he reached into his shirt pocket and pulled them out.

THE FATHER, SON, AND HOLY SHUTTLE

We paddled to shore and Joe Joe greeted us. Well, "greeted" might not be the right word. He chastised us, ripping the keys from Uncle Mark's hands.

"You *pendejo!*" he said as he approached Mark on the shore.

He told us that when he realized that he didn't have a way to start Mark's truck, he had enlisted the help of a bystander to chase us down the river. I wondered what the chances were that the guy who had rescued Joe Joe had once been the object of his insults on a New Mexican road?

After making the handoff, we watched the pickup truck disappear in the direction from which it had come moments before and settled into the canoe, alone on the great Rio Grande.

"I wonder how fast we are going?" Dad asked Uncle Mark shortly thereafter as the current took hold of us again. After some back and forth, they settled on about ten to fifteen miles-per-hour. At that speed, they estimated, we'd be in Bernalillo in about two hours. We all agreed it was a splendid way to spend part of our morning on a beautiful fall day.

Almost as soon as the pickup truck that had ferried Joe Joe to us disappeared though, our speed began to slow as the river grew surprisingly wider. The first hint that we had slowed was the absence of a breeze over our skin brought on by our forward velocity through the crisp air. We began to feel the heat, the radiation from the sun pricking our skin like photonic darts shot from 93 million miles away. Amy, Laura, and I were in shorts and t-shirts. No hats were on our heads. It was getting warm. Thankfully, just as I was noticing the warmth, the river got narrower and deeper again and we accelerated. But we were still going more slowly than we had when we put into the water in the shadow of the dam, and so I began to contemplate taking a refreshing dip. A peak over the gunwale revealed a dark green-blue water with the bottom barely discernible through its crystalline clarity, a perfect spot for a quick swim. Then, Mark pointed off to our right. "I wonder what those guys are doing?" he said.

I looked in the direction of his finger. In a lovely shaded area along shore we could see about twenty Native American teens, most of them shirtless boys in shorts and swim trunks. I started to raise my hand to wave at them. But just as I was about to, around ten to fifteen of them ran into the Rio Grande as if they were starting a triathlon, kicking up white foam like stallions fording a river on a cattle drive. Once the water became deep enough, they started to swim toward us.

"What the hell are they doing?" Dad asked. I assumed the question was rhetorical. I had no idea what they were doing. To the extent we could see their faces, they didn't seem to have smiles. They looked menacing.

"What the hell are they doing?" Uncle Mark repeated as the boys closed in on us. I began to wonder if we had any documentation granting us permission to pass through the reservation we were likely now entering. Recalling that uncle Mark had sought permission for us to pass through Indian land on our journey, I suddenly wondered: how did we know the guy he talked to had the authority to grant permission? How did we know that he was even representative of the reservation? Maybe he was just some dude collecting $20 for a "trespass fee." Had we been duped? And even if he was the right guy, how in the world did he get word out to the residents of several reservations and pueblos along a twenty-five mile stretch of water to let them know that white men would be passing through and, most importantly, that we came in peace? As a young child who was a fan of old westerns made in a time when cultural sensitivities were virtually non-existent, my mind raced, and I wondered if smoke signals might have been employed.

"Let's start paddling," Dad said with an urgency in his voice that worried me a little. But the faster Dad and Uncle Mark paddled, the faster the probable marauders swam. I thought of *The Lone Ranger* television series – the closest thing to educational content about Native Americans I had ever consumed – and in that moment I wished desperately we had Tonto with us so that he could let his people know in his throaty voice, that we, "come, not seeking war, but to admire beauty of native lands." I imagined him sweeping his arm across the horizon as he spoke, each word ending with a sort of grunt that characterized the diction of all Native American English speakers from Hollywood.

"Be ready to pop those guys on the heads with your paddle if they try to tip us," Uncle Mark said, his voice showing a level of worry elevated above the baseline set earlier by Dad. I hadn't considered the possibility of being tipped. But of course, that was a danger. Once they got to the boat, what else could they do but reach up and latch on to the sides of our canoe?

The boys continued to gain on us, and our trepidation amplified exponentially. I half expected to see burning arrows fly from the foliage along the bank, the distraction of the boys making us easy targets. Poor Laura had survived a near drowning on the rafting trip in the shadow of the Tetons only to now be taken as a child slave, growing up in a teepee and eating buffalo jerky. Then, as a line of them came within a few feet of the boat, they stopped, treaded water, and started to excitedly ask questions about where we had started and where we were going.

They weren't Native Americans intent on driving us from their land. They were normal boys just like me who had seen the novelty of a canoe of five paddling by and wondered, "What the hell are those guys doing?"

We told them our plan, impressing them with our stated goal. "That's so cool," one of them said in an almost southern California "surfer dude" intonation. With that, my emotions moved from a foundation of fear to one of pride. Presumably, they knew this land better than us, yet my Dad and his brother had, like Lewis and Clark, set out on a grand adventure despite their lack of knowledge. If only I knew how uninformed we were.

We waved goodbye to our new admirers as they turned to swim back to their picnic on the shore. In the excitement, I hadn't noticed how much hotter it had become. The river was at about 5,000 feet altitude which put a good percentage of the earth's protective atmosphere beneath us, so the intensity of the UV rays was pronounced. My skin had already taken on the hue of a blushed cheek.

"Dad," Laura said, "it's really hot." Dad looked to us and could see that we were roasting. A reflective aluminum canoe didn't help our cause. Its concave shape made it like a floating Easy Bake oven – the light bounced off of the inside of the hull and cooked us in areas that usually didn't see the sun. The underside of our arms and bottoms of our legs were not spared. Dad took off his shirt and handed it to Laura so that she could fashion it into keffiyeh, Lawrence of Arabia style, or drape it over her legs. He now was totally exposed. We had no sunscreen. Why would we need that for a short float down a river in September?

As our journey continued, the river once again got wider, shallower, and slower. While I don't think we knew it at the time, the Rio Grande only drops about 200 feet in altitude from the Cochiti dam to Bernalillo. That's just a drop of eight feet every mile of our route. And given how swiftly we had moved early in our expedition, I wouldn't be surprised if 199 feet of that drop had occurred in the first 100 yards beyond the dam. The Rio Grande was less a river between Cochiti and Bernalillo than it was a very long, very thin lake. A lake with virtually no water in it.

About an hour after Joe Joe had left us, my peeks over the side showed the bottom coming into clearer relief rapidly until ... we bottomed out.

"Goddamnit," Dad said.

"You communist," Uncle Mark added, imputing a political affiliation to the river.

"Get out kids," Dad said with a sigh. We dutifully rose and stepped over the gunwale into the ankle-deep water. I was mildly concerned about getting out of the boat. Those *Lone Ranger* episodes along with installments of *Gilligan's Island*, seemed to have too many storylines that included quicksand slowly dragging a villain to his early death. It was one of those irrational fears of the sort that every kid has, but it was as real to me then as the fact that dinosaurs once roamed the rift that created the river we were on.

"On" was the right word. We literally were walking on top of the Rio Grande. Dad and Uncle Mark had each grabbed a cross bar on the canoe and lifted it to continue our trek south, hoping to find deeper water. And by deeper, I mean a lot deeper. We were traipsing through no more than three inches of the Rio Grande – in fact, calling it the Rio Grande seemed like a cruel joke. There wasn't a single thing *grande* about it. Rio Seca or Rio Árido (the dry or arid river) seemed much more appropriate. Frustration in our party started to grow. Amy, Laura, and I began to complain. The knowledge that we'd be suffering through blisters formed by the third-degree sunburns we were getting certainly didn't help.

After about a quarter mile, the water became deeper and we got into the boat again. But there was still virtually no current. The canoe became as silent as a lifeboat full of shipwreck survivors lost in the vast Pacific. Dad and Uncle Mark spoke sparingly and when they did, it was usually a profanity-infused rant about the stupidity of the idea to "float" down the Rio Grande or a quick, terse phrase such as, "River my ass!"

Amid these intermittent outbursts, Laura spoke.

"Dad, I gotta pee," she said a bit sheepishly. In the annals of the Mullane family, nobody had to piss as much as my younger sister. We were constantly stopping the car or leaving a movie so that she could piddle a few drops into a toilet or the desert sand. I was convinced that the back of her throat was connected directly to her urethra; moisture she swallowed just flowed straight through her.

"Seriously?" Dad said, frustrated. "Laura, we were just walking for twenty minutes. Couldn't you have gone then?"

"I didn't have to go then," she replied. Of course. She never had to go "then."

The bank was not conducive to an easy shore landing and, besides, at this point Dad just wanted to keep moving. So, he decided to hang Laura's ass over the edge of the canoe and let her piddle in the water. After she had removed her shorts and underwear, Dad got low in the boat to bring his center of gravity close to the deepest part of the hull and then grabbed Laura under the armpits. Lifting her carefully, he placed the back of her thighs on the edge of the boat.

She screamed.

"It's hot!" she said in a long agonizing whine. The exposed metal of the boat was like a left-on iron.

"Goddamnit," Dad said as he strained to hold her above the edge, her weight a challenge given the absence of a firm surface for him to find a sturdy base. Just as Laura started to go, Amy pointed to the water near an outcropping of rocks, her arm snapping so smartly I thought she might have dislocated her elbow.

"A snake!" she shrieked.

Dad was incredulous.

"Damnit Amy, there's no snake," he said sharply, clearly annoyed at having to accommodate Laura's constant need to urinate while in a boat he had carried half the trip, without a shirt on, under a crystal-clear sky and blazing sun, at 5,000 feet altitude. He was not in a good mood.

"A snake!" Amy repeated again.

"Goddamnit Amy! There's no –" He cut himself short and fell back into the boat with my half-clothed, five-year-old sister on top of him. "Jesus Christ!" he exclaimed. "There *is* a snake!"

He and Uncle Mark manned their paddles and stroked furiously to put distance between us and the reptile. After we were safely away from the likely harmless animal (while there are poisonous snakes in New Mexico, there are no poisonous water snakes), we all burst into laughter. What idiots we were.

Just fifteen minutes later, though, nobody was laughing. Again, we had to get out of the boat and carry it. The expedition was turning into something more harrowing than that of Lewis and Clark. At least they had provisions and their incredible guide, Sacagawea. We had a couple of canteens of water, some granola bars, and two guides – Dad and Uncle Mark – who didn't know shit about the river that would probably kill us all. The journey had become a fusion of the Shackleton Expedition and the Bataan Death March. With each arcing bend in the river (or dry bed that was supposed to be a river), we wondered, will we see the bridge at Bernalillo this time? But alas, each cruel turn just revealed another turn in the opposite direction.

Finally, about six hours after we started, the bridge came into view. We cheered and hugged each other as if we *were* the five men with Shackleton that crested the mountains on South Georgia Island after sailing 800 miles to reach civilization and secure rescue for his crew stranded in the Antarctica. We were *that* happy. We dragged the boat ashore and Dad walked up the slope to go to a gas station where he used a pay phone to call Joe Joe, who showed up about forty minutes later.

When we were all loaded into Uncle Mark's truck, we told Joe Joe of our harrowing journey – of the "attack" by the "hostile" Indians; of the need to carry our boat for long stretches; of the snake that almost bit Laura on the ass; of the sunburns we'd gotten for lack of sunscreen or proper clothing and hats. Joe Joe just sat in his seat with a coy grin on his face, shaking his head slowly.

"You stupes," he said.

CHAPTER 4: GETTING LUCKY

We left England in December of 1973 when I was five years old. Dad was going to attend the Air Force Institute of Technology at Wright-Patterson AFB in Dayton, Ohio to get his engineering graduate degree. I remember being excited to leave simply because I got to ride on an airplane.

Dayton was the home of the Wright Brothers, the bicycle shop owners whose tinkering led to the first "heavier than air" flying machine. It was strange to realize that if not for their tinkering, I would never have lived in Dayton. After all, the only reason I was there was because my father was an Air Force officer flying much heavier than air machines.

Technology had progressed at a blistering pace since the Wright's first flight. In 1903, the Wright Flyer made it to an altitude of about 10 feet and a speed of about 7 mph. My father was flying F-4 Phantoms in England that could get to 1,400 mph and over 50,000 feet altitude. Orville and Wilber had let the flight genie out of the bottle and those that came after them made innovation after innovation as if the sky would run out of air to keep their inventions aloft.

We moved into the Huber Heights suburb of Dayton. Our home was a non-descript two-story with a large backyard demarcated by a chain-link fence that tied into a network of other such fences. These barriers were very Midwestern in nature; they politely said to others, "this is my property," but not in the exclusionary way a six-foot, wooden privacy fence might. Dayton was on the eastern edge of the

Midwest and therefore had exciting times in the spring when cold air rushing over the Rockies and into the great plains would collide with warm, moist air moving north from the Gulf of Mexico and spawn enormous thunderstorms that often brought tornadoes with them.

In April of 1974, the warning sirens were blaring as storms approached from the southwest. It was my earliest memory of my father grabbing his camera to try and capture a tornado on film. He loved thunderstorms and an embedded tornado was his white whale. And he was the picture of Ahab, standing in the open as the storm approached, leaning into the wind, his shirt stretched tight across his chest and flapping behind him, his camera at the ready and a defiant look across his face as large drops of rain hammered him, hitting his skin with a heavy crack. But if Dad was Ahab, Mom was the nagging seaport beer wench, yelling at her petulant sailor.

"Damnit Michael!" she shouted from the back stoop as Dad repositioned himself, running further away from the house to see more of the horizon. "Get in here! What the hell are you doing!? Are you trying to get killed?!"

"Donna stop worrying!" he replied. "I can see what's coming. If there is an issue, I'll run into the house. I'm not going to get killed." He said it as if annoyed, as if Mom's thesis about his probability of being smote by a lightning bolt or a vortex or tornadic wind had absolutely no validity. Even I knew that she could be right. But it didn't matter; I hoped that she wasn't able to convince Dad to retreat back indoors. I wanted him to get that photo. In fact, I was hoping I could witness the moment of his triumph by joining him at the back of the yard.

But Mom would have none of it.

She shooed us kids into an interior bathroom where we listened to an AM radio station give updates regarding tornadoes on the ground in the region. I listened to the names of villages being battered by the storms and tried to remember where they were in relation to Huber Heights. As lightning illuminated the inside of the house, I'd begin to count — *one Mississippi ... two Mississippi ... three Mississippi ... four Mississippi ... five Mississippi*, BOOM! I remembered the trick I'd been taught: sound traveled about a mile every five seconds. It was getting close. (By way of comparison, the light from the distant bolt traveled at nearly 670 million miles per hour).

Dad viewed anybody who had ever seen a natural disaster of any kind as "lucky." If you saw a tornado ripping across a cornfield, you were "lucky." If you saw lighting strike the tree next to you (or possibly a friend), you were "lucky." If you were at the epicenter of an earthquake, or in a high-rise watching a Tsunami roll in, or in the plains around an erupting volcano, you were "lucky." His favorite refrain when hearing about some natural phenomenon witnessed by another human being was always, "Why doesn't anything exciting ever happen around here? Why doesn't a giant meteor come crashing down right over there?" He'd point to a location a short distance away – a location that, had a giant meteor actually come crashing down, assured Dad would have been vaporized as he started to yell for Mom to come and take a look.

When hiking with us children in the mountains of New Mexico or Colorado on a back-woods trail, Dad would often ask, as if frustrated by the fact that no real-world meteorological or astronomical event was transpiring near us, "Kids, what would you do if a giant tentacle reached out and grabbed you right now?" I could see his own imagination running wild with the possibility. In fact, the older I got, the more convinced I became that my father's frontal lobe was a continuously running 1950's drive-in movie theater, where black and white science fiction films played, one after the other. There were giant ants and crickets. There were aliens that looked suspiciously like humans in poorly made gorilla suits that had had the ape eyes replaced with unnaturally large orbs. There were large-breasted women in tattered dresses thrashing helplessly as otherworldly villains kidnapped them, always for the purpose of keeping the distressed damsel as a concubine.

The latter fact made me confused as a child – why would aliens with sexual parts and motivations that almost certainly were different from a human's, long for an hour-glass shaped woman with large mammary glands? Are boobs universally valued? And if attraction could transcend interplanetary biology, then why didn't it ever seem to go the other way? Why didn't a human man in these movies ever fall for a female alien with particularly voluptuous gills?

I'm not sure we ever answered Dad's question about the tentacle. In fact, by the time we were each six-years-old, Dad had become so predictable that we immediately tuned him out whenever he started a sentence with, "Kids, what would you do if …" Still, I loved Dad for stoking my imagination and instilling in me an incredible curiosity about the world, even if that curiosity was about an imaginary tentacle.

Dad didn't see his tornado that day. But the inhabitants of Xenia Ohio about a 25-minute drive to the southeast of Dayton, did. An F-5 tornado killed 33 people as it tore through the town. An F-5 designation means the twister had top wind speeds between 260 and 320 mph. The "F" in "F-5" stands for "Fujita," the name of a Japanese-born scientist, Ted Fujita, who devised a method to determine tornado intensity based on damage to structures on the ground. Fujita was born in Japan in 1920 and lived there until he immigrated to the United States in 1953. In a fortuitous twist of fate, Fujita avoided certain death in August of 1945 – a death that would have come to him because of the work the Wright Brothers did earlier in the century in a shop just a short car ride from Xenia.

On August 9th, 1945, three days after the first atomic bomb was dropped on Hiroshima, the United States prepared to use its relatively new B-29 bomber to drop a second bomb on its primary target, Kokura. But because of cloudy weather and smoke from a neighboring city, the group of bombers couldn't see their objective and instead diverted to attack their secondary target: Nagasaki. The residents of Kokura, where Mr. Fujita lived at the time, were spared and didn't even know it. The inhabitants of Nagasaki were not so lucky: over 30,000 were killed and 60,000 injured when the bomb named "Fatman" exploded. Temperatures inside the detonation fireball got to 7,000 degrees Fahrenheit (steel melts at around 2,500 degrees) and the shockwave created a wind speed estimated at over 600 mph. Had the Wright Brothers not flown when they did or had they not at all, perhaps the development of subsequent aircraft would have been delayed or changed in a way that would have resulted in a bomber approaching Kokura on a clear day instead of the cloudy, smoky one of August 9th. If so, Mr. Fujita would likely have perished as a 25-year-old man with a lot of promise unrealized. And the Fujita Scale for measuring tornadoes, including the one that killed 33 people near the Wright

Brother's home, would not be called the "Fujita Scale." Fate is a tricky bitch.

My father's lack of success in capturing a tornado on film did not discourage him. In the years that followed, I remember hours with him trying to capture lightning in time-exposures and filming or photographing all sorts of weather phenomenon or interstellar images.

One clear night while we were on another wilderness adventure, I was with Dad while he was playing around with his camera trying to catch some images of the night sky. At some point, he decided to take a time-exposure of the moon but with a different twist.* After opening the shutter of the camera, Dad traced the word "Donna" with it, hoping that he was blindly writing her name on the film with the light of the lunar surface. He did this a few times and then we went back to camp, quickly forgetting about our little experiment.

While Dad was at work one day and more than a month after we had returned from the trip, Mom went to pick up the developed film from a local photo shop. When she opened the envelope containing the glossy 4x6 photos, the color melted from her face. It was a sign from God! Mom was beside herself with wonder. The moon had unmistakably, if crudely, spelled her name! Forget images of the Virgin Mary in pizza dough. This was indisputably divine in nature. All those years of lighting votive candles, praying the rosary, and seeking the intercession of the saints had led to this. But what did it mean?

When Dad came home from work, Mom met him at the door, speaking almost too quickly for him to understand her.

"What are you talking about?" Dad asked incredulously when Mom said that the moon had written her name. He was clearly clueless, as was I, the disconnect in time between Dad's photographic high jinks and that afternoon too great to make a connection.

"The moon, it spelled out my name in a picture you took!" she repeated. Dad started to question her once again, still not

---

* A time exposure is a photographic technique usually used in low light conditions whereby the shutter on a camera is opened for an extended period to collect as much light as possible. If there is any movement of that light, it will trace an illuminated path on the film. Pictures of stars carving arcs in a night sky are taken using a time exposure.

understanding. But he stopped himself, his memory of that night in the wilderness coming to the fore. A quick instant of understanding on his face was supplanted by a smile and then by an uproarious laugh. I giggled along. As Mom looked at us perplexed, I wanted to ask her why God had written her name as a third grader might? Or why, if he could write her name as a "message" he couldn't write a whole message to be clearer about his intent? But alas it was just too cruel. After Dad caught his breath, he told her of his photographic wizardry, having to pause between sentences so that he could laugh some more. When he finished explaining, Mom slapped him with a dish towel and said, "Damn you!" frustrated, embarrassed, and – I'm sure – a little disappointed.

Another opportunity for meteorological excitement came in 1983 as Hurricane Alicia was bearing down on the gulf coast of Texas. We lived near the Johnson Space Center about halfway between Houston and Galveston Island. The authorities had warned that our area should evacuate, but there was no way we were going to leave our house. Dad was finally going to get "lucky." In the day leading up to landfall after preparing for the storm to arrive, Dad decided to relax as the rotating hurricane approached. He had done what he could to protect the house, had gotten some provisions, and had prepared his camera so there was not much else to do. He slipped into the backyard under an overcast but serene sky – the literal "calm before the storm" – with his bathing suit on, walked to the edge of our pool, and dove in. Mom hadn't seen him exit the house and, upon hearing the splash from the kitchen, walked with purpose to the back door, stuck her head out, and shouted, "Michael! There's a damned hurricane coming! You can't be out there in this weather!"

Dad had swum to the shallow end of the pool and was standing as he wiped his face clean of water and slicked his hair back with both hands. He looked at Mom dismissively and then raised his hands like a priest chanting at the altar, looked skyward, and replied, "What the hell are you talking about? It's beautiful out!!!" Mom was not amused and slammed the door. "He's going to get himself killed," she said as she huffed her way past me and back to the kitchen. Little did she know that he'd eventually experience things that got him much closer to death than swimming on the eve of Hurricane Alicia's landfall.

***

After just a year-and-a-half in Dayton, Dad completed his master's degree in aeronautical engineering in 1975 and we were off to Edwards AFB in the deserts of southern California where he began the Air Force's flight test engineering program.

Edwards was a boy's dream. Our home backed up to thousands of square miles of desert just beyond a cinderblock wall. I'd venture into that desert on foot to explore at every opportunity. When feeling even more adventurous, I'd take my bike into the desert and ride for hours. (The desert floor was hard – in fact, it was the hard and dry sand lakebeds around the base that the Air Force used as areas to land and takeoff experimental aircraft. The wide-open spaces offered more margin for error than did the cement runways on the base). While I know it was a different time when parents were more permissive when it came to the comings and goings of their children, it wasn't *that* different a time; looking back on my solo adventures into an unforgiving desert I wonder now if my parents were trying to get me killed.

Edwards AFB was named after Captain Glen Edwards who, coincidentally, was born exactly 50 years before me on March 5, 1918 in Medicine Hat, Canada. He was killed while testing the YB-49 flying wing in the deserts of southern California, along with four of his fellow crewmembers. Perhaps more coincidentally, when his family immigrated to the United States, they settled in Lincoln, CA, just a forty-minute drive from my own birthplace at Mather AFB in Sacramento, CA. Mather was named after Second Lieutenant Carl Mather, who was killed in the early days of aviation in a mid-air collision during a training mission at Ellington Field in 1918. Ellington was the airfield my father would call his home base for the final 14 years of his career; it was the field near Houston that NASA used as its base of aircraft operations, about a fifteen-minute drive from JSC. Ellington was named after First Lieutenant Eric Ellington who died in a plane crash in San Diego in 1913. If memorializing dead aviators through the names of military bases wasn't enough to remind us of the danger my father put himself in frequently, then deaths of neighbors and friends drove it home in an even starker way. While I was too young to remember, when we were in England our next-door neighbor and a squadron-mate of Dad's was killed along with another crewmate when their F-4 (the plane my father also flew in) crashed at the end of the runway. While we were living at Edwards, Lt. Col. Michael Love was killed, also while flying an F-4. Later in that same year, Dad would have his own brush with death in a crashing airplane, the first of many such close calls I came to remember.

I was outside constantly at Edwards. In a place that got just 6 inches of rain a year (the national average is 39 inches), there was plenty of sunshine inviting my sisters and me outside. One day I was with some friends and Amy in the front yard playing hide-n-seek. A boy and I snuck into our front garden to hide behind some bushes while the "seeker" hid his eyes behind a small tree and began to count. I was creeping along the outside wall of the house trying to squeeze myself into a shady spot to find both better concealment and some relief from the heat.

"Pat, don't move!" my friend said to me in a shouted whisper.

I looked back at him and his eyes were wide, looking to the ground near my feet. I followed his gaze to a rattlesnake coiled up inches from my front sneaker. It began rattling its tail. I backed away slowly, my heartbeat in my chest almost drowning out the sound of the rattle.

After getting out of the flowerbed, I ran to find my parents.

"Show me where he is," Dad said when I explained to him in a rush of excitement what we'd found. I took him to the garden and pointed from a short distance away. The snake was still there.

"It's a Mojave green," he said as he forcefully pushed my sisters, friends, and me back from the tight circle that had formed around the rattling reptile. Mojave Green rattlesnakes got their name from their common habitat and the green tint of their scales. Among rattlesnakes they are not the biggest, growing on average to the length of a yardstick. But their venom packs a punch. It's the deadliest of the rattlesnake family and some contend it's deadlier than many other venomous snakes from other parts of the world, including the Cobra.

"What are you going to do, Dad?" I asked, wondering if he would find a way to kill it. Or maybe he would just let it be and hope that it made its way back to the desert.

I was so naïve.

Dad disappeared for a few minutes and then reemerged from behind the house with a shovel and an empty Folgers coffee can. By now my mother had joined several neighborhood children and me in the front yard to view the reptile from afar.

"Michael, what are you doing?" my mom asked

"Michael?" she asked again when he didn't respond.

I wonder how many times my mother asked that question of Dad over the course of their marriage (now over fifty years strong). She had to know what I had figured out already in my short life: if you had to ask the question, you didn't want to know the answer.

Dad remained silent as he put the can on the ground and started to maneuver around the snake with shovel in hand assessing its position relative to the house and the bushes. He was trying to understand how best to approach the snake. I wasn't sure I wanted to hang around. Seeing Dad pummel a snake—even a dangerous one—to death with a shovel sounded horrible. I took a step back.

"Michael!" Mom said again.

He finally answered, annoyed by her front yard interrogation.

"I'm going to catch it and take it to the survival school." He said it calmly, almost quietly and as if it was the obvious course of action, as if he might finish the sentence with a "duh!" and a roll of his eyes at her. Edwards had a desert survival school that kept some live specimens on hand to help aviators learn about the sorts of things they might run into should they have to parachute to safety over the desert. Some of those specimens became dinner as instructors showed pilots how capture, cook, and consume the vermin.

"That's insane!" Mom said. I didn't speak, but it was hard to disagree with her assessment.

As Dad slid the shovel under the snake, he must have assumed it would stay coiled, like a tiny compressed spring. But as the rattle grew louder, the snake unwound itself and began to slither over the blade of the shovel, now looking more agitated than ever. Those of us gathered to watch were tense and silent, unconsciously and slowly moving back from the scene, growing the circle around my father. I was enthralled. It was like a live version of *Mutual of Omaha's Wild Kingdom* which I watched religiously each week. In that show, the hosts, Jim Fowler and Marlin Perkins sought out, interacted with, and filmed wild animals in their natural habitats. They always seemed to have a convenient excuse to intervene in the lives of the wild creatures they filmed. The jaguar cubs were in a flood zone and needed to be relocated. The mountain lion had killed some cattle and needed to be transferred to another region. And, of course, there was a lot of "tagging" that would somehow aid in the research of a particular critter's mating or migration habits. I suspect the only real need was some interesting footage for each week's installment of the popular program. The other reasons were all horseshit.

As my dad tried to steady his shovel and move the blade toward the coffee can, I imagined the voice of Marlin, narrating the scene in his folksy carnival voice:

My colleague, Mike Mullane, an Air Force officer with absolutely no training in ecology or conservation, approaches the Mojave Green with the respect it deserves. He assesses the situation, charting his path of ingress through a residential garden to the venomous snake's location beneath a typical bush. He plans to capture the rattler and has therefore retrieved the best tool for the job: a standard flat-blade shovel with a forty-four-inch handle. It's the perfect implement for corralling an angry snake. He's slowly sliding the blade under the snake now. As you can see, the Mojave Green is becoming agitated. His rattle is a warning; if you should hear that sound while in the wild, do not do what Mike is doing. That would be insane.

Oh, now he's done it. The snake has uncoiled on the blade and is slithering around. He is flicking his tongue quite a bit now, trying to gather information about the environment around him. He undoubtedly senses Mike and the gaggle of children gathered around him.

Mike has prepared his reptilian trap device. It's a standard steel coffee can emblazoned with the Folgers logo and still smelling of that rich, smooth odor that indicates its previous use as a storage device for ground coffee. Another perfect tool for the job.

Mike is moving slowly. He has the snake balanced well on the blade. Now, watch as he slowly swings that blade to the coffee can. Okay he's in position now. And…he's got it! Watch again in slow motion as the snake twists at the last moment in an attempt to elude the can below it. What wonderful luck! As you can see, the snake almost made its escape, and if it had, would certainly have threatened the cohort of children encircling the scene. Another close one Mike! Quickly, Mike has covered the can and entrapped our Mojave Green friend, bringing another exciting episode to a close.

After getting the snake securely imprisoned in the Folgers can, Dad then did the next most obvious thing: he took it to the Air Force survival school at Edwards … on the back of his bicycle. Rather than drive the snake to the on-base facility, and for reasons that are still a mystery to me, Dad strapped the can to the back of his bike using Bungee cords and pedaled his way through residential neighborhoods.

To this day I'm not sure how the handoff went. Did Dad just hand a coffee can to some unsuspecting airman and say, "There's a green in there"? And if he did, why didn't some senior officer tell my father, whom the military had spent a fortune to train and educate, that chancing a deadly or debilitating snake bite put all that training and education at risk? My gut tells me those conversations didn't happen because the guy who took the coffee can probably said, "Cool! You caught a snake with a shovel and a coffee can?!"

You would have thought that the close call with the snake would have made Dad shy away from such encounters in the future. That was not the case. I was hiking with him as an adult in the Sandia Mountains outside of Albuquerque one hot summer day and we both came upon a rattler just to the side of a trail. We had almost stepped on it before we heard the warning from its tail. After a surge of adrenaline that made us both jump back, my dad gathered himself. He then grabbed his walking pole to poke at the snake as he asked me to pull out my phone and get a video. As in the case of the broken throttle cable, I put my health at risk to comply. What else could I do? Finally, we had gotten "lucky."

***

My parents had both been raised very Catholic and they reared Amy, Laura, and me in that same tradition. Mass every week. Rosary together once a week. Mass after mass during holy week. The sacraments became mile markers on the road of life: baptism, confirmation, first communion, confession. While I would have identified my parents as ardent Catholics, their comfort with church doctrine only went so far. Both felt that their upbringing in Catholicism had saddled them with guilt and angst around issues related to sex.

Their kids, by God, were not going to suffer the same fate. And the first step in ensuring that did not happen was talking openly and honestly about it early in our childhood.

While living at Edwards and when Amy and I were the tender age of eight-years-old, Mom and Dad sat us down in the family room one evening and put a large picture book between us. *Where Did I Come From?* used straight-forward language and a cartoon family to tell the story of how every person began. One of the many things I remember from this traumatic evening was how the husband and wife had been drawn in the book. They were plump; this couple was not hitting the gym very often. The nose on the man looked more like a penis than his penis and the woman's breasts seemed too perky for her body, hinting at work done at a younger age. The book's use of cartoons and light-heartedness made it seem like a little-more-serious Dr. Seuss book. I wonder sometimes how it would have read had the master of children's stories written this seminal work:

Mr. McDoozle puts his long straight pupfloozle into Mrs. McDoozle's furry pouchkoozle,
He then shuffles and duffles on the one he loves singly,
Til his firm long pupfloozle gets warm and all tingly,
Mrs. McDoozle feels really good too,
If Mr. McDoozle does the job he should do,
Until finally Mr. McDoozle's stiffy pupfloozle shoots creeklecumsnoozle in her hairy pouchkoozle.

Mom and Dad turned the pages slowly, as if they had steeled themselves to go through the material in a deliberate manner. As I recall, Dad did most of the talking. On one page, there was a drawing of the naked couple standing and holding hands. On the facing page, the author describes differences in the bodies of the two characters. Reading that page now, it seems like the story was written in 1940 instead of 1973. In a short review of terms for a woman's breasts, the first that comes to the author is "bosom." Interesting…in my time since puberty, I never recall a buddy saying to me, "Check out the bosom on that girl." Of course, being cruder might have led one Amazon reviewer's negative assessment of the book to be even more critical. In 2004, "Heather" wrote that the book is very "male perspective dominant" – I suppose that could be true, but it certainly wasn't something that entered my mind back at Edwards AFB. Another one-star reviewer mentioned that it left out the role of consent in sex. While important to be sure, I think the anonymous reviewer misses the point of the book and the target audience. After all, for most eight- to ten-year-olds, consent of the woman implies she might *want* to have the man's pupfloozle near her pouchkoozle.

As for creeklecumsnoozle, at the point in the story when ejaculation is described, Amy looked up from the pages at Mom and Dad, horrified.

"Ewwwww!" she said in disbelief.

"That's so gross! Mom, can you feel it going in?" she asked.

Mom shook her head, no. Then, Amy turned to Dad.

"Dad, can you feel it coming out?" Dad laughed as if somebody had just told him the best-ever fart joke. He looked at my mom knowingly and she blushed and smiled.

"Yes honey, I can feel it," he said after gaining his composure.

From that day forward, my parents were relatively open about sex. While that would have been uncomfortable for any child if that openness manifested itself in clinical discussions about the ovulation cycle of a girl or the purpose of testicles on a boy, more often than not in our home it took the form of embarrassing reminders from Dad about the fact that Mom and he "did it."

When Dad was in an amorous mood, he would talk about "squeaking the bed" with Mom – one of us had noted that the springs on their old mattress seemed to be audible at times in a rhythmic "eek, eek, eek" and my father, always eager to make us cringe, took up the "squeak the bed" euphemism with gusto. It was also common, while Mom was bent over at the waist loading the dishwasher, for Dad to sneak up behind her, grab her hips, and pretend like he was doing her from behind as we kids cleared the table.

It got worse when we were older. No longer did he just stand behind her and say something like, "Let's go squeak the bed." Now, he augmented the performance with a scene mimicked out of the 1981 movie *Quest for Fire*. In that film, a caveman couples with a cavewoman who's bent over at the waist getting water from a river. While he's humping away, a rival clan attacks from across the water. The Neanderthal looks up in surprise and half speaks, half grunts, "Huh?!"

Dad took to reenacting this scene over and over again – a few half-hearted thrusts at my Mom's backside finished off with a gaze across an imaginary body of water and an exaggerated "Huh?!" Unlike the cavewoman in the movie, Mom let out a frustrated sigh and shooed Dad as if she were a jockey whipping a horse's hindquarter as it came down the final stretch.

"Damnit Michael!" she would say with frustration. While many might have found these displays in front of children inappropriate, they were important for my sisters and me to see. Part of a healthy relationship is wanting your partner. There should be no shame in that. But in fairness, there might be ways to demonstrate the desire you have for your spouse that don't include pretending to be a Neanderthal surprised by an attack while in the middle of coitus in front of a dishwasher.

CHAPTER 5: BULLIES, BASKETBALLS, AND BOWELS

In 1977, we moved into a small bungalow in a neighborhood in Fort Walton Beach, Florida close to Eglin AFB. Eglin once had an air force pilot stationed there named Henry John Deutschendorf Sr. Henry had become a minor celebrity in the Air Force in 1961 when he flew a B-58 Hustler bomber about 1,300 miles at an average speed of just over 1,000 mph, setting six new speed records. The B-58 was the sort of airplane that showed up on the cover of 1960's comic books. It had a sharply pointed nose and an iconic delta wing that made it look like flying equilateral triangle. Its four large engines hung under the wings like testicles, giving it a testosterone-fueled look that made it seem both powerful and nimble even when standing still. It belonged in a science fiction movie, dropping nukes on giant ants wreaking havoc on downtown Cleveland.

Deutschendorf's love of flying was passed on to his son, Henry John Deutschendorf, Jr. But junior didn't join the military like his dad and it's not clear that he hung model airplanes from his bedroom ceiling as I did. What is clear is that he spent some time in his youth playing a guitar he received as a gift when he was eleven years old and then shortened his name after he dropped out of college to make it easier to promote his singing gigs at small venues around the country. Deutschendorf Jr. chose as a stage name the capital city of his favorite state, Colorado. John Denver went on to sell millions of records and die at 53 while doing what his father loved to do – fly.

My father almost met the same fate as John Denver while stationed at Eglin – and for almost exactly the same reason. Denver died when he ran out of fuel from his primary tank while flying a small aircraft off the coast of Monterey, California. When trying to switch to a secondary fuel tank using a lever in an unorthodox location, Denver lost control of his airplane and crashed into the sea, dying instantly.*

Unlike Denver, my father was in an airplane with an ejection system. After completing a test mission over the Gulf of Mexico, he and the pilot realized they were dangerously short of fuel. Concerned that he might run out of gas, the pilot rushed the landing attempt back at Eglin AFB and lost control of the airplane over the runway. My father, sensing death was imminent, pulled the ejection handle and the entire cockpit of the airplane rocketed away from the rest of the craft and parachuted to safety. The plane broke apart on the centerline of the runway and burned. I still have a picture of its charred carcass and remember upon first seeing it that my father could have been a charred carcass himself. But the fact that he survived made the whole experience another cool factor when it came to the bona fides of my father. It made him a real test pilot … even though he was "just" a navigator.

While my dad was cheating death in Florida in 1976, we hadn't yet made it to Ft. Walton Beach. I was living in New Mexico with my mother and sisters. Dad had to get to his new assignment at Eglin, but our household goods weren't set to arrive in the sunshine state for some time. So, Mom, my sisters, and I moved in with Nonnie and Joe Joe and we kids were enrolled in St. Charles Catholic Elementary School near the University of New Mexico. On a Wednesday afternoon after being picked up at school, Mom told us of dad's daring escape. I

---

* In the shuttle heydays before the *Challenger* disaster, John Denver was being considered as a potential passenger on the shuttle – the first musician in space. His name was floated along with several other, shall we say, "nontraditional" astronaut candidates. According to a 2016 Smithsonian.com article, one such candidate was Big Bird of Sesame Street fame. The article notes though that NASA canned the idea noting that "at eight feet plus – he'd be hard to squeeze into the shuttle." Putting the merits of this idea aside, I wonder if anybody ever considered that Big Bird was not a real person with a real height and that it would be possible to put a smaller Big Bird on the shuttle?

don't recall being too frightened by what she said but I also don't remember being too surprised. We knew what Dad did was dangerous. In addition to friends of my parents getting killed flying airplanes, one of Dad's groomsmen, a West Point classmate, was killed on the ground in Vietnam shortly after Mom and Dad tied the knot. This military business was a dangerous one. But in youth you don't believed mortality applies to you and, I learned, you extend that belief to those you love. The lessons regarding death at the hands of high-performance machines was one I would learn again ten years later in a more tragic and public way.

Living in New Mexico during that brief period between our move from California to Florida, was, for the most part, a wonderful experience. For a kid who loved to visit his grandparents, actually living with them for a more extended period was like being on permanent vacation. While time out of school was spent enjoying the endless fascinations of Joe Joe's basement and bewilderment at his rants about the Mexicans messing with him, time in school wasn't as pleasant.

The full name of our school was St. Charles Borromeo School; it was named after a cardinal who served as the archbishop of Milan. I don't remember being told much about St. Charles while attending the school that was his namesake but some research later in life was revealing and likely explains why we didn't delve into Mr. Borromeo's resume. St. Charles was a key figure in the "counter-reformation," a term used to describe resurgence in Catholicism in reaction to the Protestant Reformation. If "counter-reformation" were interpreted literally as "doing the opposite of reforming" then St. Charles did his part. During a visit to Switzerland in 1583, Borromeo came upon a village where witchcraft was the religion du jour. Unpleased with this revelation, our Catholic hero decided to send a signal to others who might contemplate a mysticism other than that offered by Catholicism: he had the offenders burned at the stake.

Sometimes I thought the fate of those heretics was better than mine. I hated the required weekly masses at the school's chapel. Like many Catholic children, I came to believe that if suffering demonstrated the highest order of commitment to Christ then I was pretty devoted given the torture of being asked to sit still and be quiet while a man in robes spoke meaningless sentences for an hour or more, especially when all I wanted to do was run outside and burn some ants with my magnifying glass.

That's not to say I didn't try to be a good Catholic. I tried really hard at times. I'd kneel on the kneeler, squeeze my eyes shut, and fold my hands, fingers interlocked tightly, and pray the prayer all eight-year-old boys prayed: to have a superpower. If God would just give me the ability to make myself invisible, then I'd never again sneak into the kitchen in the middle of the night and drink the Hershey's syrup right from the can – something that had become a bit of a habit for me. After making my request, my mind wandered to the day I'd be granted the superpower. What would I do first? Unlike many other boys in the school who were likely beginning to feel the urge to sneak into the girls' locker room, I remember thinking it would be fun to stow away into the back seat of a fighter plane on a bombing run. I can't help but think that even God was disappointed with my lack of imagination. "I gave you brains and hormones and this is the best you could come up with?" he'd say to himself. No superpowers for me. Instead, he later gave me horrible acne and a unibrow.

While the masses at St. Charles were a special kind of drudgery, a bully at the school made my time out of mass even more harrowing. One day on the playground, this particularly large Hispanic kid began to harass my sister and me. His aggression was unprovoked and so I wondered if he might be part of the Mexican conspiracy that phoned and hung up on Joe Joe. Maybe the ethnic cabal had shifted its tactics and was trying to get to Joe Joe through me? Back at his house the day before his assault on us, I imagined The Bully's dad talking quietly around a table to a group of male neighbors as my classmate lingered in the shadows, longing to be part of the grand scheme.

"The calls aren't working," The Bully heard one of them say. "We've got to change our tactics."

"But what can we do?" exclaimed one of the caballeros seated at the table. "We have no other options! The only way to get to him is through the phone calls!" Then, slamming his right fist into his open left palm: "We must increase their frequency!"

"No!" The Bully's father shouted back. "We cannot keep doing what does not work! There must be a better way!" A pregnant pause ensued.

Sensing his moment was at hand, The Bully stepped forward into the light.

"Papa, I think Joe Joe's grandkids go to my school," he said sheepishly. Always looking for ways to make his distant and demanding father proud of him, The Bully had given up the goods. His father smiled and called him to the table, wrapping his arm around his shoulder as the boy stood proudly before the council of men tasked with punishing Joe Joe.

"I'm proud of you *mi hijo*," his father said. Then, looking to the group around the table, he smiled and added, "Men, this is our chance! If we can't get to Joe Joe with our incessant phone calls and subsequent hang-ups, we can get to him through those he loves." He stood up abruptly, his chair falling behind him, held up a *cerveza*, and shouted, "*Viva México!*" Then, he threw his head back and laughed a slow laugh that built to a crescendo as the other men joined in.

Back on the playground the next day, The Bully was doing his job. He was harassing Amy. As his teasing escalated and Amy started to show signs of fear and embarrassment, my Irish blood began to boil until adrenaline and a sense of duty led me to act. I snuck up behind him and pushed him in the back with both hands as he taunted Amy. He turned around like a bull that had just discovered the rodeo clown behind him, and he charged. I, like a rodeo clown, tried to find a barrel to jump into. I was on my ass in a heartbeat and he was kneeling over me throwing punches into my shoulders. Fortunately, probably knowing that the ever-watchful eyes of the staff were not far away, his blows were not very effective, and he didn't try to smack me in the nose. It didn't matter though; I began to cry. While I was still pinned to the ground, he looked up to the horizon after two or three punches. He may have noticed a collar-clad priest whisking his way across the playground like one of the dust devils that swept through the area on a daily basis. Whatever he saw made him jump up and walk quickly away toward the farther reaches of our desert playground.

Amy came to me with tears in her own eyes and asked if I was ok. "I think so," I said through sobs, trying to sniff snot back into my nasal cavity lest I look like I was really crying.

Despite the fact that Amy and I could go at each other at home in the cruel way many siblings do, that day I saw the part of her that put family before all else – a part I would see in dramatic ways later in our lives. After I got up and brushed myself off, I looked to her. Behind the tears welling in her own eyes, she had a fire in her pupils that reminded me of lava coming from a crack deep in the ocean floor. She turned her head and watched The Bully walk away. I thought he might be a marked man.

Later that evening, we told the story of the drama on the playground at the dinner table. Joe Joe was particularly interested.

"You need to show that kid who's boss," he said to me. Nonnie sat quietly at the table smiling as usual from behind her horn-rimmed glasses, puffing on a cigarette, looking up frequently from her mystery novel.

"Sock him back," Joe Joe added, as if clarifying for me how to establish that I was "the boss."

I just nodded. I never had much of an appetite for fighting and hoped my ambivalence showed that I had not committed to anything in the way of retaliation. I was also worried that if the conversation continued, he'd ask me if the kid was "Mexican." Even at my tender age and under the influence of Joe Joe, I wasn't concerned with The Bully's race. He fell into one category for me: jerk. It's a category that I've since learned is replete with members of all races.

The next day, I avoided any situation that might have me run into The Bully and something told me that he was avoiding me too. After all, he had won the fight and was likely elevated in stature among his peers. Neither of us had anything to gain by reengaging in fisticuffs.

Later in the afternoon, Joe Joe came to pick up Amy and me at school. He parked his car haphazardly; the left two tires were on top of the white line demarcating one side of a spot. It was as if he was daring somebody to challenge him (although, in his defense, that Town Car was massive). He sauntered across the parking lot like John Travolta as Danny Zuko in the movie *Grease*, arriving for the first day of school after a summer fling with Sandra Dee. Joe Joe had a spring in his step. He was on a mission.

Amy and I were waiting in the designated "pickup" zone along the sidewalk in front of the school. As he got closer to us, I could see him scanning the horizon and I knew what he was doing – trying to pick

The Bully out from the crowd based on my very thin description the night before.

"Do you see that *pendejo*?" he asked. Did he somehow know that the boy was Hispanic? Or was he just using his favorite insult? I'm sure he had used it several times driving his Town Car the short distance from his home on Las Lomas Road to the school. Any road that allowed him to change lanes was like a trigger mechanism for a special type of vehicular Tourette Syndrome.

"No, Joe Joe. Shhh!" He was a giant among the kids, and he was biologically unable to whisper. He was drawing attention to us…quite deliberately. I looked down and away from him as he asked me again.

"Which one is he?"

I changed my tactic. "Ready to go?" I asked as I secured my backpack on my shoulder, hoping he'd take the hint and walk us back to the car.

"Is that him?" he said raising his chin in the direction of a classmate.

Holy shit! It was him! How did he know? How did he know that the slightly overweight kid in a *Jaws* t-shirt was the son of the imaginary Mexican prank caller?

"Or is it him?" he added looking in another direction.

Phew, he didn't know.

Any relief I had at realizing he was just taking stabs in the dark were fleeting. "Which one of these kids beat you up?" he said mostly rhetorically and very loudly. Children on the sidewalk – and their parents – looked at him a bit bewildered, unsure of what to make of his seemingly random commentary.

Seriously?

"Joe Joe!" I said, glaring at him in anger while widening my eyes, imploring him to stop. He was chuckling now. When Joe Joe smelled blood in the water, even the blood of his own family, he, like the shark on The Bully's t-shirt, went in for the kill.

"That kid looks like somebody who might beat you up," he said, now pointing at another suspect. "Was that him?"

I was pissed now and stomped off toward the car, violating the rules of the school that said that we couldn't leave the sidewalk without an adult escort.

"Hey, where are you going?" Joe Joe called after me. I looked back at him with scorn and he chuckled. He was having a grand ole time. I was beside myself. It was enough that I had to deal with The Bully at school. It was quite another to be living with one who happened to be my grandfather.

We got into the car. I took the front seat and Amy got into the back. I buckled up with a huff and turned to stare out the window as we drove back to the house. Once there, Joe Joe put a pot on the burner and began cooking. I sulked at the kitchen table as Nonnie and Mom talked to Amy and me about our day. Nonnie asked if The Bully had bothered me. I started to answer when Joe Joe cut me off.

"He can handle himself," he said, giving me a knowing wink.

***

I was happy when we finally moved to Florida to join my father in Ft. Walton Beach. At this point in my life I had already lived in six different places – and I was only nine years old. Yet I have no memory of being worried about the changes. One thing that life in a military family teaches you is that the world doesn't end if you leave a school and friends to go somewhere else; there are always new schools with new friends. I had heard once that if you put a pin in the map where a random human was born, that that person would likely die within fifty miles of that pin. I thought of how sad it would be to be such a person. I had been born in the land of the adventurous forty-niner gold miners. I had lived in the desolate high deserts of Idaho. I had almost stepped on a rattler in the Mojave Desert. I had been to a school in England. I had been to the top of the Sandia Mountains in New Mexico. I had seen tornado-laden thunderstorms in Ohio. I had spent weekends on the beach by the Eglin AFB Officers' Club in Florida. I had done more living in less than a decade than most humans manage in a lifetime. And I owed it all to my father, his profession, and his expansive wanderlust.

While living in Florida, I attended Kenwood Elementary school. It was the first time I remembered being identified as "smarter" than some other kids. Kenwood had a gifted program that required me to leave my usual classroom and go to another room where students with a knack for academics would gather to do more advanced lessons in various topics.

I hated it.

Well, that's not true. I actually liked the classes. What I hated was the fact that I was pulled out of class by the gifted program teacher to attend the special sessions. He would come by each Tuesday and Thursday and knock on my classroom door, pop his head in, and say to my teacher, "Ms. Riley, it's time for Patrick to come with us." I sheepishly stood and turned to walk to the door as other students' snickering generated a whisper of white noise. I was "special" – as in "special education." It didn't help that I had a particularly large egg-shaped head, a bowl cut, and a single eyebrow traversing the lower part of my forehead like an insect commuting from my right ear to my left. *There must be something wrong with him*, my classmates likely thought.

While I was indeed a bit of a bookworm and teacher's pet, I wasn't the stereotypical braniac. I liked athletics and was a particularly fast runner in my elementary and middle school days. At the Kenwood Elementary field day one spring, I earned six blue ribbons in six events. I was so proud of those ribbons. I lined them up on my dresser like soldiers and reviewed them every morning like their general inspecting his troops. Later, when I moved to Houston in the fifth grade, I ran the mile in the Junior Olympics. But by that time, I had come to hate being a miler. I practiced every day after school with the track team but wished I was home instead building a model airplane or drawing X-wing fighters.

I made it through the local Junior Olympics vetting process and secured a place in the large regional race that would determine who would go to the state-level championships. From the get-go, I had much against me. My lack of enthusiasm due to nerdy distractions like *Star Wars* figurines and model building was the least of my problems. A couple of weeks before the race, my mother bought me some neon green sneakers. I put them at the foot of my bed and admired them and the speed they implied until I dozed off each night. But a couple of days after buying them, I became violently ill. As I rushed to the bathroom down the hall trying not to vomit on the floor, I passed those shoes, the neon appearing alive in the night as if putting a curse on me. After about my fifth race to the commode, my brain made a connection between my sickness and that neon green trim. Like a kid who ate a gallon of warm mint chocolate chip ice cream with a hair in it an hour before barfing his guts out and then came to associate the ice cream with the sickness, the sight of those shoes from that point forward drew a burning bile from my stomach to my throat.

So, there I was – I didn't like to race, and my shoes made me want to throw up whenever I bent over to tie them. Not a good start on the path to becoming a world-class athlete. But even those things might have been surmountable if not for my third affliction: before races, nerves would make my bowels sap every bit of moisture from my body and turn it into a smelly stew of explosive diarrhea. I'd be in the stadium bathroom until minutes before it was time to line up at the start line. And in Houston, in August, in an un-air conditioned and unventilated cinder block bathroom under the bleachers, the painful diarrhea cramps that culminated in shotgun explosions out my ass were accompanied by profuse sweating.

As I relieved myself with one messy surge, I'd bow my head between my legs to try and will away another episode but instead got hit by a stench that seemed to come from the Grim Reaper's own sweaty ass crack after he had bicycled through Haiti in a black robe on a hot summer day. And then I'd see those shoes – it was all I could do not to puke. By the time I finally made it to the start of the race, I was whiter than a sea-sick albino, dehydrated, and clenching my ass cheeks tightly in an effort to keep a tiny Hershey surprise from sneaking into my Lycra running shorts as I tried to slip a fart around a tiny turd. It was not exactly a recipe for a world-record time.

But the amazing thing is this: I ran well. The top three finishers would make it to the state finals. For most of the race, I hovered between the fourth and fifth positions. But in the last quarter mile, I heard the crowd and kicked my legs into another gear. I slowly gained on the kid in third place and by the time we crossed the finish line I was only a nose behind him. I came in fourth but by less than one second with a time of 5:15. As I collapsed in the heat beyond the finish line, I realized I had just missed the cut to go to the next level and felt immense relief. It was the best outcome possible; I had tried hard and done my best – something my parents always encouraged – but I had fallen a hair short of the top three. I could now retire from track with my head held high and turn my attention to other things, like preparing for the release of *The Empire Strikes Back*.

But a week after the race, I got a call from a representative at the Junior Olympics. He told me that the staff was so inspired by my spirited surge at the end of the race that they were going to make an exception they had never made before and let me participate in the state competition. I was heartbroken. But I hid my disappointment and said thank you. Weeks later, I ran the race but was well to the back of the field. My track days, thankfully, were over.

***

My father was selected as a new category of astronaut, called a mission specialist, in January of 1978 while he was stationed at Eglin AFB. Mission specialists were not pilots or commanders of shuttles. Those slots went to those who had been pilots in military roles. Since my father was a "back-seater" he wasn't eligible to sit in the two front seats of the shuttle but instead was tasked with many of the mission support duties on a flight. Mission specialists operated the robot arm on the shuttle, launched satellites from its cargo bay, did spacewalks, and operated on-board experiments.

My father, twenty-eight other men, and six women (the first U.S. female astronauts) made up what NASA called "Astronaut Group 8." The seven groups before Group 8 spanned the original "Mercury Seven" (which included John Glenn and Alan Shepard) through those that flew on Apollo and Skylab. Group 8 gave themselves the moniker "TFNG" which, in their incarnation of it anyway, meant "thirty-five new guys." While it would be nice to assume that "guys" was used in its more universal sense, political sensitivity in 1978 was not so pervasive and, in any case, "TFNG" had an entirely different meaning in the military world, a world that many in the new group of astronauts did not know – several of the TFNGs were civilians, including all of the women. The real meaning of the acronym was "the fucking new guys" – only slightly less offensive by today's standards.

I recall little of when I found out that Dad had been selected to be a part of the TFNGs. Interestingly, I remember a fantasy about it more than the reality of it. Upon hearing the news, my imagination took up the visuals and plot lines I had come to know watching re-runs of one of my favorite shows: *I Dream of Jeannie*. I saw myself in the white marble entry of a home in Cocoa Beach (where Jeannie lived) near the Kennedy Space Center (KSC), a live-in maid with a cleavage-enhancing white dress and a face that looked like Barbara Eden (whom I had an enormous crush on) comforting my sisters and me as Air Force generals counseled my mother in an adjoining room about the perils my father faced in orbit.

Alas, this was far from reality. I, like many Americans, had been fooled by the show. Astronauts like Jeannie's master, Major Tony Nelson, and his sidekick, Major Roger Healey, didn't live in Florida near KSC, they lived and did their training in Houston. Audiences could be forgiven for assuming that astronauts lived near KSC. It would have made sense for them to train at the same location where the launch facilities were located. And while there were a number of sites considered when deciding on where to put the base for manned space flight operations, including one in Florida, politics got in the way. Lyndon Johnson, a Texan, was Vice President while the decision was being made. Sam Rayburn, another Texan, was the Speaker of the House. Coincidence? I think not. Future generations would hear "Houston, the Eagle has landed," not "Tampa, the Eagle has landed."*

Moving to Houston after Dad's selection by NASA introduced me to oppressive heat and humidity. While I had lived in warm and humid Florida for two years before moving to Clear Lake City just outside of the Johnson Space Center, Houston (of which Clear Lake was an annexed town) had a special kind of wetness and heat that seemed to defy the meteorological laws of science. It was like walking around in a steam room at a spa, except in Houston (most of the time anyway) you couldn't walk around naked. A walk to your car was like hacking your way through the Amazon rain forest sans the machete. But the bugs were comparable; cockroaches the size of small dogs would scatter when the automatic garage door rose in the night and the headlights of our car hit the pre-historic creatures. While cockroaches were creepy, at least they couldn't hurt you. Fire ants, on the other hand, could. These very tiny ants built mounds around our yard and, if stepped in, instantly swarmed the foot and lower leg. The evil insects would bite to hold on to you and then deliver poison from their abdomen into your skin. The pain was excruciating. Getting them off

---

* Tampa was, in fact, the location in Florida being considered. The space center would have been at the site of where MacDill AFB now sits.

of the skin quickly is critical, particularly if you have an allergy or are small and weak; babies and tiny pets have been killed by fire ants. Suddenly, the old science fiction movies I loved where giant black ants roamed the streets of Peoria grabbing army soldiers in their pincers didn't seem so scary. A black ant didn't work with his comrades to take you down, it didn't sting you with fire-hot venom, and it could be killed with a nuclear weapon dropped from a plane John Denver's dad was flying. Fire ants, on the other hand, were like their cockroach brethren: ubiquitous and indestructible.

***

My parents bought a brand-new home in the Brook Forest subdivision of Clear Lake City with the help of a loan from my great grandmother. Great Grandma Pettigrew, Grandma's mother, lived in Wichita Falls, Texas. She was born in Minnesota in 1897 and traveled by wagon to Texas at some point early in her life. She had survived the great Wichita Falls Tornado of 1979. An F4 tornado, it killed 58 people in and around the north Texas town. Her home was completely destroyed in that storm. She told us all later that she heard the warning sirens blaring across the rooftops and knew that a "cyclone" was coming (she didn't call them tornadoes).* But she was in the middle of doing the dishes and, being one who was committed to completing a task once it was started, finished rinsing, drying, and putting away the plates and cutlery before making her way to a central hallway where she stood and said the rosary while the home was torn apart around her, leaving her unscathed. I saw pictures later of her demolished home – pictures of nothing more than a foundation, really – and recall thinking that there was some sort of protective gene being passed down in my family bloodline.

---

* According to the Hurricane Research Division of the Atlantic Oceanographic & Meteorological Laboratory, Great Grandma was not correct to call a tornado a cyclone. While both are "atmospheric vortices," tornado diameters are on the scale of hundreds of meters while tropical cyclones (also known as hurricanes or typhoons depending on where in the world the storm is) have diameters of hundreds of kilometers. Still, I could see why Great Grandma used the term. "Cyclone" just sounded like a word born for use in Texas like "steer" or "flapjack."

The house she helped Mom and Dad buy was a new construction grey brick, two-story home with a pool in the back yard and a two-car garage. The driveway was large and flat and would come to be my escape as a young teen, a basketball hoop above the garage providing endless challenges. I remember thinking that the home was large and we were rich. And by most standards, I suppose we were. But on a visit to Laurelfield Drive many years later, I realized that a house is kind of like a penis – it seems larger when you are smaller.

I enrolled in the fifth grade at Armand Bayou Elementary School, the fifth school I had attended in my short life. I walked or rode my bike the mile or so through the master-planned community each school day, dodging construction vehicles and wood and nails in the road. The Brook Forest subdivision was only about thirty percent complete when we moved there, and new houses were going up in every direction. I rode down Running Springs Drive across Clearcrest Drive, Mesa Verde Drive, and Larkfield Drive on the way to classes in a flat-roofed, single story building that looked like a school the Brady Brunch might have attended when not at home dealing with the high jinks of Alice, the maid. The neighborhood dripped with a kind of generic but pronounced Americana found in movies like *Poltergeist* and *E.T. the Extra-Terrestrial*, both of which were released in 1982 and both of which I probably saw three or four times. I wondered if any of the houses was built on a Native American burial ground, disturbing the spirits of the dead like those disturbed to the point of kidnapping a young Heather O'Rourke in the movie *Poltergeist*.

Steven Spielberg and his buddy George Lucas spoke to me in a way that cannot be underestimated. My imagination was already stoked daily by the ruminations of my father on everything from giant tentacles to asteroids hitting the earth. Steven and George took it to another level by bringing to life on screen the fantasies and fears that were always lurking in my mind, ready to come to the fore with the slightest encouragement. Indiana Jones and Luke Skywalker were who my father would have been if he had been born in a different time and place. I wanted so desperately to be like them, to save the world from evil in a dashing and unexpected way.

When there were no cars in the garage, I would park my bike in the very center, front wheel facing the door. I'd sit in a lawn chair near the bike, sweating profusely while reading a comic book or browsing an *Estes Model Rocketry* catalog as I pretended to wait for a distress call to come in from somewhere in the neighborhood. I had a walkie-talkie that never worked but it didn't matter; a few times each summer day, the handheld radio would come to imaginary life and I'd hear a call come in from somewhere in the neighborhood pleading for help to vanquish some form of evil. I'd hit the button to raise the garage door and hurriedly jump on the bike, racing out the front of my emergency response headquarters before the door was even completely up, ducking my head as my feet found purchase on the pedals. I'd make a siren sound – "*woo, woo, woo, woo!*" – as I built up speed and took a left on Laurelfield. I'd find a quiet home construction site and run into the half-built frame, locate a piece of wood on the ground, and take it in hand pretending it was a lightsaber. At times my foe was a Stormtrooper sent by Darth Vader or a Moroccan wielding a curved sword. I can't imagine what passers-by must have thought had they seen me race up to a home foundation on my bike, squealing like a tortured cat as I mimicked a siren, and then stopped to pick up a piece of wood and start stabbing randomly at the air with it. It perhaps says something about the innocence of the time that anybody who did see me didn't call the real authorities to come with real sirens blaring to haul me away in a straitjacket.

***

During my early years in Houston, I fell in love with current events. A strange passion, it was borne of my father's habit of sitting down in front of the T.V. at five-thirty every evening to watch ABC's *World News Tonight*. The show's anchor was Frank Reynolds, a journalist and World War II purple heart recipient born and raised not far from where I would eventually go to college, the University of Notre Dame. Frank was my other father (as was Peter Jennings after him) and I eagerly anticipated my thirty minutes with him each day. That anticipation peaked when I'd hear the grating, grumbling sound of Dad's '72 VW station wagon pull into the driveway at 5:25. Dad would walk in, kiss Mom, grab a cold beer from the fridge and plop down in front of the T.V. We didn't have a remote control and so my dad would use me as a remote. I was the human version of today's Amazon Alexa but with more sophistication because not only could I follow a direct command

– *Pat, turn on the T.V.* – but I could also infer my dad's wishes from a statement – *Pat, the sound is a little loud*. I'd dutifully get up from the floor and turn the dial on the front of the tube counterclockwise until he nodded at me silently, swallowing a mouthful of his brew. A few years later, I remember visiting a local electronics shop when Dad was looking for a new T.V. The salesman was trying to convince Dad that he needed to pay a premium for a remote-controlled television. My father replied, "What the hell do I need that for? I have a son." (Years later the guy who said he didn't need a remote control would go ballistic if he couldn't find the remote.)

I relished news time with my father and watched the stories that Frank brought to us from the far reaches of the globe in awe of all that I hadn't seen in the world despite the number of travel miles my young body had amassed. In a day before instant access to information, each telecast was like opening a gift every evening, unsure of what would be in the box. Unfortunately, while news is always bad, even today (if it bleeds it leads), the news in the late 1970s and early 1980s was consistently really, really bad. There was always a pile of shit in the box.

In the waning days of Jimmy Carter's presidency, everything Frank told me seemed to indicate the country – and the world – was falling apart. As Frank spoke, my father added his own commentary on everything from the Iranian hostage crisis to trends in interest rates (topping 15%) to gas shortages. The term "commie" was thrown about liberally and jumped off Dad's tongue in a way that made it seem as if his beer had gone bitter and vile. The term was used so liberally, in fact, it was easy to forget that its original meaning was centered on an economic and political philosophy. Yes, the Soviets were "commies." But so too were unions, hurricanes, Castro, and Jimmy Carter himself. The time with Dad watching *World News Tonight* brought me closer to the world and closer to him. Even when he couldn't be home for the news – which could be often given his travel and training schedule – I'd watch without him and then fill him in when I could, taking pride in sharing with him the latest dispatches from the middle east, Washington D.C., or Central America.

It turned out that watching news with Dad helped me become involved in an activity at school that only fed my desire to learn more about the world. Each week, a booklet with questions about current events would be shipped to my school and the teacher would read them aloud to a set of four to five volunteers assembled in seats in a line in front of the chalkboard. We were asked to raise our hands as quickly as possible if we knew the answers to the questions. Correct answers yielded points and he or she with the most points won. I always knew the answers.

"This week, an American Airlines DC-10 crashed after taking off from what Airport in Illinois?" The teacher looked up from the booklet and scanned the room. Up shot my hand.

"Patrick?"

"Chicago O'Hare," I answered with what, in retrospect, was a sort of smug confidence. Aviation ... please ... the category was child's play for me.*

The questions got harder as we went.

"The Shah of Iran flew to Egypt after being force from power and was greeted by what Egyptian leader?"

"Patrick?"

"Anwar Sadat."

Winning enough of the competitions in the classroom meant you earned a spot in a quarterly trivia death match that occurred in the school cafeteria against others who had made it through the first rounds in their own classrooms. This was my Superbowl. I'd watch the

---

* That DC-10 crashed in 1979 when one of its three engines fell off the plane during take-off. The root cause of the accident was traced to two months earlier when routine maintenance was conducted improperly, causing strain on hardware that held the engine to the wing – strain that worsened as the aircraft was flown more. When the engine eventually came free after two months of flights, it damaged the wing and caused the airplane to roll almost inverted in the direction of the missing engine. One of the victims of the crash was Leonard Stogel, a successful record producer and promoter. A tragedy to be sure. But even more tragic: both of Leonard's parents were killed seventeen years earlier on another American Airlines flight when the Boeing 707 they were on also crashed shortly after takeoff from New York, also rolling nearly inverted into the ground. If ever there was a ranking of happenings that demonstrate the unfairness of life, the tragedy that befell this family would have to make the short list.

news with Dad every evening in the weeks leading up to the capstone competition and commit all I could to memory. When the day came to assemble in the auditorium, I took my seat on a raised platform with four others in front of a couple hundred of my classmates. I forced myself not to get too worked up, afraid that my nerves would lead to the spasming bowels and liquefied stools I'd experience in the moments before running a race at the track. But I never soiled myself. Perhaps I was just more confident when it came to current events than to running. I often won the school-wide competition.

***

My twin sister, Amy, was in the same grade as me but we kept a cordial distance from each other. Our interests were divergent, and we had few friends in common, so there weren't many reasons for our lives to become too intertwined. Even so, the respect and love we had for each other followed us around like virtual secret service agents, ready to spring into action when adversity presented itself. Amy's relationship with Mom mirrored, in some ways, the one I had with Dad. But there was one major exception: while I lived vicariously through Dad, Mom lived vicariously through Amy. She took an interest in Amy's social life that she didn't show in mine. When we were in high school, she enjoyed spending time with Amy and her boyfriends, socializing with them frequently while I went off to play basketball or build a new remote-controlled airplane.

When I wasn't pursuing my own hobbies, I did chores around the house, often unprompted, trying to earn the approval and attention of Mom. While those efforts worked, any notice I got was short-lived. I came to see that I could never be what Amy was – a reincarnation of the young Donna Sei that gave the older Donna Mullane a chance to see what life would have been like if she had not grown up in a stern Italian Catholic family where daughters were cloistered and controlled. Still, while this might explain Mom's closeness to Amy, it didn't explain the distance between her and me. By any standard, I was a good kid. I got good grades. I stayed out of trouble. I was polite. I couldn't help but feel as if I was missing something, as if there was some fog between us.

Laura was likewise living a life that didn't intersect with mine. The three years between us, particularly when Amy and I were eight to ten years old, might as well have been thirty years. She was still a little kid in our eyes. Even when we got older, three years was just enough to keep our social circles from never really intersecting. But while Laura and I didn't share friends or interests, we did share one thing – the distance from Mom. Strangely, I thought I could explain Laura's tenuous relationship with Mom better than my own. She was turning thirteen around the time that Amy was becoming a beautiful high schooler. Amy had little trouble attracting a boyfriend while Laura (much like me) was an awkward teen with braces and short hair. This alone might have been enough to spawn jealousy, but it was exacerbated by Mom's closeness to Amy. While I couldn't quite pin the tension that existed in the relationship between Mom and me, at least I could tell myself that as a boy I was just not somebody that Mom could relate to that well. As a girl, Laura didn't have this excuse and she must have wondered why Mom didn't live vicariously through her. Whatever the reasons, Mom and Laura were often frustrating each other.

We had all spent our young lives living nowhere near extended family owing to Dad's profession and its requirement for migrating from one assignment to another. It would seem on the surface that this isolation from blood relatives would have forged tighter bonds between Amy, Laura, and me – like shipwrecked passengers on a desert island coming together to survive the perils of a hostile new world. But in reality, it worked the other way around, especially given how different we were – we each sought out friends in our neighborhood and our schools. And while those little communities we built around ourselves served us well, there was still an invisible strand that tied us together like a tether tying each of us to a space station.

***

I entered middle school (grades six through eight in Texas) in 1981. It was the year of the first space shuttle launch and my trip with Pop Pop and Grandma in the motor home to California for the landing of *Columbia*. Astronauts John Young and Bob Crippen returned as heroes – if not to the nation then to those of us in the space-crazy community abutting the Johnson Space Center. There was a new buzz in the town as people became more comfortable with the idea that this shuttle thing might work.

It was during my middle school years that I made some friends who loved to play basketball. One of them had a hoop mounted on the stretch of roof over a breezeway that connected his garage to his home. It was about two feet lower than a regulation hoop and so I loved to go over to his house (as did half the neighborhood) and try to slam-dunk over defenders. Playing basketball with those friends got me hooked on the sport and one day at dinner I was telling Dad and Mom how much I loved it.

"Why don't you try out for the team at school?" Dad suggested.

Dad's comment was not grounded in some delusion about sports someday being a ticket to a free college education or, more ambitiously, a pro career. He didn't even suggest it in the context of creating some good college application fodder. Other than the Army-Navy football game, which he was only marginally intrigued by, Dad didn't have a scintilla of interest in anything sports related. In fact, when I was well into adulthood, I took my father to a Red Sox game at Fenway Park in Boston. He had lost some of his hearing and so he spoke loudly. Between innings, Dad pointed to some numbers on the balcony of right field seats and practically shouted, "What are those numbers over there?!" I could sense people around us listening.

"I think they are retired numbers of great Red Sox players," I replied.

"Do you know any of them?"

"I don't know many of them," I said, then pointed to number nine, "but I think that one is Ted Williams."

Dad contemplated my answer as he chewed on some peanuts. He looked confused.

"Ted Williams ... Ted Williams," he repeated the name, his brain clearly working. Finally, his thought was formed. And he shared it with me and (unfortunately) all of those around us.

"Ted Williams? Wasn't he the guy that died of Lou Gehrig's disease?"

The tightly packed fans around us giggled. I was mortified.

"No Dad," I said, "that was Lou Gehrig."

No, Mom and Dad weren't suggesting I try out for the basketball team because they were sports enthusiasts who had dreams of raising some super-athlete. They were simply interested in keeping us occupied and driving home the "you never knew until you try" life lesson. My sisters and I heard this over and over again any time we expressed doubt in our chances of succeeding at something. Unfortunately for us, our father, a relatively nerdy underachiever in high school and mediocre student from West Point (winning his spot at the academy as a third alternate – two others before him backed out) had used this philosophy when he applied to become an astronaut.

"Look at your father," Mom would say. "If he hadn't applied, he wouldn't have become an astronaut."

Sometimes having a dad as an astronaut could be very annoying. But their logic was sound.

I resolved to try to make the sixth-grade team. Dad worked all day one Saturday to mount a regulation-height goal above our garage. Tryouts for the middle school were only a couple of weeks away and so I didn't have much time to get very good before I had to report to the school gym for what I hoped was the first day of a two-day tryout. Whatever skills I thought I had while playing with my buddies on a non-regulation goal and on my own setup in the driveway of our house did not translate when I got to the tryouts. I was outclassed in every respect. I came home down about how the tryout had gone but convinced that since I had tried really hard, I would make the team based on grit alone. Reality hit the next morning when I returned to the school to see a sheet posted on the door outside the gym with the names of those who had made it to the second round. My name was not on the list. I fought back tears as I left the school. Trying hard mattered. But trying hard and having skill mattered more.

At home that evening Dad and Mom were sympathetic but didn't allow me to dwell in my pre-pubescent misery. Mom suggested that I dive right back into practicing and then tryout again the following year. And after a short period of mourning, that's exactly what I did. When I wasn't watching the news, or studying, or building model airplanes, or collecting *Star Wars* figures, I was out on the cement dribbling past imaginary defenders to score the winning shot for the Clear Lake Middle School Eagles. Dad even helped make the defender less imaginary. Using PVC tubing he built "Hakeem" – named after center Hakeem Olajuwon of the Houston Rockets NBA team – for me. Hakeem was a PVC stick figure with arms raised as if he were being robbed by a gun-wielding opponent. He was mounted on a flat plywood platform with caster wheels so that I could easily move him around the driveway. News of Hakeem spread quickly and soon neighborhood boys were showing up at my house to marvel at the seven-footer. I'd shoot over Hakeem's outstretched arms until after the sun set, only coming in when my mother started hollering at me to get washed up for dinner or when I couldn't move fast enough anymore to keep mosquitos from chewing on my legs and arms.

A year later, the two-day tryouts rolled around again. This time, the first day was nothing like the same day on the previous year. I was on fire. I performed in every way. At the end of the tryout, Coach Saxe gathered all of us together. A tall man with a bit of a belly, he was every bit the stereotypical coach. He wore the polyester coaches' shorts that fit too tightly and rose too high and had a whistle around his neck even when he was walking the hallways of the school. He said that the first cuts would be made that evening and that the next day many of us would be disappointed. Then he called me forward, put his arm around my shoulder, and turned me to face the rest of the boys.

"For those of you who will be cut," he said, "I want you to take a lesson from Pat here. He tried out last year and got cut after the first day. But he worked his butt off since then. Those of you who saw him play last year know how much he's improved. And because of that dedication and improvement, this year he is going to make the team."

I was dumfounded. I wasn't even going to have to go through the two rounds of agonizing eliminations others would have to endure. I had made the team.

If coach had handed me a ball at that moment, I would have been able to slam it home like a pro player on a fast break. I caught a ride home from a friend and burst through the front door shouting that I had made the team. Mom and Dad cheered over-enthusiastically and each gave me a hug. As satisfied as I was about becoming the newest member of the Eagles squad, much more of the satisfaction came from knowing that I had made my parents – and particularly my father – proud. Dad's pride was always of the quiet variety that made it poignantly more powerful than the braggadocio evident in the fathers of my friends. He spent his energy on letting his children know they had done well by radiating pride back into the family, not wasting it on noisy proclamations to the outside world. I went to bed that night feeling more accomplished and loved than probably anybody else in the world.

CHAPTER 6: FLYING THE FRIENDLY SKIES

While my sisters, parents, and I frequently traveled to Albuquerque during holidays, we also spent quite a bit of time at a ranch south of Dallas owned by cousins of my father. Comprised of about 2,000 acres, we called the property "The Ranch" as if it were a tony, branded resort outside of Aspen which, to a kid, it might as well have been. I loved going there. The Ranch was managed by Peggy and Barry Austin. Peggy was my father's cousin – a Pettigrew – and Barry was her baritone-voiced, six-foot-five, thick-boned husband. Barry was more Texan than Sam Houston and often spoke as if he belonged in an earlier century, riding with the Texas Rangers or defending the Alamo against the Mexicans whose progeny now tormented Joe Joe with crank calls. He once bought a property abutting The Ranch that had a home on it several miles from the main cluster of homes on the original property. Somebody had been breaking into the house and Barry was incensed. He was venting about the larceny in front of my father and me one day.

"If I catch that sonofabitch, I'm going to put a bullet through him."

Dad knew that Barry was serious. He had an arsenal of weapons and the motivation to carry out his threat.

"Barry," Dad said, "I'd be careful. Shooting a guy inside the house is one thing, but if you shoot him in the yard or on the road, you could end up in jail."

No jury empaneled within biking distance of a town named Gun Barrel City (really – that's the name of a town near The Ranch) was going to indict a guy who shot an intruder in his own home. But even in Texas, Dad and I knew that hunting down a thief who wasn't inside the four walls of the home he burglarized was different territory altogether.

Barry looked at my dad. His eyes narrowed to intimidating slits. "Don't you worry," he said, a Cheshire cat grin spreading across his face, "they'll find him in the house."

The Ranch was less than a four-hour drive north of our home in Houston. The drive to Albuquerque was fourteen hours, so if we wanted some time with the extended family, The Ranch was the option of choice. My sisters and I eagerly anticipated days when we would pack up the Chevy Citation (our first car with air conditioning) and hit the road. We marked the progress on the voyage by the exits to towns that were quintessentially Texan in both history and name.

Just north of the city limits we passed through Conroe which, for a short time in the 1930s according to the Texas State Historical Association, boasted more millionaires per capita than any city in the country due to profits reaped from oil claims. About a third of the way into our trip, we passed through Huntsville where the Texas correctional system had its oldest prison. We often talked about the town and the prison as we flew by its exits off of I-45. There was good reason for the chatter: with the reinstatement of the death penalty in Texas in 1982, the prison, which acted as the state's execution facility, took up its new mission with gusto: as of 2018, death row in Huntsville had carried out more executions than any other death chamber in the United States. With less than two hours left in our trip, we'd fly through Buffalo, Texas. The town was established in 1872 on a railroad line and was named after the buffalo that roamed the area before they were all slaughtered by rifle-toting hunters. Finally, we'd exit the freeway and take winding two-lane roads through the country, cross a cattle guard with a rumble on the tires, and pull into the dirt driveway of Peggy and Barry's. In the distance was another home. It belonged to Barry's parents, Orv and Bernice.

Several times while living in Houston, we made the trip to The Ranch for the Thanksgiving holiday. I was once outside of Orv's house playing alone on one such visit when he stepped out from his modest home. Orv was a more muted and older version of the character "Cousin Eddie" played by Dennis Quaid in the 1983 movie *National Lampoon's Vacation*. Like Cousin Eddie, Orv had a prominent beer belly, but in Orv's case it was made more prominent by his propensity to wear a white t-shirt tucked into his jeans. The primary factor that contributed to the Cousin Eddie comparison, though, was both men's constant beer drinking. I don't believe I ever once saw Orv without a Budweiser can in his hand. On Sundays, while the rest of the family prepared to go to nine o'clock mass, Orv was in the kitchen getting ingredients together to make us brunch for when we returned (Orv never went to mass with us). When we got back from mass, he'd be whisking eggs in a bowl with one hand and sipping on a beer with the other. He was a one-man band, moving deftly between laying out bacon in a frying pan and pouring pancake batter onto a griddle like a robot on an assembly line. The pancake batter was next to him in a bowl on the counter and, as he flipped the flapjacks in the pan, he alternately took a sip from his beer and then poured a dash of the brew into the uncooked batter. Say what you will ... we were all convinced that the precise measures of beer Orv delivered to the batter gave his pancakes their trademark fluffiness.

"Hey Pat," Orv said when he found me in his yard playing, "can you do me a favor?" He was standing in the cool November air in his white T-shirt, a Budweiser, as usual, stitched into his right hand.

"Sure!" I said enthusiastically to his request. Orv was a man of few words, at least with me, and I found myself excited to have been recognized by him and enlisted in some yet-to-be-named task.

"Come here," he said and motioned for me to walk with him in the direction of a pen that held a pet turkey. The pen was a wire-framed cage about four feet high. The turkey was a big one, with claws on it that looked like they could hold a beer can twice the circumference of the one in Orv's hand.

Orv opened a small gate on the pen. I looked at him quizzically.

"Get in there and shoo that Turkey into that corner over there," he pointed to a place in the pen to his left. I unquestioningly complied and bent at the waist to enter the pen. I stopped part way in as I heard him close the gate behind me, confining me in the enclosure with the

Turkey which, at this point, was nervously gobbling and walking away from me toward the corner Orv had designated.

Now, you, the reader, may see where this story is going. It was November. It was the Thanksgiving holiday. I was in a cage with a "pet" turkey. It doesn't take the rocket scientist I so longed to be to get a sense of how this might end. But for whatever reason, in that pen with that turkey on that cold late autumn day, I never gave two thoughts as to why I was doing what I was doing. An adult had asked me for help. I had been taught to obey. Like a drill instructor who trains his recruits to execute orders without protest, my mother's ways had made me exceptionally compliant. If a possibly intoxicated man asked me to get into a cage with a turkey that weighed more than me and shoo it into a corner, I was going to do it, even if that turkey could slash me across the abdomen with a sweep of its claw, spilling my intestines onto the hard Texas ground.

I tentatively worked my way toward the bird, my arms outstretched to increase my size and guide him to the point where the metal mesh came to a corner. Orv was shadowing me on the outside of the cage, walking slowly as he sipped his beer. After just a few moments, the Turkey was trapped. I tilted my head to the side and raised my eyebrows as I did my best in the confining space to train my eyes on Orv.

"What now, Orv?" I asked.

Orv didn't answer – at least not with words. Instead, he reached behind himself slowly with his beer-less hand and pulled a pistol from his waistband. Then, in one fluid motion, with me just feet from the bird, he placed the barrel of the gun through the fencing just inches from the head of the clearly concerned gobbling animal and …

Blam!

Most of the bird's head was gone in an instant. I felt vaporized blood on me as the rest of the turkey now began to flail about like … well, like a chicken with its head cut off. I was paralyzed in shock and fear, still standing with my arms outstretched – not that the turkey could see me making myself large and intimidating, his eyeballs were likely in Louisiana by now.

I caught a glimpse of Orv in my peripheral vision calmly placing the pistol back between his jeans and underwear. By the time he had the gun back in its improvised holster, he was shouting at me to grab the turkey. I, needless to say, was incredulous. The headless turkey was flapping its wings and running about like a football fan that had just watched its team throw a touchdown on the last play of the game.

"Grab it!" Orv was shouting at me. His voice mingled with the ringing in my ears caused by the discharge of his pistol feet from my head. Again, I obeyed as if there was no alternative. I started following the turkey around the pen, still hunched at my waist. I didn't too aggressively make a move toward the bird. I thought that any second it would collapse into a lifeless, feathered mass. After all, how long can an animal make do without a head? Apparently for quite a while. I unenthusiastically and unsuccessfully reached for its body, trying to grab the outstretched wings which spanned a distance greater than my arms fingertip to fingertip.

"Don't grab the body!" Orv shouted. "Grab his legs!"

I wanted little to do with the dying bird's claws. Orv's request was tantamount to asking me to grab an agitated rattlesnake by its fangs.

"Its legs!" he repeated.

The bird was now in the corner opposite the one where I had seen his head liberated from his body. It continued to flap its wings, but its motions became less spasmodic and less intense. I got lower and, like a wrestler trying to gain advantage by securing the legs of my opponent, I dove at his ankles – if a turkey has ankles. I got one of the legs in my hand and held on for dear life. His other leg continued to clutch at the air as if he was hoping to find his own head lying about somewhere in the pen. I didn't notice at the time, given the shock I was experiencing, but the leg I didn't grab was scratching the hell out of my forearm.

I finally wrestled both legs into my hands as the last twitches of life fled the bird. Covered in its blood and my own, I dragged the turkey to the door of the pen which Orv had now opened to let me out. I was suddenly exhausted.

The next day, I enjoyed that bird with stuffing and cranberry sauce and took pride in the fact that I had helped put the food on the table.

***

Dad was assigned to his first shuttle mission in 1982 when I was fourteen years old. He would be flying on the twelfth attempted launch, the first launch of the newest space shuttle, *Discovery*. The first four launches of the shuttle program, all of them using the orbiter *Columbia*, had been considered test flights that would validate the fundamental assumptions about the viability of the launch vehicle as a "bus" that could take astronauts and payloads into space as frequently as every two weeks.

Declaring the system "operational" after just four test flights and subsequent pressures to prove that it indeed was a cost-effective way to get into space would be the first ominous guideposts on the way to the loss of *Challenger*, *Columbia*, and their fourteen crew members. While Dad later talked about how he and many of his astronaut colleagues had grave concerns about the pace of the program and dangers it presented, none of those concerns were evident to me as a young teenager. And in any case, those grave concerns only went so far. He and his astronaut peers just wanted the shuttle to keep flying so that the line to get into space kept moving. I watched launches ahead of Dad's scheduled mission with my breath held knowing what he did – that a catastrophic failure early in the program might lead to its demise and he would have to return to his Air Force career, remaining an astronaut in name only. As those missions preceding his returned safely to earth, his own training picked up in earnest. He was working late and traveling more. I watched missions launch and return, launch and return, still not believing that Dad's turn would ever come.

The same year Dad's mission assignment brought joy to the family, the death of Nonnie, the mob boss's wife, brought melancholy. I remember crying at the news and the realization that I never really knew her. We saw her and Joe Joe no more than two times a year. The separation of about 1,000 miles meant that visits were infrequent. And, in contrast to Joe Joe, her more muted existence of cigarette smoking and novel-reading at the kitchen table meant that memories of her were more muted too.

It says something that when she did die the memories that most involved her were ones of her and Joe Joe fighting. As a child, I thought their epic fights – which they had no reservations about engaging in with the children present – were more humorous than bothersome. One favorite family story regarding their quarrels revolved around Joe Joe, a stove top, and the mystery of the "moved" pot.

Joe Joe's role as the primary food preparer had him standing at the stovetop for about an hour each evening making up a delicious dish. During a visit to our home in Houston, Mom helped Joe Joe cook one day, but other than setting and clearing the table, we kids were allowed to relax as he made the meal. During that free time, we sat with Nonnie and played cards at a round table nestled into a nook framed by bay windows that looked into our backyard. One evening, Joe Joe had gotten the ingredients of a supper into a pot and put it on the stovetop to cook. He then left the room for a moment. After returning to the kitchen and futzing around working on an appetizer for several minutes, he noticed that while the pot was on the stove and on a burner, it wasn't on a lit burner. Once again disregarding the principle of Occam's Razor, Joe Joe didn't gravitate to the most likely – and simplest – explanation for why the pot wasn't hot: he had turned on the wrong burner. In his mind, that couldn't be the explanation because he was never wrong. So, he did the only thing he could do; he blamed somebody else.

"Amy," he said, calling Nonnie by her first name, "why did you move that pot?"

Nonnie rolled her eyes a bit as she dealt the cards to Amy, Laura, and me. "I didn't," she said, mustering a very matter-of-fact tone.

"Well then why isn't it on the burner that I turned on?" Joe Joe asked.

Notwithstanding the fact that Nonnie had been in her chair at the kitchen table with me and my sisters the entire time he was fixing dinner, I found Joe Joe's firm belief in what had happened as confusing as the certitude he had about people calling him and hanging up. His accusation made no sense.

Nonnie took a long draw on her cigarette as if to prepare herself for the answer we all knew was coming. As smoke glided out of her nose in swirling dual streams she said, "Maybe the pot isn't hot because *somebody* turned on the wrong burner."

I could see Joe Joe's jaw clench. I giggled a little inside. Her use of the word "somebody" was too much and I almost found that giggle in my head escape me for the rest of the world to hear. Nonnie wasn't going to admit to an imaginary transgression, and Joe Joe was having none of it. He banged around the kitchen for a few moments as Nonnie turned her attention back to my sisters and me at the table. We all knew the matter wasn't done though, and Nonnie seemed to continue our card game with her guard up, knowing that another verbal artillery shell was going to be lobbed into our little circle.

Joe Joe continued cooking, not saying anything for the next several moments but certainly letting us know he was there and not pleased. Drawers were closed a bit more forcefully, the door to the oven was dropped when opened, a used serving spoon was thrown into the dishwasher utensil basket with a loud clang. I watched him warily from the kitchen table, peaking over my cards like a Vegas pit boss keeping an eye on a troublemaker at the blackjack table.

After several moments, he said nothing and the tension in the room seemed to dissipate. I thought that maybe the argument was over. Then this:

"Really Amy. Why *did* you move the damned pot?!"

Nonnie took another deep drag on her cigarette. Her eyes narrowed to match the frame of the glasses she wore. I could see her waiting for the nicotine to palliate the stress induced by Joe Joe's obstinacy.

"I *didn't*," she said with a raspy retort, the words squeezing from between her teeth along with the residue of another exhaled puff of smoke.

At that, the discussion ended.

I was going to miss Nonnie and her steely, quiet resolve in the face of Joe Joe's conspiracy theories big and small, her love of cigarettes and dime-store novels, and her willingness to teach Amy, Laura and me all manner of card games. And given the tears that I saw in Joe Joe's eyes after her passing – the only ones I ever saw him shed – I knew that he would miss his wife of 48 years, even if she wouldn't admit to moving that pot.

***

Now that Dad was assigned as "Mission Specialist 1" to a crew, he spent a lot of time with those who would ride *Discovery* with him. Some of that time was at our home, having beers after work under a pergola by the pool.

THE FATHER, SON, AND HOLY SHUTTLE

The team that would fly on STS-41D* included Hank Hartsfield (Commander), Mike Coats (Pilot), Judy Resnik (Mission Specialist 3), Steve Hawley (Mission Specialist 2), and Charlie Walker (Payload Specialist 1). Judy would be the second American woman in space after Sally Ride, who happened to be married to Steve Hawley. I always liked Judy. Perhaps because she wasn't married and didn't have any family in the area, she seemed to take on her NASA colleagues as her kin. My mom and dad invited her for dinner and drinks frequently. She struck me as the feisty little sister playing opposite the pesky older brothers and, as would be expected with somebody playing that role, she dished as much as she got. No ingrate comment in her presence by Dad or another one of his male military colleagues was left without a rejoinder from Judy. I'd often hear that verbal sparring; nobody seemed too concerned about teenagers being a witness to the crude jokes being lobbed across a table scattered with Coors Light beer cans, half-eaten bags of tortilla chips, and splotches of spilled salsa.

Because members of the crew were at the house occasionally, their spouses were too. Sally Ride sometimes joined for the after-work beverages in our backyard with her husband, Steve. She had already become a celebrity after her first space shuttle mission in 1983 but she was a reluctant one to be sure. In fact, I found Sally to be a quiet person who, through the eyes of a young teen-aged boy anyway, seemed to be a foreigner in the world she occupied. The environment she had known before joining NASA had been very different than that of Dad, Hartsfield, and Coats, all of whom had been military flyers – like much of the TFNG astronaut class. She had been an academic and was

---

* "STS" stood for "space transportation system" and was a term used to describe the shuttle, the solid rockets, and the external tank together. The "4" in "41D" referred to the year in which the launch was expected: 1984. The "1" meant that the launch would be out of Kennedy Space Center. Plans were in work to launch a shuttle from California, and so there was a need to specify which launch site the mission flew out of. The "D" represented the anticipated sequence of the launch in a given year. "A" would be the first launch, "B" the second, and so on. So, STS-41D was planned to be the fourth mission launched out of KSC in 1984. After the loss of *Challenger* NASA returned to a simpler sequential numbering system as they had used in the Apollo days.

insulated from the raucous locker-room culture that permeated military brotherhoods of the time – and still does today in many quarters. She was very different from Judy.

While it was not publicly known at the time (although I learned later many astronauts suspected it), Sally was gay and almost certainly knew that such a revelation would have quashed any chance she had to fly in space, much less earn the opportunity to become an American icon in the process.

Some measure of enlightenment with respect to homosexuality was still years away and any progress being made took a big step backward with the discovery of new disease and its association with the gay community. The Centers for Disease Control (CDC) first used the term "AIDS" in 1981, the same year as the first space shuttle launch, but it became a household term four years later when Ryan White, a hemophiliac boy in Indiana, contracted the disease through a blood transfusion. He gained notoriety when he entered a protracted legal battle to return to his school after leaving it to be treated for infections brought on by his failing immune system. The association between homosexuality and the virus added additional fuel to the anti-gay fires already burning in the culture at the time. In 1980 Bob Jones III, then president of Bob Jones University (a school founded by his grandfather) said that the problem of homosexuality would be "solved posthaste" if gays were stoned.* The same year Sally flew her first mission, Pat Buchanan, an advisor to President Reagan, said in reference to the surge in AIDS cases, "The poor homosexuals – they have declared war against nature, and now nature is exacting an awful retribution." Even Bob Hope added some commentary on the matter. At the rededication of the Statue of Liberty in 1986 he joked, "I just heard the Statue of Liberty has AIDS. Nobody knows if she got it from

---

* Mr. Jones had strong feelings on a number of topics. Until 2005 (*2005!*) the university he led did not allow interracial dating because, "God had separated His people for His purpose." In an article for a Bob Jones University magazine written shortly after Pope Paul VI's death in 1978, he wrote that the Pope was "the archpriest of Satan, a deceiver and an anti-Christ," and that he "has, like Judas, gone to his own place." He is famously known for saying, "The most sobering reality in the world today is that people are dying and going to hell..." We'll save a place for you Bob!

THE FATHER, SON, AND HOLY SHUTTLE

the mouth of the Hudson or the Staten Island 'Fairy.'" While these comments drew outrage in some quarters, in the early eighties homosexuality was still something in the shadows and the public's views on gay issues were less than accommodating. Early in the decade, no more than 10% of adults believed that same-sex marriage should be allowed (a 2017 Gallup Poll showed 64% of Americans supported gay marriage) and so more ubiquitous condemnation was not forthcoming.

No, Sally couldn't have been who she really was and be an astronaut. While I'm sure some of the quiet distance I observed in her during her visits to our home were indeed due to the secret she held and the disconnection it made her feel from the aviator community she was a part of, I'm sure some of what I saw was an obdurate resolve to chase a dream no less important to her than the same dream my father held: to fly in space. And as difficult as the road had been for Dad on his way to the cabin of a space shuttle, Sally's road had been twice again as hard and, in some ways, immensely more treacherous. While she is known as a hero for becoming the first American woman in space, perhaps the more meaningful accomplishment was doing what she did as an astronaut while knowing something she couldn't control and wouldn't affect her performance could have killed her dream in the cradle and marginalized her for much of the rest of her life. For taking on that burden and still finding success, she's a hero to me.

***

The crew of STS-41D would need a new mission patch and when they went looking for somebody who could do some initial renderings, they wondered: who has a love of aviation and a passion for drawing aircraft and spaceships? Dad thought of me and asked if I would be willing to draw some concepts.

Are you kidding? I thought.

I was born to draw mission patches. I was the Van Gogh of aviation drawings; in fact, I would have cut off my own ear as part of a plea to be the artist that helped design a mission patch. My father asking me to help was like a pro baseball player asking a little league player if he wanted to be the batboy for a professional ball club. Like that batboy, I became part of the team, if only tangentially. And being a part of the community that Dad occupied was more gratifying to me than being part of some "in crowd" at school.

Discovery was a name that had a long history tied to a number of exploratory vessels. English Captain James Cook commanded a ship christened *Discovery* in the latter half of the eighteenth century during his exploration of the South Pacific, an exploration that led to the "discovery" of the Hawaiian Islands.* A ship used by Henry Hudson while trying to find a northern passage between the Atlantic and Pacific is also credited as a namesake to the orbiter my father would take into space. The 41D crew had an idea that the patch should pay homage to the sailing vessels that preceded the space vessel and so the crew asked if I could draw something that would include a ship like that of Cook or Hudson. I went to the library at my school and sought out the reference section to scan volumes of the *Encyclopedia Britannica* on the shelf. The librarian asked me what I was up to and I told her with pride, but cryptically, that I was doing research on a project (all very hush-hush, you know) for my father's upcoming space shuttle mission. She rolled her eyes. My school had a number of astronaut children so the novelty of my relationship to a star sailor – "astronaut" broken into its Greek roots – was actually no novelty at all.

The *Encyclopedia Britannica* was first published a few years before Cook landed in Hawaii and, in its totality, was only three volumes. The set I walked along, head tilted to the side seeking out the right book for my research, was more than thirty volumes long. I found what I was looking for only three spines in – the book that covered topics between *Ceara* and *Deluc*. I found James Cook in the first third of the pages. In the entry about him were some photographs of paintings showing the ships he had commanded, three-masted and regal. Dad and his crewmates had an inkling that the patch should show the ship of the past being connected to the shuttle of the future in some way. Twelve stars on the patch would denote the twelfth shuttle mission. I drew no less than fifty different variations of the main theme and bounced them off my father as I went. I also drew a humorous piece

---

* While precision is elusive when it comes to timing the arrival of those that *really* discovered the islands for the first time, it was likely sometime in the early to mid 1200s. The settling of Hawaii by seafaring explorers who "island hopped" across the vastness of the Pacific in relatively small boats not knowing if they'd ever see land again makes the idea of astronauts as "explorers" seem laughable.

that showed an old sailing vessel of the kind Cook commanded inhabited by caricatures of each of the crewmembers taking on personas they had adopted after being named the "zoo crew" by an office secretary. My dad was Tarzan; he was seen swinging from a vine tied to a cross beam of one of the masts. Judy Resnik was Jane. I drew her in a bikini-like ensemble that today would land me in sensitivity training. The commander, Hartsfield, was the zookeeper and was shown with a whip in his hand. Mike Coats, the pilot, was Superman owing to his boyish good looks and blue eyes; he was seen in a cape flying about the ship. Drawing that sketch and giving it to the crew filled me further with pride – I was even more "in" since I knew of their secret identities. I can't help but wonder if, in retrospect, they saw me as a dingleberry – a tiny piece of fecal matter hanging on for dear life in a desire to be close to them. If they did, I don't blame them. I'm sure I was.

***

As Dad was preparing for his first space shuttle mission, I was finding my footing in high school. Each class at Clear Lake High School, home of the Falcons, had about 700 students. The freshman class was in a building across the street from the rest of the school. The balance of about 2,100 sophomores, juniors, and seniors were in a single-story, sprawling building with an office and cafeteria at the center and wings of classrooms radiating from that locus like the legs of a spider. The school had four basketball courts, a large swimming pool, and a theater that could hold around 1,000 people. In many respects it was like a small college. While the stereotype of all things in Texas being big was a bit overblown in my mind, it seemed to be true when it came to the size of schools. In 2017, the largest school in Texas, just north of Dallas, boasted an enrollment of 6,664 pupils.

Finding an identity in a high school so large was difficult. I had continued to play basketball and that was about the only thing keeping me from being the strange nerd nobody wanted to hang out with. "Lake" – a truncated pseudonym for "Clear Lake" – was known for its prowess in the sport with all the credit given to our authoritarian coach, Bill Krueger. Coach Krueger had a bulbous nose, close-set eyes, and a pursed mouth that made him look angry all the time. And that might be because he was. He lorded over a cadre of coaches with a team for every grade. He was the mayor, police department, and preacher at the school, holding as much (or more) sway than the senior administrators at the central office. Coach Krueger yelled about everything as he strutted about the basketball court, leaning at the waist as if his head was anxious to get somewhere before the rest of his body did. As much as I feared Coach Krueger, I longed for his approval, hoping (as other boys did) to become one of his "chosen ones," destined to play on the state-ranked varsity team. During the summers, he would open the gym in the afternoon and boys from all over Clear Lake would show up to self-organize games. I'd ride my bike the mile and a half from my home to the school, already drenched in sweat by the time I arrived, hoping I wasn't too late to be a part of the first pick-up game. Little did I know at the time that by my senior year I'd be on the sidelines as the only male cheerleader in the entire district, possibly in the state of Texas.

In a stroke of luck, I was able to feed a passion other than basketball during my regular school day since my high school offered—as a for-credit class—the Federal Aviation Administration's (FAA's) ground school. In the class, I learned about the physics of flight, the parameters of controlled airspace, how to read the instruments of an aircraft, and a myriad of FAA regulations. The final exam for the course was the FAA written exam – effectively one half of the work needed to become a private pilot (the other half being actual "stick time" in an aircraft). I only took a few formal flying lessons with an instructor since that could get expensive and, in any case, my father had gotten his private license and would bring me along with him whenever he rented a plane. Flying with Dad was where I got my flight training.

Dad rented our planes at Ellington Field, the same airport that he flew T-38 jets out of with his fellow astronauts. The Cessna 172 models we rented were nothing like the sexy, two-person, tapered-waist, white and blue jets that Dad flew. The 172 was a single-engine, propeller-powered workhorse of flight training and leisure flying. In fact, more 172s have been manufactured than any other airplane in the world. On the nights before he and I were to go for a flight together, I couldn't sleep, hopped up on anticipation of the adventure that would start the next morning. We'd wake up early and head to the airport, the Houston air heavy with moisture, a low fog hanging along the ground. By the time we got to Ellington Field the sun was an orange ball on the eastern horizon and its radiation began to burn the fog into an ever-thinning network of ankle-high vapor rivulets. Dad and I would check in at the rental desk and then walk to the airplane across the tarmac. I could see the T-38s and other military-type aircraft parked in the distance and imagined myself as a pilot in the UK making my way to a fighter that would escort a phalanx of bombers set to deliver their bombs to Dresden or Berlin.

Dad taught me how to do the preflight check; I took great pride in moving around the outside of the plane, feeling like a real aviator as I checked the fuel to ensure there was no water or sentiment in the tank, wiggled the control surfaces to verify free movement, and released the tie downs. After the walk-around, we got into the two front seats – Dad in the command position on the left and I in the co-pilot seat to the right – and continued with the rest of the pre-flight checklist. Dad would read out the items and I'd take action and respond:

"Throttle open."

"Check."

"Mixture rich."

"Check."

"Carb heat cold."

"Check"

Several items later, we'd get to the step to start the engine and Dad would open the window and shout "Clear!" to ensure no passersby was in danger of losing a limb or worse. Seeing nobody in the area, he turned the key and the airframe vibrated as if shivering off cold and the propeller took two lazy arcs before the motor found its pace and roared to life. Dad contacted the tower asking for clearance to taxi to the active runway and we'd be on our way.

Breaking the rules of the aircraft rental agreement, Dad let me, his sixteen-year-old son, do most of the flying. I don't think he was aware of what this tiny act of rebellion and trust did for me. Sons want nothing more than to be connected to their fathers through their dad's vocation. The farmer's boy driving a tractor. The carpenter's son swinging a hammer. The pilot's son flying an airplane. I have in my later years wondered what gave me the confidence to do so many things that I'd later attempt. Much of the answer to that question was found in those weekend flights with my dad.

I put my left hand on the throttle, pushed it slightly forward, and then released the brakes to begin our taxi. As the plane moved forward, I steered using the rudder pedals under my feet which turned the nose gear. When we got to the runway threshold, I would push on the top of the pedals with my toes to engage the brakes as we waited for final clearance from the tower to take off.

"November six seven kilo, cleared for takeoff, runway one-seven right. Winds one six zero at five knots."

The designation "November six seven kilo" referred to the ID of the airplane which was painted on the fuselage's side. The full ID on our plane was N5467K but it was common to shorten your plane's call sign to the first letter and last three characters. All the planes we flew had an "N" at the beginning of the identification. This was the prefix assigned in the early days of flight to aircraft registered in the United States. In aviation and the military, a word was used to represent each letter (the phonetic alphabet): "N's" word was "November" and "K's" was "kilo" – thus the designation "November six seven kilo." The use of a word rather than a letter ensured no confusion was sown due to crackling radio transmission where "N" might sound like "M"; "S" might sound like "F"; and "T" might sound like a "B." My favorite phonetic words were "Yankee" (for the letter "Y") and "Foxtrot" (for the letter "F"). They had a special cadence to them that, if sound could take on a physical form, felt like testosterone soaked in jet fuel and wrapped in a jockstrap. The words "G" and "H," on the other hand, were less inspiring. I prayed we wouldn't rent a plane that would require me to say "Golf" or "Hotel."

Dad let me pull the plane onto the runway and I pushed the throttle forward to begin our takeoff roll. There were two control yokes that were tied together – one in front of him and one in front of me – as were the rudder pedals under the instrument panel. Dad kept his hands and feet loosely on the yoke and pedals adding tiny corrections as we reached "rotation speed" (about 65 mph) and I raised the nose of the plane with a pull back on the yoke. The thrill of becoming disconnected from the earth was something I never got tired of. Succumbing to the gravity that kept feet firmly planted on the ground was something that normal men allowed. Not aviators. Not me. Being airborne made me feel uniquely powerful and doing so with my father made that power feel somehow more intimate, as if he and I alone had secretly conspired to defy the laws of God himself.

We also were defying the laws of man by having me fly the rental plane without a pilot's license. I was badass – like Indiana Jones. *Raiders of the Lost Ark* had been released in 1981 and I had seen it somewhere near a dozen times. Indy taught me the value of taking action to advance a cause even if that sometimes required breaking the rules. To be sure, Dad and I weren't fighting the Nazis by renting that plane, but it didn't matter. What mattered is that Indy would have flown illegally with his father in his youth – and he grew up to fight the Nazis.

We climbed out of Ellington Field and headed south toward Galveston Island. Dad would find one of the small airports that dotted the flat swampland between Houston and the gulf coast and we would practice landings. One time, we stopped at a single-runway airfield to go to the bathroom and grab a snack. When we got back in the plane to head back to Ellington, we noticed that our radios weren't working. While this was not that big of a problem if we stayed in the airspace around one of the very small uncontrolled fields like the one we had stopped at, it presented a much bigger problem if we were to fly the plane back to Ellington field and its controlled airspace where not only civilian aircraft like ours were landing and departing, but where high performance jets were as well.

Dad cursed – godDAMNit! – and got out of the plane to return to the small building just off the tarmac. I followed him into the structure relishing the fix we found ourselves in. We had a real anomaly like one of the many that might have been thrown at my dad and the *Discovery* crew while they trained in simulators at JSC for hours on end. Except this wasn't a simulation. This was real!

Dad found a payphone and dialed the number of the control tower at Ellington Field, which he found written in the aircraft's checklist. He explained to the controllers on the other end of the line that we would be approaching the field from the south in about half an hour but that we did not have functioning radios. I listened to one side of the conversation as Dad spoke:

"Light signals?"

Pause.

"Okay. And what runway should we expect?'

Pause.

"One-seven right?" He made a note on the checklist.

We'll be landing to the south, I thought.*

"Fifteen hundred feet...yeah, got it."

Pause.

"We'll keep a lookout for the signals. See you in a few."

Dad hung up.

"Well," he said, "let's head back." In my head, I heard an imaginary version of music composed by John Williams of *Star Wars* fame. It was at once ominous – hinting at the danger we faced – and inspirational – signaling the resolve Dad and I had to overcome this shitty card fate had dealt.

As we got back to the plane and began our preflight checklist, Dad explained that the tower at Ellington would use a light gun to send us signals to help us safely approach and land at the airport. He said that after we took off, he'd be flying the plane given our emergency (an emergency!) and that it would be important for me to play copilot (copilot!) and keep an eye out for the beacons from the control tower.

"As we approach, look for either a steady red or blinking green light from the tower," Dad said.

"I don't remember what they mean," I replied. I had studied the signals in my FAA ground school but had never considered it would be important information to retain. How often do two radios fail?

"Steady red means we should enter a holding pattern away from the field – that they aren't ready for us to enter the pattern yet. Flashing green means we're cleared to approach the airport and a steady green means we're cleared to land."

---

* Runways are numbered based on how they are oriented relative to a compass where north is 360°, east is 90°, south is 180°, and west is 270°. The last number in the heading is dropped so a runway that runs east-west has one end of the runway labeled "9" and the other "27." If you are landing on runway 9, your compass should show your direction as 90°, or due east. Knowing this makes watching movies unbearable at times; in *Catch Me if You Can*, a character references runway 44. No such runway could ever exist. Sometimes being a nerd made it hard to suspend disbelief.

"Got it," I said.

(A real emergency was cool enough to get my adrenaline going. But my fertile mind couldn't help creating a story around our misfortune. We weren't a father and son in a pokey civilian plane with radios out. We were two special forces commandos – my codename was *Dragonfly*; Dad's was *Neptune* – flying at night into occupied France to supply the resistance with guns and grenades. Our contact in France – codename: *Liberté!* – would guide us to a clandestine grass landing strip with light signals so that we would not give away the mission with intercepted radio transmissions. In the cockpit, I had a picture of my girl, a soft-focus headshot of a Clear Lake High School cheerleader, wedged into the tiny gap between the glass of our altimeter and the metal of the instrument panel. I was fighting this lousy war to make the world a better place for her and all the dames back home who would rather die than live under the jackboot of the Nazi oppressor.)

Once back to our plane, we taxied out to the runway, took off, and turned northeast. Dad showed me an aviation map once we were airborne explaining as he pointed to landmarks that we would be approaching the field from the southeast. I studied the map so that I could have a sense of where to look for the tower once we were in range of the airport. The air was thick with a humid haze and I worried a bit, as did Dad, about our ability to see the airport clearly. After being airborne about twenty-five minutes and using landmarks below, we knew we were nearing the field and I began to peer intently out the front left window of the cockpit.

"You keep an eye out for the signal, and I'll watch for other air traffic."

"Will-do," I said.

Many moments passed as I squinted into the glare of the sun, hoping to see the signal.

"There it is!" I said, pointing across my dad's field of view.

He looked to his left.

"A blinking green. Good," he said. We were cleared to approach the airport.

"I'm going to head north on a heading of three-five-zero for our downwind. When we get abreast of the threshold of one-seven, let me know so that I can start thinking about turning base." Dad was giving me his plan for how he was going to make a sequence of turns to line up with the runway.

"You keep watching for the next signal," he told me as he pulled back on the throttle to begin our descent.

"The steady green?" I asked.

"Yep."

A few moments later, I told him we were abreast of the end of the runway. He flew for a bit longer then turned left on a heading perpendicular to the runway. Our next turn would be to one-seven-zero degrees to line up for landing.

Just as we began to turn to that heading, I saw the steady green light from the tower.

"Cleared for landing," I said.

Dad looked toward the tower.

"Good," he said.

"Give me some flaps," he asked. I moved the flaps lever down. Flaps made the wing more curved which allowed it to create lift at slower speeds. I felt myself get pulled forward in my seat as the airplane slowed.

"Keep an eye out for any traffic," Dad said. "I don't want us to die in a midair collision because some asshole wasn't listening to the tower."

Even though we had faith the controllers would do what they could to ensure other aircraft were staying away from our area during our landing, we had both seen pilots ignore the instructions of the tower. Always better to be safe than sorry. I scanned the sky.

"Can you see the windsock?" Dad asked. The piece of tubular cloth on the field would give us an indication of the direction of the wind.

I spotted it in the distance and told Dad, "It looks like you've got a quartering cross-wind from the left." I felt Dad apply a little more rudder upon hearing this. We were a team. I doubt in retrospect he needed me to execute the landing, but in that moment, I believed otherwise.

We crossed the threshold of the runway and, as the plane settled, Dad began to pull back on the yoke to raise the nose. The warbling sound of the stall warning* began to fill the cockpit just as the wheels touched the ground. Dad eased the throttle back further and popped open his window. I did the same. The cockpit filled with air that, while hot, felt cool given its movement over our sweating skin.

"You have the airplane," he said, giving me permission to taxi to our parking spot. I took over and brought us to a stop in line with other rentals on the tarmac and shut down the engine.

"Cheated death once again!" Dad said triumphantly. I laughed. "You did good," he added.

"So did you," I said.

---

* Contrary to what most people think – and with no help from an equally ignorant press – when a stall is referred to in aviation it has nothing to do with an engine. It references a condition in which the airflow over the wing of an airplane has gotten so slow or disrupted the wing is no longer producing enough lift to keep the airplane airborne. According to the Aircraft Owners and Pilots Association, unintentional stalls account for nearly 25% of fatal accidents.

CHAPTER 7: DAD'S TURN

April 13, 1984 was a big day in our family. That was the day that STS-41C, the eleventh space shuttle mission, returned from orbit. That meant that my dad and the rest of Zoo Crew were the "prime crew" – the next up to launch. The patch concepts I had drawn up when Dad and his five comrades were chosen for the mission had been tweaked and given to a professional artist to create the final product. I felt incredibly proud that the main themes of the drawings I had made earlier in the year had survived the final cut and the patch looked much like its early incarnations. The shuttle was swooping to the foreground trailing a red, white, and blue line that circled a globe in the distance before terminating at the bow of a silhouetted eighteenth-century ship. In the wide part of the line streaking from the back of the orbiter, the word *Discovery* was written. Twelve stars denoted the twelfth mission. From the cargo bay of the shuttle, a large solar panel was seen deployed, a facsimile of one of the payloads *Discovery* would carry. The last names of the crewmembers circled the imagery with my family name at the nine o'clock position on the outer circle. Mullane. Wow.

Dad's first launch attempt was set for June 25th, so his training was now at a crescendo as the crew tried to tie up any loose ends before heading to Cape Canaveral for the launch. Mom was busy lining up accommodations for us in the Cocoa Beach area and purchasing airline tickets for Amy, Laura and me to fly to Orlando, the closest major airport to the Kennedy Space Center. Surprisingly, while NASA would fly my mother to the Cape on a business jet, little was done (actually, nothing was done) to help the children of astronauts get to Florida for the launch. Monthly pay for an Air Force Lt. Colonel in 1984 was around $3, 500/month or $42,000 a year. While a decent salary even by today's standards ($42,000 is about $104,000 in 2020 currency), buying three airline tickets and purchasing accommodations in Florida, especially when launch delays could make the expenses creep up relentlessly, was a real hardship. Fortunately, Amy, Laura and I would be out of school for the summer by the time the launch rolled around. So at least we didn't have to deal with missing a class.

Joe Joe flew down to Houston to escort my sisters and me to Orlando on a commercial flight. He loved the excitement around the coming launch and was proud to be associated with an astronaut. He would often try to use my father's illusory celebrity to help us gain special treatment from some poor sap – he'd lean over to me and, in his not-a-whisper whisper, say with a nudging elbow, "Tell them who your dad is." I'd find it terribly embarrassing even though I had pride that surpassed his.

Once, we went to a crowded restaurant where a hostess told us we'd have to wait for a table. When Joe Joe predictably pulled out his "tell her who your dad is" refrain, she heard him and looked at me critically, trying to decide if I resembled the son of some celebrity. I decided to go on the offensive against Joe Joe and rather than saying, "He's an astronaut" (which probably wouldn't have mattered anyway), I simply said, "Mike Mullane" knowing the name would fall flat. She paused for a moment trying to determine if it was a name she should know. Making no connection, she said to Joe Joe dismissively, "The wait will be about fifteen minutes." Joe Joe was not amused and gave me a disappointed glare. My sisters and I laughed softly, hands to our mouths.

The crew entered a quarantine a week before heading to KSC to ensure they wouldn't contract an illness in the days leading up to liftoff. A head cold or stomach bug could result in a delay in the launch at best or removal of a crew member from the mission at worst. This was no small concern; Astronaut Ken Mattingly had been removed from the Apollo 13 crew after he had been exposed to German Measles. In the weeks before my dad was to leave for KSC for the launch, I wasn't feeling well and so Mom took me to the flight surgeon at NASA where a throat culture was taken that showed I had strep throat.* Since the flight surgeon I saw knew my father was part of "prime crew," he told my mother to tell my father to come into the office for a throat culture as well. If Dad had strep throat, it was highly unlikely that NASA brass would let him strap into *Discovery* several weeks hence. The tension between my parents in the days after Mom took me to the doctor was palpable. Dad was furious that Mom had taken me to the flight surgeon, wondering why she would do something that could threaten his chance to fly in space. "At least," he said to her, "you could have taken him to a goddamn civilian doctor outside of NASA!" I recall being annoyed too. As miserable as I was with the virus, I'd be more miserable if Dad didn't get to space. His dream had become mine and if I had to be on my death bed to help him get to orbit then, by God, I'd take one for the team.

After avoiding calls from the flight surgeon for several days, Dad eventually did have to give a throat culture and we waited nervously for the news. Thankfully, it was negative. He apologized to Mom.

On the day Dad went into quarantine, he took Mom, Amy, Laura, and me to the crew quarters at JSC where he and the rest of the *Discovery* astronauts would live before heading out to KSC in their T-38s. A "double wide" mobile home trailer inside of a larger building would be their dormitory for the coming week. This would be the last time Amy, Laura, and I saw Dad before the launch. NASA would allow the crew to have visitors, but they had to be over eighteen-years-old and also had to have been through a physical with the flight surgeon to ensure they weren't harboring a communicable illness as I had several weeks before (thankfully I had fully recovered from my strep).

The time with Dad at the crew quarters was stilted; we all knew the tour of the facility was leading to a goodbye. My sisters and I had lived now for over a decade with a man who had cheated death flying in combat and while testing aircraft. We had seen Mom and Dad mourn the loss of colleagues who had been flying machines much less

---

* A flight surgeon is a medical doctor specializing in care for those that fly in aircraft or spacecraft. The cadre of them at JSC were the astronauts' doctors but they doubled as family physicians, treating spouses and children too.

complicated than the space shuttle — and their machines had ejection seats that gave them a shot at escaping some calamity. The shuttle didn't have any means of escape. Dad and the rest of the crew were going to be prisoners during their entire mission. These thoughts occupied all of our minds like an unwelcome house guest as the goodbye loomed.

I've never seen my father with tears in his eyes, and I didn't that day. But I could tell he was emotional. Dad used humor to mask discomfort and the frequency and silliness of his jokes were like a Geiger Counter — higher frequency and more silliness meant more nerves and emotion. The nerves/emotion Geiger Counter clicked like crazy that day. Those nerves were well-founded; our intuition about the danger he was soon to face was spot on. The loss of *Challenger* was just two years away and would kill Judy Resnik, whom we said goodbye to in the crew quarters that day as well.

The time finally came to say goodbye. My sisters hugged Dad first. Laura smiled as she hugged him but my twin, Amy, always the more emotional of us, had tears in her eyes. After Amy and Laura had finished with their goodbyes, I stepped forward and gave Dad a brief but tight squeeze. While Dad never cried, he wasn't cold. He freely and frequently told us he loved us. And he did so in the crew quarters that day. In the seconds I held him I wondered if it would be for the last time and in turn wondered if saying, "I love you," was enough. The three words seemed too feeble for the moment. Shouldn't we recount all of the times we had shared, bonding us as father and son? Shouldn't we re-live our time flying together around south Texas or corralling a slithering rattlesnake into a coffee can? Shouldn't we talk about what was expected of me if Dad did indeed die somewhere over the coast of Florida? These questions raced through me in an instant as Dad's embrace tightened, mirroring mine. But as quickly as they emerged, they evaporated as Dad released me, put his hands on my shoulders, and looked me in the eye and said, again, "I love you." In that moment I realized that, yes, those words were enough.

***

Amy, Laura, and I made it to Florida where Mom had already arrived on a NASA jet. She and the rest of the wives (since Judy Resnik was unmarried, there were no husbands) met the crew on the tarmac adjacent to the runway at KSC. Images of that greeting appeared on local television broadcasts and on the front page of space-coast newspapers. Norman Rockwell painted many works related to U.S. efforts in space and, had he not died three years before the first shuttle launch at the age of eighty-four, he might have captured my mom in oil, walking toward my father with her arms out, ready to embrace her husband, who was frozen in a purposeful walk, the black heel of his right boot striking the cement, a joyous smile making his blue flight suit bluer and his white airplane whiter. I sought out pictures of the arrival in every paper I could, clipping them to save for a family scrapbook.

We stayed at condominiums along the beach in Cocoa Beach, just south of KSC on highway A1A and not too far from Ron Jon Surf Shop, which later became the largest surf shop in the world. The town was founded in 1925 in an area that was previously called, with a hint of mysticism and a tip of the hat to the ancient Greeks, Oceanus – a.k.a "Titan of the Ocean." For the next thirty-five or so years it was a relatively quiet, sparsely developed community. That changed with the advent of manned space flight programs and the establishment of KSC. In 1940, the population of Cocoa Beach was forty-nine. In 1950, it was 246. By 1970, thanks to the Apollo program, it was just under 10,000.

If not for modern cars on the road, a visitor plopped down on Cocoa Beach's main drag today would be forgiven if they thought they had been transported to a time just a few decades after Cocoa Beach's founding. The homes in the area, many of which were built during the boom of the 1960s, conform to a template of flat roofs, stucco sides, and single-auto car ports. The retail establishments are festooned with stylized neon signs from an era past. There is probably no town in the world that has such a mismatch between the glory it is responsible for – meeting the timeline Kennedy laid out in a speech to a joint session of congress in 1961 to land a man on the moon – and the lack of glory it projects. Cocoa Beach has a workingman's feeling to it; it's the Allentown of central coastal Florida, not the Greenwich. It's more Lehigh Valley than Silicone Valley.

To some extent, it was foreordained that launch facilities would be at Cape Canaveral. Physics and safety dictated it. If the orbit of a spacecraft allows, it's always preferable to launch to the east and as close to the equator as possible. This is because the earth rotates to the east and so any rocket launching in that direction will get a boost from the spin of our planet. That boost is not insignificant and increases the closer to the equator you get. At Cape Canaveral it comes to around 900 mph, a little more than 5% of the needed speed to get to orbit (the boost at the equator is about 1,000 mph). But you can't just launch to the east from anywhere. For example, it's possible to get the same 900 mph boost from a launch near Houston. But a shuttle blasting off from there might pass over New Orleans or Atlanta. If the vehicle exploded, fire and metal could rain down on suburbs, setting them ablaze. Even if things went perfectly, the solid rocket boosters would be jettisoned and might crash into a school in Alabama. These constraints then – launching to the east as far south as possible and inside the U.S. without jeopardizing populous centers – pointed to somewhere on the east coast of Florida as the logical location to establish a launch facility. KSC was born.

When we arrived in Florida, many of our friends and family were already there, some in the same condo complex as us. In addition to Joe Joe, a significant portion of the extended family had made the trip. Grandma and Pop Pop were there, having driven their motorhome almost 1,800 miles from Albuquerque to Cocoa Beach. Pop Pop had never taken an airplane anywhere during my lifetime. I once heard one of my uncles nagging him to do so. Pop Pop kept demurring until he finally said with more emotion than I was used to, "*I can't.*" While there are many practical reasons this might have been true – not the least of which was the question of how he would easily get around once he got to his destination with no ramp-equipped vehicle – the passion of his response seemed to hint at something else. Did flying take him back to one of his last rides on an airplane? The one that possibly infected him with polio and sentenced him to his wheelchair? I later told the story of Pop Pop's reaction to Dad. He brushed off my hypothesis saying that it was all about mobility when he got to where he was going. To this day, I'm still unsure if that was the whole story.

In addition to Joe Joe, Grandma, and Pop Pop, my great grandma Pettigrew (who had survived the tornado in Texas) made the trip along with a gaggle of other extended relatives. Great-grandma Pettigrew was the definition of a cute old lady. At 87-years-old she had a slight bend at the waist and a face that looked like one of the Cabbage Patch Kid dolls that were popular at the time; it appeared sewn together in a way that exaggerated her features and tied them together. Two deeply stitched dimples seemed to cause her cheeks to puff out in apple-like bulbs of rosiness framing a nose barely prominent enough to hold her glasses. Her full head of white hair topped off a rounded but tiny frame. I did not get to see her very often and so having her with the entire family to enjoy the time together was wonderful.

During excursions to the grocery store or on other errands, we would see messages of support on signs in front of drug stores and souvenir shops. "God speed *Discovery!*" "Good luck STS-41D crew!" "Go for launch!" I was over the moon with excitement. At the theater in town, four huge summer hits were being shown: *Star Trek III: The Search for Spock*, *Ghostbusters*, *Indiana Jones and the Temple of Doom*, and *Karate Kid*. But the proprietor found room for a message to the crew: "Safe Travels *Discovery!*" To see a reference to my father's mission next to the name "Star Trek" and alongside the title of an Indiana Jones adventure was almost tear-inducing. It was as if I were a small-town parish priest seeing his name next to the Pope's on a jumbotron at the Vatican. Once back in our condominium, we would tune into the local and national news. Images of Dad and the rest of the crew were everywhere. The shuttle program was still in its infancy and I knew that on launch day networks would break into broadcasts to show the launch live.

One afternoon in the days before launch, Grandma and Pop Pop asked if I wanted to go to the KSC visitors center with them. I jumped at the chance. I had been to the center a thousand times but never tired of the surplus rockets standing like sentinels in the "Rocket Park," the display cases showing a chronological history of the U.S. space program, and the gift shop where pictures of the crew and the mission patch (the one I helped create!) were on sale.

I pushed Pop Pop around in his wheelchair as we meandered through the museum. He sat cross-legged, his thighs and calves so small and thin they fit neatly into the seat slung in the center of the metal frame of his chair. He wore a baseball cap on his head, the brim decorated with "scrambled eggs," the name given to gold, leaf-shaped ornaments famous for their use on formal military head gear. At the center of the hat was Dad's mission patch. The adjustable clasp in the back was buttoned too tightly to fit the circumference of his skull but for whatever reason, he didn't expand it, so it balanced on the top of his mostly-bald noggin, one whisper of a breeze away from being blown into the alligator swamps that abounded on space center property.

He also wore a t-shirt with a gaudy piece of painted art showing *Discovery* leaping from the launch pad, smoke billowing into an American flag, and the crew names suspended in metallic-looking letters, glinting in a painted sun. It looked like a work of art meant to promote a professional wrestling match. While I sound critical, it's not because of what was on the shirt, it's because I was wearing the exact same one. While both of us were proud, I was still a teenager worried about my own "coolness" – or lack thereof – and so strolling through the space center looking like twins separated by fifty years wearing the same ostentatious shirt didn't help me wash the stain of "nerd" from my back.

After we were done with our visit, we got back into Pop Pop's motor home in the baking sun. He drove at his customary glacial pace made all the more glacial due to speed bumps in the lot. We didn't need a speedometer to measure our speed; we needed a calendar. Eventually, we pulled to a stop at Kennedy Parkway where we would turn right to head south and off of the KSC property. Except we didn't turn right. Instead, Pop Pop took a left, heading north toward a security checkpoint beyond which loomed the massive Vertical Assembly Building (VAB), the Launch Control Center (LCC), and launch pads 39A and 39B, the ones used to launch space shuttles. *Discovery* was on 39A, the same launch pad used to launch the Apollo 11 crew to the moon.

"Hugh, where are we going?" Grandma asked, stealing the words from my own mouth.

He ignored his wife.

"Pat, come here," Pop Pop said, inviting me to the space between the captain's chairs at the front of the motorhome. He spoke with his pipe clenched between his teeth, the words escaping from a small opening at the corner of his mouth. As I made my way forward, he took the pipe into his right hand and held it by its round end as he pulled down on the car hand control with a few of his fingers. Pulling down on the handle made a rod – through a series of linkages –press on the accelerator pedal; pushing in on the handle caused the brake to be applied. Pop Pop did a lot more pushing in than pulling down.

"Where's that badge you have?" he said.

The badge he was referring to was my "Astronaut Dependent" badge, something I had shown him earlier. By modern security standards it was hardly a badge. It looked more like something a young boy would get from a kiosk at Disney World for $5. About the size of a playing card, it had a picture of me at fifteen affixed to the front – that alone should have made any checker-of-credentials balk at granting me access to a restricted area. The picture showed a boy with acne and a haircut like one the Beatles might have worn … except by 1984 it wasn't a "cool Beatles cut" it was an "asshole Bowl cut." My unusually small mouth smiled slightly asymmetrically; the sagging right side of my bottom lip made me look like I was a very young stroke victim.

This image was laminated to heavy stock paper with "ASTRONAUT DEPENDENT" stamped to the right of my image just under "MULLANE." On the back, to the left of my full name, there was a stern warning about the badge being the property of the U.S. Government and that "use or possession by any other person is unlawful and will make the offender liable to heavy penalty (18 USC 499, 506, and 701)." A badge number was also on the back. Mine was 00143. I wondered, was I the 143rd astronaut kid or spouse to get a badge? I suspected I was. I took pride in the number. It was a relatively small one and made me feel a part of the nation's early space exploring history. I loved that badge – I memorized the government warning on the back of it. I was carrying it with me that day out of an abundance of caution. I worried some interloper at the condominium complex might take it and try and pass themselves off as me, violating 18 USC 499, 506 and 701. That said, deep down I knew the badge was pretty meaningless. It simply allowed me to get on the JSC premises back in Houston for visits to the flight surgeon.

"What do you need it for?" I asked as I wedged the badge between Pop Pop's thumb and the bowl of his pipe.

"I want to tour the base," Pop Pop answered. I looked at Grandma nervously. She sensed my worry.

"Hugh," she said, "I don't think that's a good idea."

Pop Pop took his hand off of his controls and waved off grandma. The motorhome coasted without his palm's weight on the control arm.

"Marge, Pat has an official badge, our son is going to be riding a rocket put together right here, and our tax dollars pay for all this!" He swept the horizon with his pipe through the front windshield where the VAB and LCC grew larger in our field of view. Say what you will about Pop Pop's chutzpa, his logic was always just good enough to make you think: *Well, he does have a point.*

Grandma looked at me as if to say, "I tried," and settled back into her seat. Pop Pop put his hand back on his controls and the motorhome accelerated slowly. I had pulled out a lawn chair from the back of the camper and perched myself between the two of them at the front of the vehicle (seatbelt laws were still a long way off). My sphincter tightened as Pop Pop pulled up to a checkpoint that blocked access into the outer perimeter of security that included the VAB and LCC. The guard at the gate was a NASA contractor. He did not look intimidating. In fact, his uniform made him look like he worked a night shift as a mall cop and had taken the NASA job because they would allow him to man the day shift at KSC without changing his clothes. He didn't have any sort of weapon – just some handcuffs and a walkie-talkie.

Pop Pop rolled down his window and transferred my badge to his left hand.

"How can I help you?" the guard said, stepping out of his air-conditioned shed.

Pop Pop grabbed my shoulder – I was slightly behind him and elevated – and pulled me forward.

"This is my grandson," he said while shoving the badge into the guard's face and pulling harder on my shoulder, bringing me into view of the gatekeeper as if I was a hostage being forced to show my face for proof-of-life. "His dad – my son – is going to be on that shuttle" – Pop Pop motioned to the distance with his left hand, my badge flapping between his fingers – "when it blasts off. We'd like to take a drive around."

THE FATHER, SON, AND HOLY SHUTTLE

I wanted to die.

The mall cop took my badge from Pop Pop. He stepped forward slightly, raised on his toes, and leaned forward to get a peek inside the cabin of the motorhome, letting his gaze linger for a moment on the vehicle's hand controls and then looking to each of us in turn. All I could think about was the matching t-shirts. We looked like redneck tourists on our way to a NASCAR race.

After taking a quick look into the camper, he rocked back on his heels and inspected the badge more closely. He seemed perplexed. I could tell he wanted to make us turn our sorry asses around. But, for those who didn't know Pop Pop to be the brash New York bullshitter he was, he said enough things, in just the right order, with just enough certitude to be just convincing enough to get his way. I'm certain it helped that he was in a wheelchair and clearly the age of somebody who was in their prime during World War II. Who was going to question a crippled war hero? A war hero whose son might be an astronaut?

"You'll see there," Pop Pop said motioning at the badge across his body with his right hand, holding the pipe again by the bowl, "that it is an astronaut dependent badge. Pat, my grandson here, is the dependent of an astronaut." I was so embarrassed.

The guard still didn't say anything. Pop Pop took the time to grab his lighter from the center console of the motorhome and light his pipe. He showed no concern. In fact, he showed confidence. He didn't look at the guard but instead stared out the front window as he inhaled a lung-full of sweet smoke and then exhaled, letting the cloud linger around his head. He squinted through the smoke into the distance, as if he were pondering the route he would take to the launch pad, knowing that the review of the small, laminated document was a formality that would shortly end with a flippant wave encouraging us to move under a raised gate.

The guard looked at the flip side of the badge. *It's just a warning to return it if found*, I wanted to interject, hating the awkward silence. *I've read it a thousand times*. But I kept my mouth shut. I was too afraid of Pop Pop and his enormous forearms.

I saw the guard reach for his radio. I was sure he was going to call us in. I could see the headlines the next day: "Disabled Father of

Discovery Crew Member Arrested Using Grandson's NASA Badge, Violating 18 USC 499."* And then, in a subtitle in slightly smaller font alluding to the picture on the badge: "Acne-Riddled Son of Astronaut Taken into Protective Custody." But my concerns were unfounded. He simply turned down the radio at his hip to mute some chatter.

Then, the miraculous happened: he handed the badge back, stepped into the shack, pressed a button to raise the gate, and waved us through. Are you kidding me?!! I wanted to let out a *wohoo*! and almost did. But Pop Pop didn't seem to be excited at all and so I held my emotion in check. He didn't think he had duped anybody. He thought he had used legitimate government documentation to gain legitimate access to a restricted area. I was blown away. Was I the one who was out of touch? Did my ASTRONAUT DEPENDENT badge have power I never before knew? That must be the case.

"Where should we go first? Pop Pop asked matter-of-factly, as if wondering which attraction to start with after passing through the front gates of Disney World.

He drove even slower now and I felt like yelling at him as if I were a thief that had just robbed a bank and Pop Pop was the worst get-away driver in the history of get-away drivers. Surely, they'd be coming for us. I got up to walk to the back of the RV and look out the rear window. The guard shack disappeared in the distance as the mall cop took a seat and picked up a magazine inside the shed's air-conditioned confines. No blue lights were fired up and closing in on us. No helicopters were tailing us from overhead. In fact, there was virtually no activity at all. It was hard to believe that preparations for a launch were even underway.

The benign view out the back of the camper helped my paranoia slowly recede. In its place, a growing confidence took root that I had a right to be inside the security perimeter. I returned to the lawn chair

---

* 18 U.S. Code Section 499 says, "Whoever falsely makes, forges, counterfeits, alters, or tampers with any naval, military, or official pass or permit, issued by or under the authority of the United States, or with intent to defraud uses or possesses any such pass or permit, or personates or falsely represents himself to be or not to be a person to whom such pass or permit has been duly issued ... shall be fined under this title or imprisoned not more than five years, or both."

between Grandma and Pop Pop and settled into it, taking in the view out the front window.

I noticed the road we were on was called "Saturn Causeway," a reference to the massive rocket that took Neil Armstrong and eleven other moonwalkers to the surface of the moon. Pop Pop took a left onto Utility Rd. and we inched toward the enormous Vertical Assembly building. The structure, as the name implies, was the place were NASA stacked its rockets. Originally built to accommodate the Saturn V Apollo rocket, it stood 526 feet high.

There are plenty of buildings that are taller than the VAB but standing in the Florida flatlands with nothing else large around it made it appear massive beyond its specs, as if an alien civilization had built it eons ago to placate their own gods. Stepping inside of the VAB (as I had the opportunity to do once while I was an Air Force officer) made you realize that the scale of the building couldn't truly be fathomed from the outside. To understand its size, you had to stand in its 129 million-cubic-foot cavernous interior. Yes, there are plenty of buildings taller and wider than the VAB, but they aren't *empty*. The VAB is, for all practical purposes, a shell. You can't see the ceiling at the very top of the of the Empire State Building while standing on the bottom floor. But you can see the ceiling of the VAB from 526 feet below on its bottom floor.

I leaned forward in my lawn chair, craning my neck to see the VAB more clearly as we drove around it. I removed the "handicapped" placard hanging from the rearview mirror to give me clearer lines of sight. Pop Pop circled back in the direction from which we'd come, and we found the LCC to our left. The Launch Control Center stood with its long side facing the east toward launch pads 39A and 39B. Firing rooms on the top floor housed controllers who were responsible for launching rockets out of KSC. Manned flights only used these control rooms until vehicles left the launch pad. Then, control switched to the MCC – Mission Control Complex – in Houston. I'd be standing on that roof in a couple of days to watch my father attempt his launch in *Discovery*. The roof provided not only a great vantage point from which to watch the launch, but it also isolated the families from the press and others in the event something catastrophic happened.

Speaking of *Discovery*, it now was in view three miles to the east. Actually, the shuttle itself wasn't visible. But the launch gantry was, its grey metal topped with an enormous white lightning rod. So was the rotating service structure (RSS) that encircled the shuttle. A gargantuan swinging gate with a cocoon built into the side of it, the RSS was rolled around the space shuttle after it was placed on the launch pad. In addition to protecting the orbiter from the elements, it allowed access to some space shuttle systems and the sixty-foot long cargo bay while the shuttle was vertical on 39A. Shuttle payloads could also be loaded while the orbiter was on the launch pad via RSS access. About twelve hours before launch, it would be rolled to the side, revealing the orbiter hanging on the large, orange external tank book-ended by the solid rocket boosters. I couldn't wait for that to happen. We were scheduled to join our astronaut escorts for a drive out to a viewing area near the pad the night before launch to see the shuttle bathed in lights, naked to the world. It was something I had heard other families talk about as an almost religious experience. I couldn't believe it was almost my turn to see that spiritual sight.

"Where's the shuttle?" Pop Pop asked as we came abreast of the back edge of the LCC.

"It's out there," I said, pointing to launch pad 39A. "But you can't really see it. The gantry is sort of between us and the shuttle and, besides, the RSS is around it so it's really hard to see any of *Discovery*." Hours upon hours of trying to be a part Dad's world had made me a dictionary of NASA acronyms and a repository for minutiae useful to a sixteen-year-old boy only if he was giving a tour to his grandfather at KSC in the hours before his father's space shuttle launch. It was a very narrow skill to be sure.

Pop Pop didn't understand my technobabble. I explained the RSS function to him.

"Balls!" he said at the realization that he couldn't see the shuttle. It became clear though that *Discovery's* relative obscurity wasn't going to keep Pop Pop from trying to get a closer look. He turned back onto Saturn Causeway which, to the east, became a service road that paralleled the giant track the massive "crawler" used to transport the rocket stack from the VAB to the launch pad.* Another guard shack loomed in the distance. But this time I was less concerned about the checkpoint. I had my badge. My ASTRONAUT DEPENDENT badge. I sat up straighter in my lawn chair both out of pride in my status and so that the guard becoming larger in the front window could see the government ID clipped to my t-shirt.

This guard was more special forces than mall cop. He was wearing tactical gear – cargo pants with too many pockets to count, a holster with a side-arm, aviator sunglasses, dark gloves. An automatic weapon was slung round his neck for use in the event that a small caliber sidearm couldn't get the job done. The rifle laid flat across the lower part of his chest and he used it as a sort of shelf, letting his arms rest atop the stock and part of the barrel. As we inched forward, he stepped slightly into the road and held up his gloved hand. That's when I noticed another identically outfitted guard emerge from the shack.

Without being asked, I gave Pop Pop my badge. Despite the more intimidating nature of the duo of security personnel now between us and the launch pad, I was unconcerned. They were just doing their job. There were a lot of nut jobs out there who might try to gain unauthorized access to the pad, including space nuts who wanted to be close to machinery; protesting environmentalists disturbed by the number of birds and other wildlife fried by the ignition of the solid rocket boosters;[+] and tourists who wanted to capture that perfect

---

* The crawler was enormous. It needed to be to move the space shuttle to the launch pad. Weighing six million pounds, it had tank-like treads rather than wheels. Each of the treads was made up of fifty-seven linked metal pieces – called "shoes" – that alone weighed almost 2,000 pounds each.

[+] In a 1990 *Orlando Sentinel* newspaper report, it was noted that the Air Force was going to be conducting studies during its launches just south of pad 39A to determine if its rockets threatened wildlife. The article noted that it was estimated that over a four-year period, launches killed 400 Florida scrub jays and 12,000 southeastern beach mice. Also mentioned: "The animals may die from toxic exhaust from the rockets or intense heat in the area, or would suffer hearing loss from noise levels that reach 170 decibels." No word on funding for tiny hearing aids for the afflicted.

picture. We didn't fall into any of those categories given the credential I had and the security wicket I had passed through to get it – namely being born to somebody who became an astronaut.

Pop Pop pressed gently on his hand control and the RV came to a stop. The guard in the road walked from the front of the vehicle to the driver's window while the other strolled in front of the windshield and disappeared down the passenger side, inspecting the motorhome as he walked. Pop Pop rolled down his window to once again present my badge to secure passage. The guard took it from him but didn't look at it right away.

"We just want to take a drive around," Pop Pop said preemptively, sounding more confident than ever.

"Drive around the what?" the guard said. I thought the questions was silly – the road that stretched out before us had no intersecting byways and terminated at the launch pad. Where else would we be going?

Pop Pop answered gruffly, "The pad out there."

I thought I saw the guard smirk – or at least I thought it was a smirk. In an instant, part of me considered that it might be a smile he was trying to kill on his lips.

"What's this?" special forces man asked, holding up my badge to Pop Pop. At this, Pop Pop again grabbed my shoulder and pulled me forward into full view of the guard.

"It's my grandson's badge. His father is my son. Astronaut Mike Mullane."

The second guard had now completed his circumnavigation of the motorhome and took a position next to his partner outside of Pop Pop's window. They both looked at the badge after Pop Pop's explanation. Their faces showed not a scintilla of recognition. They showed something else though. Something that stoked an uneasiness in me I just couldn't place.

"Sir, we can't let you pass with this badge," special forces guy number one said abruptly with hardly a passing glance at the laminated credential in his hand. Now he was smiling. It was the smile that bothered me. At first, I couldn't understand why. Then it came to me: it was a pitying smile.

In a nanosecond, my bravado turned to shame.

We had no business trying to get past this checkpoint. We probably had no business getting past the first one. My grandparents were a cute old couple and I was the nerdy, hapless grandson; a troika sure to be the butt of their jokes later in the evening when they got off duty and shared beers and belly-aching laughs at Cheaters or the Inner Room – two strip clubs in Cocoa Beach on A1A. I wanted to crawl into a hole. I was a relatively secure kid, not easily ruffled even at sixteen. But while the barbs of classmates at school were easy for me to brush off, knowing that members of the space community I so revered and longed to be a part of were literally trying not to laugh in my face stung me deeply.

It was about to get worse.

The guard handed my badge back to Pop Pop. In his mind, the discussion was done. I'm sure he fully expected my grandfather to roll his window back up, put the RV into reverse and, using what was sure to be a forty-five minute three-point turn, get us pointed back west. But that's not what happened.

"Now listen here," Pop Pop said, removing his pipe from his mouth. "When they light that candle in two days, my son will be on a dangerous E ticket elevator ride into space! We just want to see her on the pad."

"Light this candle." "Elevator ride." "Dangerous E ticket."* Pop Pop was talking like an over-the-top screenwriter for *The Right Stuff*, a movie that had come out less than a year before chronicling the history of the original "Mercury 7" astronauts. I could see the smiles grow on the faces of both guards now. I wanted to take my badge, crawl into the tiny closet that was the RV bathroom and flush myself into the blue liquid of the holding tank.

---

* The term "E ticket" is courtesy of Disney. In the early days of Disneyland theme park, coupons of varying value were sold which granted access to the park's attractions. The coupons were designated with the letters "A" through "E" where E tickets granted admission to the newer, most popular rides. The term worked its way into popular culture and eventually came to be used more generically in reference to any great ride. After her space shuttle mission in 1983, Sally Ride said, "Ever been to Disneyland? ...That was definitely an E ticket!"

"Sir, I'm sorry. But even the most senior people at NASA are not allowed past this point when a shuttle is on the pad so close to launch." There was little doubt in my mind that he was telling the truth. The kindness with which he said it somehow exaggerated the embarrassment. We were children being lectured.

"Hugh," Grandma said, "I think we should probably go back."

Thank God. One of the adults in our little exploration party was talking some sense.

"Good luck to your son, sir," the guard said, trying to put a definitive end to the discussion.

"You boys stay safe out here," Pop Pop said, as if the previous exchanges had not happened. "Keep an eye on that bird for me," he added raising his chin to the east in the direction of *Discovery*. His comment harbored no ill-will. There was not a hint of embarrassment in his voice or demeanor. Pop Pop was as collected and unfazed as a man that had just been told the road ahead was closed due to some repaving underway.

He handed my badge back to me, put the RV in reverse, and began his interminable three-point turn to get us pointed back toward the VAB. As we drove the service road back to the first checkpoint, Grandma said, "Hugh, do you want to pull off on the way back to the condo and have a turkey sandwich? How about you Pat?"

Pop Pop and I both said yes. I was famished.

During that drive, my embarrassment evaporated slowly, like sweat in the humid air. Pop Pop asked me about landmarks along the way and we talked with giddy anticipation about the upcoming launch. As we rolled along at Pop Pop speed – I was sure the crawler that carried the shuttle to the pad could cover the same distance in half the time – I found myself marveling at my grandfather. While his actions and words could embarrass the hell out of me in the moment, the audacious confidence that led him to do and say the things he did was something I couldn't help but admire. His legs may have been taken from him but the disease that atrophied his body did not do the same to his spirit. He lived fully and unapologetically – maybe *because* the ability to walk had been stolen from him? And why not? Were those guards at either of the NASA checkpoints going to shoot us? What was the worst that could happen? Even today, I wish I could be more like him, the New

York Irishman who, without actually saying it, lived by a credo of "fuck it." Life is short – it would be too short for him; he'd die four years later at 66-years-old. I committed to myself that I would be more like him and remember that I had an ASTRONAUT DEPENDENT badge that gave me license to really live.

∗∗∗

The night viewing of the space shuttle on the launch pad the evening before launch lived up to the hype. Mom, Amy, Laura, and I drove out to KSC in a government van, with our astronaut escorts, Dick Covey and Brian O'Connor. Dick Covey and his wife lived just a couple of blocks away from us. Amy and I frequently babysat their daughters. I liked Mr. Covey a great deal. His kindness seemed evident even with just a glimpse from a distance. He was thin with a boyish look and light demeanor and carried a perpetual smile beneath a neatly trimmed mustache. Had I not known him and met him on the streets of Houston, I might have surmised he was a mild-mannered accountant or a priest, not the accomplished fighter pilot and test pilot that he was.* He had flown 339 combat missions in Vietnam, almost three times the number my father had, and had thousands of hours of flying time in all sorts of aircraft – many of which I had drawn throughout my youth in my personal book of aviation art. Bryan O'Connor was less well known to my sisters and me since he didn't live nearby and was selected in an astronaut class after my father. He was a U.S. Naval Academy graduate and Marine Corps officer. Also a test pilot, he seemed too young (even to a sixteen-year-old) to be an astronaut. Given everything that both men had seen in their careers, they exuded a confidence that felt like a warm blanket smothering any fears we had.

Both Mr. O'Connor and Mr. Covey were wonderful to have as our tour guides through the days leading up to the launch and they were especially fun to have at the night viewing with us. As we stood in the

---

* Mr. Covey would end up being the CAPCOM – mission control's point of contact with a crew in orbit – during the launch of *Challenger* when it was lost. It was the only time I ever remember him appearing anything less than cheery. Pictures of him looking forlornly at a video feed from his position in mission control showed up in newspapers around the world.

salt-infused evening air, we were all giddy with the sight of the vehicle about a half mile to the northeast. *Discovery* was so blindingly white, it looked like its skin was made of porcelain, not more than 24,000 silica tiles. While the orbiter was indeed like a new car in a showroom, yet to be soiled by the grime of regular use, the xenon lights bathing it were so spectacularly bright, they would have made a soot-covered spacecraft look equally luminous.

The shuttle looked regal, solid, and simple. But I didn't let its looks seduce me. I could see the main engines, which together produced 37,000,000 horsepower and had turbo pumps that could suck the water from a family-sized swimming pool in 25 seconds. In several hours, its external tank, which hung between the solid rocket boosters (SRBs), would be loaded with fuel, meaning Dad would be sitting on top of nearly 4 million pounds of explosive propellant. From our viewing spot, I could see clearly a rib running down the length of the solid rocket boosters. Dad had once explained to me that the feature was essentially a long stick of dynamite that would be detonated if the shuttle went out of control during launch and threatened a population center. If the command to destroy the shuttle had to be sent, the crew would have no way to escape. No, I wasn't going to be seduced by the regal queen on her throne. She was dangerous and, like a petulant and youthful queen of the middle ages, she could kill on a whim. I may have been young, but I was not naïve.

While we stood on the platform taking pictures of *Discovery*, I explained to Laura what we were going to see during launch the next day, pointing out the pieces of the rocket as I did so. I had been to the launch of STS-4 two years before and used that as a basis for my expertise. She didn't ask for the briefing, I just needed to talk. I explained that the three engines on the back of the space shuttle would light about six seconds before *Discovery* lifted off the pad. This was because these engines, fed by liquid oxygen and liquid hydrogen flowing from the big, orange external tank, could be shut down if they weren't operating properly. Not so with the SRBs. Once they were lit, you were committed to leaving the launch pad. So, during the time between ignition of the main engines and that of the SRBs, computers would check the main engines to ensure that all was going well. She just shook her head as I spoke. I doubt she registered any of it given the nerves that had already begun to consume each of us. But I also think she appreciated the distraction nonetheless.

On the drive back to the condominium in the van, I could see the realization of what was coming start to take root in our souls; the invasive cloud held at bay by the distractions of moments before was now drifting freely into our minds. I thought of Dad, who was likely in his bedroom at the KSC crew quarters attempting to get some sleep. Undoubtedly, his mind was trying to find a path to reconcile the excitement borne of a lifelong dream about to come true with the realization that that dream could kill him.

My emotions mirrored his. I had lived on the periphery of that dream in my sixteen years, finding ways to connect to his experiences in small but meaningful ways. Certainly, some of that desire to connect was an almost instinctual urge written into the DNA of boys through the ages who want to engage with their fathers on an intimate, emotional level. But for me it was more than that. My father had *been* somebody and I wanted to be somebody too. He was changing the arc of history by being a part of history. And he was doing it as the pop culture heroes of my world – Luke Skywalker, Han Solo, and Indiana Jones – were teaching me the values of the greater good above self, of bravery in the face of danger, of steady chivalry no matter the circumstances. Evenings spent watching the news with Dad convinced me that these traits would be valued above all others.

Good and evil were blessedly simple to identify through the lens he had given me. The Soviets were evil. The United States good. My Catholic upbringing added a further layer of clarity about the virtues of sacrifice in a world where there was no room for ambiguity. Right was right. Wrong was wrong. The self was secondary to the community. Yes, I longed – like any boy – to have a relationship with my father and thankfully we had one, a rich one. But more than anything, I wanted to be somebody, somebody who mattered. As I thought of the dangers to come, I couldn't help but remind myself that dying prematurely is always a sad and heartrending thing, but dying a nobody having not striven to leave your mark on the world – that was so much sadder. I vowed that I, like Dad, would not die a nobody.

THE FATHER, SON, AND HOLY SHUTTLE

Mom and Dad. Dad would ship off to Vietnam less than two years after this photo was taken. One of Dad's groomsmen was killed in combat before Dad even made it to southeast Asia. This military business was dangerous ... as was NASA's business.

Dad in Vietnam. I longed to be what this image conveyed – a brave hero staring down America's enemies.

The Mullane clan near Edwards AFB in 1979. While playing in the yard of our military housing at Edwards, I came within a shoelace of stepping on a "Mojave Green," a very deadly rattlesnake.

My Catholic confirmation photo – a confirmation of my pristine nerd credentials.

Showing my skills as a "Lake" cheerleader. Making the varsity cheerleading squad changed the arc of my high school experience in unexpected ways.

THE FATHER, SON, AND HOLY SHUTTLE

All grown up on a family trip to Cocoa Beach in 2013. Just a few miles away, Dad's dream was realized in 1984 and, by extension, mine was as well. (Left to right: Amy, Mom, Dad, Laura, me)

Three generations of Mullanes (my son, Sean, is between Dad and me) sending *Discovery* off to the Smithsonian in 2012.

CHAPTER 8: LAUNCH?

The alarm went off early the next morning, the eastern horizon not yet aglow with the rising sun. Mom, Amy, Laura, and I ate a light breakfast. The family bus and police escort were waiting for us in the parking lot of the condominium complex. When we stepped into the early morning air, we all looked skyward. As expected, the weather looked good. The launch wouldn't happen with excessive cloud cover or any other number of weather phenomena. Assuming the cloudless sky held, that, at least, wouldn't be the reason for a scrubbed attempt.

We were the first on the bus and we said our "hellos" to the other bleary-eyed families as they boarded. The Mullanes were always early. Mom was like a NASA engineer in her conservatism when it came to planning arrival times during the course of a journey. Flight leaves at noon? Let's work backwards. We should be at the gate at least an hour before flight. That puts us at 11:00 am. It'll take about thirty minutes to get through security so let's say 10:30. Add a safety factor in case one of the x-ray machines goes down. Make it 10:15. Time to check bags and walk to the security check point: probably thirty minutes. But you never know – those ticket counter lines can be long at that time of day (and it was always "that time of day"). Add another thirty minutes just to be sure. We are now at 9:15. It'll take about thirty minutes to drive to the airport and find parking and make our way into the terminal. But traffic is such a wild card and what if parking is full and we had to go to the long-term lot? Let's add a buffer of another thirty minutes. Looks like we should leave the house at around 8:15. But, we have yet to add time for bathroom breaks. Probably should shoot for 7:30 a.m. Before we knew it, we were leaving four-and-a-half hours of time for a process that consistently never took half of that. If we were going to fly to Dallas from Houston, we could have walked the distance in less time given Mom's pre-flight ritual.

The bus pulled away from the condo onto A1A and headed north. As we neared the Kennedy Space Center, we could see cars parked along the road as tourists and locals secured viewing spots for the launch. Dad would be on just the twelfth space shuttle flight. There was still much novelty about the program and the buzz around a mission, while not Apollo-like, hummed a bit louder in those days. Those lining the streets saw the lights of the police cars leading and trailing us and walked to the edge of the road to wave as we rolled by. I suspect they had no idea who we were. Hell, some might have assumed we were the astronauts, unaware of the protocols regarding where the crew stayed in advance of a launch. I didn't care, it was awesome. I wondered if those assembling along the causeways and rooftops of Cocoa Beach had the same trepidation we did? Did they know the dangers that *Discovery's* launch posed for the crew? Were some of those present secretly hoping to witness a catastrophe, securing a story to rival those of their friends when asked, "Where were you when *Discovery* blew up?" I didn't want to know.

After passing through several checkpoints, (including the one Pop Pop used my ASTRONAUT DEPENDENT badge to transit) we unloaded at the LCC and made our way to the top floor of the building where we took up residence in the Launch Director's office. He wouldn't be needing it as he'd be in the launch control center for launch and, in any case, his office was one of the few places large enough to hold all of us in comfort. The room was outfitted with a closed-circuit television and audio sources that, already, were filled with the chatter of launch-day technobabble. Coffee and pastries were provided. On one wall was a large whiteboard and the younger kids were encouraged to use it to doodle as they whiled away the hours

THE FATHER, SON, AND HOLY SHUTTLE

before launch.* Windows in the office faced the east, toward the launch pad, but nothing was really visible. The sun had still not illuminated the eastern sky in any meaningful way and so the glass reflected any light inside the office too brightly to see what was outside.

I walked to the windows and cupped my hands around a small portion of the glass, put my eyes inside of my make-shift shades, and took a look. Pad 39A was visible in the distance, still bathed in the light of the xenon bulbs. I could see a venting mist coming from near the top of the external tank – liquid oxygen was boiling off as the tank was filled with fuel and its low temperature was condensing the moisture in the atmosphere, creating a dancing fog that gave the impression the machine was breathing. † A lone helicopter swooped overhead. The sights seemed more Hollywood than reality. I left the window and took a seat in the office, chatting frequently with our escorts and the other family members as the horizon, over the next hour, lightened with a deep red glow that hinted at the humidity saturating the coastal air. Condensation started to build on the outside of the windows and drip down the panes in lazy rivulets.

"Pat," Mr. Covey said, "Take a look."

He pointed to the television where a recording was playing of Dad at a table with the rest of the crew in an awkwardly staged breakfast meal – a meal where nobody was eating. The photo opportunity probably felt even stranger than it looked. The rectangular table had one long edge – the one facing the camera – unused so that the entire crew could be seen. They looked like actors in a play, arranged on a stage so that the audience could see all of them clearly. In a way, that's exactly what they were: actors playing the part of the cool and collected

---

* Later in the shuttle program, those whiteboards were framed after each launch to be preserved and hung along hallways in the LCC and, eventually, other KSC locations.

† Liquid oxygen boils at -297° Fahrenheit, meaning it will turn to vapor at any temperature above that. When the oxygen is mixed with the liquid hydrogen in the combustion section of the main engines, it produces a hot expanding gas that is shot through the nozzles to create thrust. The mixing of the two elements creates water vapor (H_2O). The shuttle main engines expel 3,000 lbs. of invisible water vapor every second when at full power.

American hero, knowledgeable about the danger they faced but unconcerned with the probability of their demise being hours away because, by God, they had a job to do, one that would further establish the hegemony of the United States in the twentieth century. I knew, having had many conversations with Dad about the risks of a shuttle mission, that it was, indeed, all an act – each of them had hearts that were beating with a different cadence as the shuttle's tanks were being topped off three miles away. They deserved Academy Awards. Despite the fact that we in the families knew it was a show, we clustered with our respective clans and talked excitedly about how they all looked so loose, happy, and well-rested. We told ourselves lies to help the time pass.

The footage then transitioned from a recorded to a live shot. The setting on the screen was one that had become familiar to me. Since the Apollo days, this had been the location where the public first saw astronauts outfitted for launch as they made their way in their space suits from the crew quarters to the "Astrovan" – not the horribly uncool Astro Van made by Chevy that would be released a year later – but the astronaut-van, a souped-up Airstream motor home.* The Astrovan would take them to the launch pad using the road that Pop Pop had tried to access by way of the guard gate manned by the special forces guys.

I could tell Dad and the rest of the crew were about to emerge from deep inside the Operations and Checkout Building as flash bulbs from reporters assembled off-camera began to illuminate the area. Then, they appeared. The *Discovery* crew had changed from the slacks and golf shirts they were wearing at breakfast into their trademark

---

* I suspect that many astronauts had no idea of the connection Airstream had to aviation beyond the Astrovan. The man credited with the distinctive design of the Airstream RV, Hawley Bowlus, was also a designer of manned sailplanes. Bowlus Gliders were a respected and well-known brand. His knowledge of aircraft design led to a role as the superintendent of construction for the *Spirit of St. Louis*, Charles Lindbergh's aircraft for his flight across the Atlantic. Bowlus had a long association with Lindbergh, having given him gliding lessons. I'm sure that for many who rode in the Astrovan through its history, the drive to the launch pad was filled with as much anxiety as Lindbergh had leading up to his historic flight.

NASA powder blue flight suits. Unlike astronauts of earlier eras, they would go into orbit without wearing a pressure suit. That really bothered me, but not because of the extra level of safety that pressure suits gave the crew (if the cabin sprung a leak at high altitudes, the suits would protect them from unconsciousness or death), it was because … well … the flight suits just weren't that cool. Neil Armstrong had walked down that same ramp at the checkout building wearing a large, white pressure suit with metal ports on the front that allowed umbilicals to be connected for various purposes. There was a "Communications / Electrical" connector, a "OPS O2 In" port, a red "Purge Valve" connector, a "PLSS Water In/Out" ring, and a red "PLSS CO2 Out" connector. Not only did Armstrong, Aldrin, and Collins get to wear these science-fiction-like suits, they carried a portable air conditioning device that connected to the rings on the front of their suits, enhancing their "walk on the moon" fashion. To top off (literally and figuratively) this look, they wore large, bubble-like polycarbonate helmets. The *Discovery* crew's helmetless heads and baby-nursery-colored coveralls just didn't evoke the "Right Stuff" image of days gone by. They looked like painters in a family business setting off to paint a single-family home in the suburbs of Orlando.

As the six of them walked briskly to the Astrovan, they waved a few times to the workers and reporters who had assembled to give them an enthusiastic – if brief – sendoff. I saw Dad take a peek at the sky as I had before I got on our bus at the condominium. He too wondered if the weather would be a problem. A few others looked skyward as well and then filed into the Astrovan. With that, the door closed behind them and they were on their way to the launch pad.

The video feed transitioned to a "live" shot and we saw the van make its way to 39A on the television. A short while later, the view switched to the "white room" on the end of the access arm that connected the gantry (the launch tower) to the shuttle hatch. Dad came in and out of view as each crewmember awaited his or her turn to crawl through the side hatch and, with the assistance of a "checkout" crew member, get situated into their seat and strapped in. Dad would be sitting on the flight deck during launch, something he was immensely happy about.

The shuttle had two levels to it. The flight deck was on the top floor where the pilot and commander sat and where all the windows (save one) were located. The middeck was the "finished basement" of the orbiter and, with the exception of a small window in the side hatch, was like a solitary confinement cell. If the crew was comprised of more than four people, then somebody (or a couple of somebodies) would need to sit in the middeck during launch and landing. Thanks to his designation as "MS-1", Dad lucked out and would be sitting upstairs behind the pilot, Mike Coats, in the open area behind the two front seats and in front of the back bulkhead. In this location, he would be able to see some flight instruments and views out the windows both in front of him and (if he twisted himself into an uncomfortable position) overhead. Steve Hawley would be sitting to his left. Judy Resnik and Charlie Walker, on the other hand, would be in the middeck, blind to both the instruments telling them how the launch was progressing and the view outside where the sky would turn to black as the shuttle gained altitude and the limb of the earth would come into view as *Discovery* came close to achieving orbital velocity.

Given Dad's position, he was the third to enter *Discovery*. He shook hands with the checkout crew. There was no audio from the white room on the television, but the sentiments from both sides were clear. Dad thanked the NASA workers, knowing that they were at the end of a chain of tens of thousands whose work had led to this moment for him. The workers, in turn, wished Dad good luck with smiles on their faces that showed that they felt blessed to give him and the rest of the *Discovery* crew this gift. With that, Dad got down on his hands and knees and ingloriously crawled through the side hatch. Steve, Charlie, and Judy followed. The hatch was closed and locked and the white room vacated. Dad and his five fellow star voyagers were now sealed inside of a spacecraft that, once the motors lit, held them prisoner come success or failure. I gulped.

As the litany of transmissions among the controllers became more frequent, the families' chatter in the LCC office became less so. The clock was below three hours to launch now and would enter a planned hold at T-20 ("T minus twenty") minutes.* The holds gave the controllers slack in the countdown so that any unexpected issues could be worked. The countdown holds were moments of great conflict for those of us who's loved ones were sitting out on the rocket. On the one hand, we all wanted the hold period to last no longer that it was supposed to. Since many launches had limited "launch windows" in which blastoff had to occur due to the operational requirements of the payload or the need to rendezvous with, for example, an ailing satellite, holds could not last indefinitely without jeopardizing the launch (STS-41D's launch window was 43 minutes). On the other hand, as soon as the launch director gave the go ahead and we heard the words, "The clock will start again on my mark. Three … two … one … mark," we all felt the breath go out of us. This constant tension between "we want them to light the engines" and knowing the risks that lighting the engines implied, brought on a mental exhaustion surpassed only by that of the crew sitting on the pad. Nonetheless, when the flight director did give the go-ahead to come out of the T-20 minute hold, we all cheered and clapped. One more hold was left, at T-9 minutes. If the Launch Director let the countdown proceed past that hold, we'd be making our way to the roof of the LCC to view the launch.

Things looked good as we neared the last scheduled hold. But then, trouble. There was chatter on the communications networks about issues with one of the GPCs – the general-purpose computers. During launch, the space shuttle was essentially on autopilot all the time and the GPCs were the brains of that autopilot. While the commander and pilot had control sticks in the cockpit much like a conventional airliner, as my father once told me, "If the PLT or CDR are using the stick during ascent, then things were FUBAR." Translation: if Hank Hartsfield or Mike Coats was trying to fly the space shuttle while the

---

* The space shuttle countdown checklist, known as KSC-S0007, is five very large volumes. It's glossary of procedures includes: Predetermined Fire Indication in Crew Module, Major Leak/Fire in LOX [Liquid Oxygen] Storage Area, L02 [Liquid Oxygen] ET Vent Area Fire During Loading. With understatement only possible in a government-issued document originating from NASA, the title page has this declarative: "THIS PROCEDURE CONTAINS HAZARDOUS OPERATIONS."

main engines were burning, then things were "fucked up beyond all recognition" and the day was going to end badly. Even though the space shuttle had five GPCs and could fly on just one, NASA's culture of conservatism did not allow a launch to happen unless all five computers were up and running.

We pinged Mr. Coats and Mr. O'Connell with questions about what was happening even though I already knew enough of the acronyms to piece together a picture that didn't look good. Sure enough, the Launch Director called off the launch during the T-9 minute hold. We all groaned. We'd have to do this *again*? The feeling was probably not unlike what a death row inmate feels when given a last-minute reprieve while knowing that that reprieve may be revoked the next day. The good news: the decision to scrub happened early enough in the countdown that a quick turnaround for a launch attempt on the next day, June 26th, was possible.

I hugged Mom and asked how she was holding up as we began to gather our things to head back to the bus. "Oh, okay," she said unconvincingly. "I don't want to have to do this again," she added.

"I don't either," I said. "But look on the bright side, we get free coffee and pastries again tomorrow." She smiled weakly.

***

June 26th. Groundhog day. The movie that led to the use of the words as an indication of a never-ending cycle wouldn't come out for another nine years, but I lived it before Bill Murray did. The early wakeup call. The bus ride. The police escort. The looming VAB astride the LCC. The fourth-floor office. The coffee and pastries. The fake breakfast on TV. The drive in the Astrovan. The events themselves were enough to make me think I was living the same day over again but the sense of déjà vu was made all the more piercing not because of what I saw but because of what I heard: the verbal markers as controllers made their way through KSC-0007, the countdown checklist. The same voices made the same calls on the same communications network at the same points in the countdown. It was at once maddening and reassuring.

There was one difference that morning that I'd noticed on the drive into KSC from the condominiums. It was foggy. Really foggy. While the shuttle would not be permitted to launch if visibility was below a certain level (and the visibility five hours before launch was definitely below that level), fog was commonplace early in the morning in a climate where the air was saturated with moisture. As temperatures dropped in the evening hours, the moisture in the air cooled and condensed, turning hidden water into visible vapor. Fortunately, this process is reversed when the sun comes up and the warming air chases the fog away. But nearly an hour after the first photons of light leapt over the horizon to the east, a quick look through the condensation-soaked windows in the LCC revealed ... nothing. Pad 39A was not visible from our perch three miles away.

The countdown entered the T-20 minute hold. So far so good. No major issues were reported. I looked out the windows again and finally could see the gantry, a muted grey form lost in a sea of orange-yellow haze. It wasn't clear outside, but it was bright, the still-lifting fog scattered the glow of the sun in a way that made it appear that light came from everywhere. If launch did happen, I was worried we'd never see it lift into the milky atmosphere. This disappointed me; I wanted to see the solid rocket boosters jettisoned and the weather didn't look like it was going to allow that.

The countdown resumed and we watched digits on a monitor in the LCC office begin to move again. 19:59 ... 19:58 ... 19:57. Next stop: 9:00. The countdown proceeded smoothly down to the T-9 minute point and the final hold was initiated. Fortunately, there were still no major issues being worked. The GPCs were good. While still very, very hazy, the visibility was within thresholds set by NASA. All other systems were operating as expected. The hold was ten minutes long, so about eight minutes into it we listened intently for the voice of the launch director. After a roll-call of his controllers where he heard voice after voice say that they were "go for launch," the launch director said the magic words: "Okay everybody, we'll be coming out of the hold on my mark. Three ... two ... one ... mark." I saw the digits on the clock in the office begin their march to 00:00.

"Let's go to the roof!" Bryan O'Connor said triumphantly. Suddenly, leaving for our viewing area with less than nine minutes before launch seemed absurd. Would we get there in time? Did we know for sure that the doors to the stairwell we'd ascend were unlocked? What if somebody slipped and hurt themselves on the way?

I wanted to sprint out of that office. Nine minutes was less time than it took for me to memorize the government warning on the back of my ASTRONAUT DEPENDENT badge. Nine minutes was less than the total amount of flight time my control line airplane had before it met its demise in my high school parking lot. Nine minutes wasn't enough time to listen to the first two songs on my double LP *Star Wars* record. Nine minutes was … nothing.

I looked to Amy, Laura, and Mom to try and encourage them to get moving, but apparently they were thinking the same thing as me and were making a beeline for the office door along with the rest of the families. We entered a wide hallway lined with pictures cataloging the history of U.S. spaceflight. Our sneakers squeaked on the linoleum tiles. Mr. Covey was leading the way and opened a door onto a lower roof and then we hiked some steel stairs along a façade to a higher perch on the very top of the LCC.

The warmth and humidity hit as starkly as if we'd stepped out of the air-conditioned building and jumped into the surf three-and-a-half miles to the east. We proceeded to an area roped off with yellow twine. Speakers on stanchions were setup in the corners of our roped zone and a few folding chairs were scattered about the area. The audio coming from speakers was loud and reverberated with an amplified echo. The VAB was behind us and to the left and its looming, enormous walls ensured that noises bounced back toward us. Launch pad 39A was still barely visible. The fog had not burned off at anywhere near the pace I had been used to in many trips to the area over the previous years.

The access arm my father had crossed from the gantry to the side hatch when entering *Discovery* was being retracted into its launch position. The crew was now on a very dangerous island.

At T-5 minutes, the SRB and ET range safety devices were armed. A member of the Air Force at Cape Canaveral Air Station could now press a button to blow up the shuttle if it strayed off course.

At T-3 minutes and thirty seconds, the engines on *Discovery* were jerked through a sequence of movements to test their readiness to steer the stack into orbit. The steering had to work, or things could go south every quickly.

At T-2 minutes and fifty-five seconds, the gaseous oxygen vent arm that I'd seen exhaling vapor earlier was moved out of place. The external tank was now "topped off" with 1.4 million pounds of liquid oxygen.

T minus thirty-one seconds was fast approaching. I knew from watching earlier launches that this was a particularly important milestone. The controller in the launch control center would give a "go" for auto sequencer start. This was the point at which almost all of the control of the rest of the countdown was transferred from ground computers to *Discovery*'s. That handoff had to happen cleanly if Dad was to get to orbit.

Mom, Amy, Laura and I were standing closely together. Arms interlocked. Hands held. Shoulders squeezed. The primary voice we heard on the speakers was that of a public affairs officer (PAO) who would translate the "NASA-speak" of the launch controllers for the public. This led to a strange repeating of critical calls. A launch controller would announce to the team in the LCC, "We have a go to start the automatic ground launch sequencer," and the commentator would repeat the information with a slight spin: "The ground launch sequencer is now in control until T minus 31 seconds when the shuttle's onboard computers will take over primary function." As the countdown accelerated, it was difficult to listen to both the primary communications of the controllers in the LCC and that of the public affairs commentator translating their calls, each stepping on the other's words.

Launch controller: "T minus forty seconds."

PA commentator: "T minus forty seconds and counting."

Two-thirds of a minute. That was all that was left. Two-thirds of a minute.

Launch controller: "Go for auto sequencer start."

There it was. The clock on the roof clicked past thirty-one seconds as the countdown continued. Cheers came from far off at viewing stands beneath us as others acknowledged the momentum now building.

All morning long we had heard many different voices on the communications channel broadcast throughout and on top of the LCC. Now, there were only a few. Earlier in the day, there was a natural softness to the start and end of the words coming from both the controllers and the public affairs officer. Now, the calls came in staccato, sharp-edged bursts book-ended by periods of static-infused silence. Minds were focused. Bodies tense.

"T minus twenty seconds." My heart was in a sprint.

Five seconds of quiet.

"T minus fifteen seconds and counting ..."

God, please keep him safe. Please.

Five seconds of quiet.

"Ten – we have a go for main engine start ..." Cheers louder now from the flatlands beneath us. My eyes began to tear. I squeezed Mom harder.

"Seven ... six ..." – we didn't join in the count, but we could hear others doing so like fourth graders anticipating a fireworks show – "five ... we have main engine start ..."

I saw an orange flash through the haze. The three engines at the back of the shuttle were coming to life. Brighter and more unorganized that I expected, the light from the main engines on the shuttle brought screams of joy, fear, and anticipation from those watching.

"Go *Discovery!*" I shouted stepping on the words coming from the LCC, unable to control my emotions

It was happening ...

Then ... nothing.

The flame I had seen earlier didn't turn into a laminar slice of light streaming smoothly from the back of *Discovery* as the engines came up to full power. The cloud that we'd seen rising from the flame bucket under the launch pad didn't continue to build, but drifted away in a large, solitary billow.

"We have a cutoff," came the call from the launch control center. The voice had a hint of confusion in it. "We have a cutoff," came the echo of the public affairs commentator.

Then, quickly:

Controller: "NTD we have an RSLS abort."

PA commentator: "We have a ... uh ... an abort by the onboard computers of the orbiter *Discovery*." *No shit.*

Controller: "Okay ... uh ... NDT verify..." Fear started to slowly grip me like wax cooling around my spine. The use of verbal fillers like "uh" were noticeable. Controllers never said "uh." It struck me: they were unsure. They were confused. They were worried. My sense of foreboding became heavy.

I momentarily heard only fragments of the calls from the LCC.

"Verify ignition is safed."

God, please, please verify the vehicle is safed. The controllers were scrambling to ensure that no motors would ignite. If the SRBs ignited now, without the main engines running, it would mean certain death for Dad and the rest of the crew.

Then, I heard it ... an explosion.

Mom, Amy, and Laura had their heads down. They looked up with me abruptly toward the launch pad as a loud rumble that yawned into a groan swept across the LCC. In an instant I was sure we had lost him. A million thoughts streaked through my mind in milliseconds.

Oh God ...

"It's the sound from the ignition! It's taken a while to get here!"

I don't know who shouted it. But thank God they had. *Of course.* Sound takes fifteen seconds to travel three miles. We were hearing sounds that originated a quarter of a minute ago when the engines (some of the engines?) had come to life. Why in the world hadn't somebody reminded us of this? That sound from that distance was a window into the past? We hadn't heard an explosion, but the beginning of a launch that never happened.

Any relief I felt was fleeting.

"Break break! Break break!" somebody in the LCC shouted into their microphone using language that indicated an urgent need to communicate with the entire team – an urgency I'd never heard before during previous launches.

"GLS shows engine one not shut down!"

By now I was standing on the precipice of a panic-filled crevasse. The clear confusion and stress of the launch control team was more unsettling than the scene that had just unfolded at pad 39A. The men and women of NASA, arguably the most accomplished and well-trained organization in the world, were supposed to communicate confidence, not seed doubt and worry. But at that moment, I suspected they were having the same thoughts shoot through them that I was. If a single engine was still running, it meant that the computers were not behaving in an expected way. And in a vehicle so complex, where nearly a half-million lines of computer code was the only thing keeping Dad alive, doubting the behavior of the electronic brain of *Discovery* was beyond unsettling. I looked at Mom. She held a vacant stare and I knew she was coming to the same conclusions. Each nightmare she had had about losing her husband to his passion in the year leading to this moment was now cruelly playing back to her. What folly to think that these machines could defy the laws of physics. What hubris to think they could do so without killing men and women along the way.

"Okay, PLT?" The controller was calling the pilot, Mike Coats. "CSME verify engine one …" Translation: make sure engine one is shut down.

Coats: "You want me to shut down engine one?" Why was he asking? Didn't he know if the engine was running?

Many people were talking over each other now. I wondered if they knew how much their chatter was rattling us. I looked at Mr. Covey and Mr. O'Connor. They were focused, their heads cocked toward one of the speakers, trying to catch the dialog.

The back-and-forth continued about whether an engine was running. How could they not know if engine one was on? Then, a man – a controller in the LCC – with the slow, gentle voice of a rancher talking to an excited horse said, "All engines are shut down."

He seemed to be trying to ratchet down the anxiety that permeated the LCC. I loved him – whoever he was – for that. But there was still confusion in the cockpit. The commander, Hank Hartsfield, called to launch control: "We have red lights on engines two and three in the cockpit, not on one." The instruments he was looking at were telling him that one of the engines was still running. This led to several volleys of conversation between various controllers who I could tell were frantically picking through their checklists at their consoles to determine what steps to take next.

By now, though, the LCC team was becoming more confident in what their instruments were telling them. After several exchanges, they seemed comfortable that all of the engines were quiet and that the rest of the vehicle was safe. As concern lifted, we all finally had a chance to pay attention to each other.

Amy was emotional. She had taken a seat in one of the folding chairs, crossed her arms across her chest and said petulantly, "Why don't they just put more damn gas in the thing and try again! God!" It might have seemed like a strange reaction in any other context and while I didn't have the same sentiment, I completely understood it. Fear had been a part of our lives ever since the mission before Dad's had landed and he had become part of prime crew. That fear had been held at bay by the building excitement leading up to *Discovery's* launch and, in some strange way, the sense that no matter what, one of two things would happen: Dad would get to orbit or die in the process of trying. Once the engines lit, the logic went, those were the only two possible outcomes. None of us anticipated a sort of in-between state, not even Dad. An engine shutdown had never occurred before in the shuttle program. Now, in that state, the anguish of the realization that our assumptions were wrong and that we would likely have to go through all of this again at some point in the future had released a frustration all of us felt and that Amy verbalized.

Mr. Covey and Mr. O'Connor gave us the best explanation they could of what had likely happened. They noted that the computers onboard had probably done exactly what they should have. While checking the liquid engines as they fired to life, something "non-nominal" had been detected and the engines had been shut down lest the orbiter leave the pad with a problem that might cause something very dangerous to happen during its ascent.

We made our way back to the office unsure of what would happen next. After taking up positions in chairs we had occupied earlier, we turned to the monitor in the room where we saw shots of the launch pad from various remote cameras. Several minutes later, the fear that had begun to drift away with the lifting fog returned. There was now chatter about a fire at the base of the launch pad. Sure enough, a close-up shot of the back end of *Discovery* showed a flame licking its way up the edge of a control surface under the engines. The fire was just feet away from the external tank and its millions of pounds of highly explosive hydrogen and oxygen. Everybody leaned forward in their seats. While the access arm had been quickly rotated back into place shortly after the abort, the crew had yet to open the hatch and exit *Discovery*. I began to wonder if they would initiate an "emergency egress" by popping the hatch open, running across the access arm, and jumping into large basket-like cages that slid down steel cables depositing the crew next to a bunker where they could wait out any fire or toxic leak on the launch pad. I later learned that Dad and his companions in *Discovery* had seriously considered the option, but they decided against it. That turned out to be an incredibly fortuitous decision. Later analysis indicated that a fire on the left side of the shuttle likely reached areas near the hatch. And since hydrogen (the fuel for the fire) burns invisibly, the crew would not have known of the danger by just looking out the hatch window; the path to the emergency slide wire would have looked clear, when, in reality, it was cloaked in a 1,000° fire they couldn't see.

"They're turning on the fire suppression system," Mr. Covey said. I got the sense he didn't want to alarm us and any sentence with the word "fire" in it would do just that. But what was the point in avoiding the obvious? We saw jets of water pointed at the engine bells of the orbiter stream from nozzles ringing the entrance to the flame bucket.

The room was tense. My mind flashed back to Dad telling me about how, when he was a newly selected astronaut, he and his TFNG classmates were taken to mission control at JSC where they were asked to sit at a console and put on the headsets laid out before them. Then, audio began playing in their ears from January 27th, 1967. It included the voices of Gus Grissom, Ed White, and Roger Chaffee – the Apollo 1 crew. The audio started with the mundane back-and-forth of a test plan; the astronauts were not preparing for an actual launch but were in their pressure suits seated in their capsule to conduct a launch simulation. Quickly, though, the audio turned horrifying. A voice believed to be Grissom's shouted, "Hey!" or "Fire!" Then Chaffee: "We've got a fire in the cockpit!" Next, garbled transmissions of a panicked voice pierced the baseline of static on the tape saying, "We've got a bad fire! Let's get out! We're burning up!" The audio ended with a sickening scream of pain and horror followed by silence. A message was being sent to the new cohort of hopeful space travelers listening in mission control: this job could kill you in unpleasant ways. Know what you are getting into.

Grissom, White, and Chaffee died just six-and-a-half miles south of where Dad now sat in a seat just a couple of hundred feet above a fire now visible on the closed-circuit television in the LCC office. In a sort of mental spasm, I wondered: would the fire at the base of the shuttle grow? Would it be a slow burn that Dad and his crewmates would be aware of, leading to panicked calls for help – like those from the Apollo 1 crew? If so, we'd hear it all unfold in real-time over the communications radios we'd been eavesdropping on all morning. Or would the fire slowly melt the aluminum of the external tank, igniting the liquid hydrogen and oxygen contained within in a brilliant, nuclear-like explosion, killing all onboard instantly? All possibilities were too horrifying to imagine.

We all were glued to the monitor, watching the fire suppression system douse the pad. Then it was turned off. But I could still clearly see a fire dancing on the body of the shuttle near the engines. Why didn't they just leave the damn thing on? I wondered.

The public affairs commentator then said, unbelievably, "We didn't have confirmation that there was a – a uh fire or anything in the region of the aft end, but we did have a couple of fire detectors that were on so, as a precautionary measure, we went ahead and turned on the heat shield water which – again – is being sprayed into the three engine bells of the shuttle main engines."

What the fuck was he talking about?

I was getting angry now. In aviation you are taught to trust your instruments, not your senses. But Jesus! There was a goddamned fire right there on the monitor! Your fire detectors were working! I didn't know if the commentary was just meant to keep the public calm even though controllers knew of the danger or if they were simply unaware of the fire. Neither explanation was particularly comforting. Watching the video feed and listening to the controllers while having information I thought was helpful *(there is a fire!)* but having no way to communicate the information to those that could do something about it was like watching a horror movie where the killer was sneaking up behind the teen in the tool shed and all I wanted to do was yell, "Turn around!" But this horror movie was real, and my father was the hapless teen.

After many minutes of dousing, the flames were extinguished, and the fire suppression system was shut off again. But the flames had seemed stubbornly persistent. I worried about them coming to life again. I just wanted Dad out of *Discovery* and off that launch pad. Some of the tension started to lift yet again.

"Exciting morning," I said to nobody in particular. Like my father, I used humor to cut through tension. Or tried to anyway; only Mr. Covey and Mr. O'Connor smiled. Mom looked like I felt – spent. Amy and Laura also appeared gaunt with the residual effects of nearly an hour of intense anxiety. I felt weak all over as the adrenaline coursing through me moments before thinned in my system, leaving behind what felt like a shell of a body.

The crew had been working through some shutdown procedures to safe the vehicle but those progressed quickly. Just thirty-eight minutes after the abort, we saw Judy Resnik on the TV emerging from the cabin into the white room with the assistance of the checkout crew who had raced to the pad to help. The rest of *Discovery's* crew followed.

When Dad emerged, he looked like we all did: exhausted and disappointed. I also saw a hint of anger. He knew how close he'd come. He was already projecting scenarios into the future, just as I was doing. Would this abort lead to a shuffling of the space shuttle launch manifest? Would his mission slip into the future or be scrubbed altogether? If he and his crewmates did lose their place in the line to orbit, would the loss of another shuttle mission and its crew due to some fatal failure cause a cancellation of the entire program before he ever got a shot again at realizing his life-long dream? There was no way to know. And not knowing what the abort meant for the future while still recovering from the fear and disappointment of the engine shutdown introduced a new kind of slow-burning anxiety that I knew we'd all deal with for weeks to come.

***

That afternoon, Dad didn't go back to Houston right away as some of the crew had. He had been convinced by Mom to come to the condominium complex where virtually all of our extended family – just hours after the failed launch attempt – were having a "lubricated" reunion by the pool. All of those in attendance were happy just to be together and, while I'm sure most would have loved to see Dad make it to space that day, they seemed equally enthusiastic about having an unexpected reunion with each other and, more importantly, with him. But when Dad arrived at the impromptu fête, it was clear that his mood was not celebratory. While those drinking beers and laughing boisterously in the breezes coming off the ocean meant well, they seemed oblivious to the trauma he had just gone through. Sure, he hadn't gotten into orbit, they collectively seemed to think. But he will in a few months, so what's the big deal? This accidental callousness seemed to ignore the fact that he had seen a lifelong dream slip from his grasp by just four seconds (the time frozen on the countdown clock when the abort occurred) and he had sat for nearly forty minutes on top of four million pounds of explosive fuel wondering if the fire underneath him might instantaneously dismember him. It was as if he were a minor league baseball player who had been called up to the majors and, while on a flight to Los Angeles to join his major league team, he got a message notifying him that they actually didn't need him, that he could go back to the minors in Gary, Indiana. Then, while still trying to deal with the disappointment of a big-league dream not realized, the plane caught fire and, for forty minutes, the pilot struggled to get it safely on the ground. Given that scenario, I don't think our friends and relatives would have expected that baseball player to be in the mood to party an hour after his harrowing landing, but they seemed to expect it of Dad. Nonetheless, he did his best to be cordial, smiling while he enjoyed a beer even while his eyes were glassy and distant, as if a close friend had just died.

In the early evening, Dad snuck away to get some well-needed rest and escape the joviality he just couldn't feel. At 5:30, a number of us gathered to tune into *World News Tonight with Peter Jennings* (Frank Reynolds had died the year before, so I was still getting used to hearing world events from another voice). As we all huddled around the television, Peter told us of the day's happenings. The lead story that day was from the Kennedy Space Center and told the tale of the *Discovery* crew's harrowing ordeal. The excitement I initially experienced at seeing Dad on television and hearing his name mentioned turned into a sudden melancholy. It was a sad irony that the first time I ever heard his name or saw his face on our favorite news program he was not by my side to watch with me.

CHAPTER 9: WAGES AND WOMEN

We all returned to Houston a few days later and waited to hear the fate of STS-41D. The engineers at NASA had figured out fairly quickly what had caused the abort. A main fuel valve didn't open as expected using a primary control system, so the machine had defaulted to a backup controller. Since launch rules didn't allow the shuttle to leave the pad running on that backup system (it was there to handle an in-flight failure), the computers did what they were supposed to do and aborted the launch. While the cause was known, the impact to the STS-41D crew was not. NASA was still working to determine the engine fix and, once a course of action was decided, they would then determine what it meant for the launch schedule.

I returned to Houston to enjoy the summer and try to forget my disappointment by burying myself in work. From a very young age I had been expected to keep busy and was generally excited to earn money to feed my model-buying habit. In addition to the job I had later in my high school career at the model shop, I worked in several other roles before that.

One of those jobs was as a fourteen-year-old at the Baskin Robbins Ice Cream shop in a strip mall about two miles from our home. I'm not sure it was legal to be working at that age and suspect that the owner knew that. Federal minimum wage in 1983 was $3.35 per hour. I was making less than $2 per hour, but I didn't care. It was money. The owner was smaller than me, but he scared me nonetheless. A native of Vietnam, he'd bark orders with an accent that made him seem more authoritative. Often those orders were directing me to "practice my scoops." We were required to scoop ice cream from the tubs under the glass display case and weigh them so that we'd have a natural feel for the optimal size of an orb lest we "over-scoop" and cut into profit margins. After weighing, we were instructed to place the balls of frozen confection back into the tubs, giving the impression that the ice cream had been shipped "pre-scooped." All that practice scooping had gotten my right wrist lean and strong ... or it could have been the teenage masturbation, we'll never know.

What my Vietnamese boss didn't know was that all the money-saving, scoop-weighing in the world wouldn't make up for the fact that while he wasn't around and the store was without customers, I'd take a tasting spoon and eat directly from the tubs under the glass, sometimes even going to the hot fudge warmer and placing a dollop of the warm, gooey chocolate on top of my sample before savoring the cold and warm together on my tongue. My go-to treat was Rocky Road – chocolate ice cream with tiny marshmallows and almonds. I loved the marshmallows and so I would pick them from the tub, leaving the top layer looking like regular chocolate ice cream. I often had to assure customers that the ice cream they were viewing under the "Rocky Road" placard was indeed infused with nuts and marshmallows. I'm not sure how many health codes I violated during my tenure at Baskin-Robbins, but I'm sure I was "patient zero" in many flu pandemics in the area around the Johnson Space Center in the early 1980s.

During my short breaks, I'd rush to the drug store in the same strip shopping center and buy a Mountain Dew soft drink (total calories: around 170) to wash down an entire, large Cadbury Fruit and Nut chocolate bar (total calories: around 810). My diet of candy bars, sugary sodas, and ice cream, in today's day and age, would have put me at high risk for obesity or diabetes. But when I wasn't gorging myself on such treats, I was riding my bike between jobs and playing basketball for hours a day, easily burning more calories than I took in. In fact, despite my diet, I was exceptionally thin and spindly with a mop of hair so large that, from a distance anyway, I looked like a life-sized bobblehead doll worthy of display at the National Bobblehead Hall of Fame and Museum in Milwaukee, Wisconsin (it really exists).

When I was sixteen and had secured my driver's license, I was able to contribute to my calorie burn with another job: mowing lawns. Jake, a buddy of mine from the sophomore basketball team, and I started our own little landscaping business and managed five or six clients. We'd load up my dad's lawnmower into the back of Jake's car along with some other equipment and drive to our customers' homes where we'd take turns between mowing and other duties such as edging the grass, cleaning up clippings, or cutting hedges. We sweated profusely in the Houston heat pushing lawn mowers through thick, St. Augustine grass, dodging hazards such as fire ants and dog shit (running over soft turds with a mower in such heat was a gag-inducing experience – we both hated mowing pet-owners' lawns).

When done with our work for the day, we'd drive to a 7-Eleven convenience store with the air conditioner on and the windows down, listening to Prince's "When Doves Cry" or Van Halen's "Jump," two Billboard hits of that summer. Once at 7-Eleven, I'd use the self-serve soda fountain to fill a 48-ounce Super Big Gulp cup with a mix of Coke, Mountain Dew, and Dr. Pepper. Jake would get a Big Gulp as well and, after purchasing a couple of bags of Doritos, we'd retire to the car in the parking lot and listen to more of the *Purple Rain* album while we washed down the yellow chips with our carbonated beverages, watching other teens come and go.

We had a particular interest in the girls that frequented the store in shorts and bikini tops. Jake, a six-foot-five-inch kid with an olive complexion and a curly tumble of hair that hinted at his carefree nature, had a phone in his car and would make a habit of picking it up and putting it to his ear whenever an attractive girl walked by on her way into or out of the store. Except it wasn't a car phone. It was an old phone that had once hung on the wall of his family's kitchen. He had placed it in the console between the two front seats giving the impression that it was a true car phone, a technology that was just making it into the vehicles of wealthy technophiles and businesspeople. He'd bring it to his ear and have a mock conversation about buying a stock for a brokerage account he didn't have or picking up a boat he didn't own.

Once, we were called out by a very attractive girl Jake was staring at as he had one of his faux conversations with an imaginary listener on the other end of the line. She exited the store with a pink Tab soft drink can in her hand and smiled at us as she stepped into the sunshine. She was going to walk between our car and the one next to us on Jake's side but stopped as she passed and backed up, stood next to Jake, put a hand on her hip, and said incredulously, "If that's a real car phone, then where is the antenna on the outside of the car?"

She had a point. Autos with car phones had small, pig-tail type antennae mounted somewhere on the outside of the vehicle, usually in the center of the top of the trunk. Jake just smiled as I sunk lower into my seat, sipping on my Big Gulp. The smile sloughed off of the girl's face as she realized we were grade-A losers. She resumed her runway model walk into the parking lot behind us and disappeared into a waiting car. As the Tab-drinking beauty drove away, Jake didn't initially say anything; he just slowly put the phone back into its arm-rest cradle. Then, after a sip on his drink and while staring out the front window focusing on nothing, he said, "What the hell does she know anyway?" He said it as if we really *did* have a working phone connected to an operating antenna. I loved that about him – he was comfortable with "ambiguities" that I was not.

One day, late in 1984, I dropped Jake at his house after we had played some basketball together and then stopped by the home of another friend, Thomas, to hang out and talk about our class schedules and basketball. Thomas was on the basketball team with me at Lake and lived in a modest ranch-style home in an older community down El Dorado Boulevard from my house. Like Jake, Thomas was tall, coming in at somewhere around six-two. He was very thin with long limbs and a way of moving that reminded me of a praying mantis. He had a cutting humor and would use it sometimes to cut me, but I liked him nonetheless, mainly because he, along with Jake and I, occupied the same layer in our school's social strata that defined the pecking order in any such institution. If the thin, top crust of that strata was where the most beautiful cheerleaders and most accomplished jocks resided, then the slightly thicker layer beneath that was the group that had a sort of adolescent charisma and o.k. – but not great – looks. My friends and I were comfortably ensconced in the thick third layer – generally unattractive nerds and nobodies that had some unique element to their resumes (ours was basketball) that kept them from the

THE FATHER, SON, AND HOLY SHUTTLE

depths of the lower layer. And the lower layer was where the outliers were. These were the goths, the drama queens and kings, the dope heads, the math geeks, the metal-heads and gearheads.

The thin crust and layer-two kids wore Jordache and Gloria Vanderbilt jeans, Ocean Pacific t-shirts, and Members Only jackets. They listened to the popular music of the day because those two classes of teens defined what *was* popular: Prince, Van Halen, Phil Collins, Bruce Springsteen. My layer was not so homogeneous. Yes, some wore the first two layer's clothes and listened to their music, but more variety started to emerge. The music of the Romantics, Thompson Twins, and Eurhythmics was now sprinkled through this largest stratum. The clothes were often knockoffs of the expensive brands the anointed ones wore. A light coat may have looked, at first glance, like a Members Only jacket, but closer inspection revealed that the telltale black tag sewn under the breast pocket actually said something like "Modest Original."

Those in the lower layer, crushed by the weight of the classes above them, calcified into their respective sub-groups, rejecting outright the tastes of their classmates. The metal-heads were blasting Queensryche, Judas Priest, and Metallica. Their wardrobe was a rotation of black concert t-shirts bearing dark-themed artwork that relied heavily on airbrush effects. The drama girls rejected the heavily feathered hair style of the popular kids and instead favored more curl, more tangle, and, often, more color in their coiffure. The drama cabal would only listen to a song that had meaning; while others up the strata listened to the cotton-candy "Uptown Girl" by Billy Joel, drama kids listened to Joel's "Summer, Highland Falls," a beautiful lament about manic depression that never made Casey Kasum's weekly top forty countdown (They say that these are not the best of times / But they're the only times I've ever known).

Thomas and I talked at great length about getting ready for the upcoming basketball season and gossiped about girls we were interested in (girls in layers above us that didn't know we existed) – discussing who had gotten hotter over the summer and who had slipped in ranking. At one point, Thomas put down his Coke abruptly, interrupted our banal banter, and said, "Pat, I can't believe I forgot! You aren't going to believe what my dad has!" He said it in a shouted whisper even though he had told me earlier that both of his parents were not at home. He walked toward the family room and waved his hand over his shoulder beckoning me to follow. We passed to the other side of the house where the bedrooms were and Thomas cautiously opened the door to a spare bedroom, peeking in before entering as if he thought his folks might be there.

Once in the room, he went to the sliding closet doors and pushed one of them open. He then reached up to a shelf hidden high in the closet and pulled down a cardboard box. He set the box on the floor, pulled apart its interlocking flaps and pushed the four flaps down. And there it was…a *Penthouse* magazine.

The periodical had gotten a lot of press in the summer of 1984. For the first half of the year, Vanessa Williams, the first African American Miss America, had been enjoying her reign. But *Penthouse* had gotten ahold of some explicit photos she had posed for during her college years and announced they would be publishing them in a future issue. Williams resigned in light of the news and waited for the magazine to hit newsstands. I, of course, was aware of the scandal – watching the nightly news almost every evening assured that I knew the story of her downfall and what had caused it. But I never thought in a million years I'd see the magazine and the pictures within.

Thomas gingerly picked up the issue, which included on its cover a picture of Williams with comedian and actor George Burns. She was a clear three or four inches taller than the bespectacled Burns, who had his right hand around her back and his left hand relaxed in front of him, holding his trademark cigar. It was a fifteenth anniversary issue and the caption next to both of them read, "Oh, God, She's Nude!" – a double entendre referencing Burns's role in the 1977 movie *Oh, God!* Burns starred in that film as the supreme being with a popular musician of the time serving as his costar: John Denver.

Thomas laid the magazine on the bed and began thumbing through the pages. My heart was beating so loudly I thought that Thomas' father would hear it from wherever he was and know exactly what we were doing. I had expected that the first time I'd see such a publication it would be the more ubiquitous *Playboy*. It was common knowledge among boys my age that *Playboy* contained images evocative of the great nudes painted by Italian artists during the renaissance – a perspective I'm sure we all shared after overhearing our fathers make such a comparison in an effort to justify their subscriptions. *Penthouse*, on the other hand, was like a gynecological medical journal edited by P.T. Barnum; "intimate" shots of genitalia interleaved with scenes containing two or more people gave it a decidedly edgy reputation relative to *Playboy*.

While black-and-white nude photos of a Miss America published in *Penthouse* would have been scandalous under any circumstances, the photos of Williams were considered even more tawdry since she was posed with another woman in distinctly sexual positions. I was stunned. In one photo, Williams had positioned herself on her knees on a stool (as one does) while the other woman, kneeling next to the stool, got into a position that allowed her to put her nose and mouth into the ass crack of Miss America (as one, apparently, also does). The crack-diver had one hand on each of Williams' buttocks as if she were holding an enormous goblet and the photographer had asked her to take a drink. What the hell was she doing? I wondered. For a moment, I couldn't help but wonder why *Where Did I Come From?* never covered this sort of sexual engagement. There were no light-hearted pictures showing the plump woman with the big cartoon nipples having her rear-end inspected by another crudely drawn lady. If there had been such artwork, I wondered how the text above the image would have begun: *Sometimes, when a Miss America loves another woman very much, they will get a stool and ...*

As Thomas flipped through the pages quietly, I stood a foot or two back from the magazine as if it was a piece of civil war ordnance we had found on the beach that might inadvertently explode in our faces. Despite my parents' openness about sex, I was a prude by the standards of most teenage boys. My conscience was in a perpetual tug-of-war between the liberalism of my parents' attitudes and the infusion of Catholic sensibilities that came by way of weekly mass and participation in St. Bernadette's youth group. The regiment of the church and its *Star Wars*-like clarity about right and wrong (and there were a lot of wrongs in the realm of sexuality) kept me nervous enough to be cautious with things related to the feminine sex.

Obedience to the rules of Rome began at seven-years-old when I experienced my first confession and communion because I had reached the "age of reason." This was apparently the age at which a child had the wherewithal to determine that eating the actual flesh of Jesus Christ and telling his or her darkest secrets to a guy behind a wicker screen inside of a telephone booth was necessary for spiritual growth.*

But my moral confusion only went so far; as I got older and "impure thoughts" started to involuntarily bounce between my synapses as if they were frenetically searching for a way out of my head, I never once confessed a single one of them to a priest. I stuck to things like being mean to my sisters and vandalizing a neighbor's pumpkin on Halloween night. And I certainly wasn't going to talk to a stranger about masturbation. Dad had been clear that if you surveyed men, 97% of them would admit to masturbating and 3% of them would lie about it. Ergo, priests violated their own temples too. Why should I have to talk to the guy in the collar about my wanking when he was running back to the rectory to spill his seed in an unproductive, sinful manner?

"Isn't this awesome?" Thomas asked, smiling as he looked over his shoulder at me.

"Yeah, cool," I said, lying. Vanessa's pictures were more uncomfortable than titillating.

I tried to engage in casual conversation with Thomas, walking a line between seeming appropriately eager to view the images while behaving as if it wasn't that exciting because, well, I'd seen stuff like this before (I hadn't). I'm sure my attempt to walk this line failed miserably, but Thomas didn't seem to care. He was too distracted by the ass-crack goblet drinker.

***

---

* I wondered how the age of reason was determined to be seven-years-old and found this answer on Catholic.com: "The Church does not define the age of reason as seven-years-old. Rather, the Church does not obligate Catholics under the age of seven to observe laws which are merely ecclesiastical ... *Code of Canon Law* states, 'Merely ecclesiastical laws bind those who have been baptized in the Catholic Church or received into it, possess the efficient use of reason, and, unless the law expressly provides otherwise, have completed seven years of age' (CIC 11)." Well, that clears things up.

THE FATHER, SON, AND HOLY SHUTTLE

While it was a rite of passage for every teenage boy to be made uncomfortable by his friends because of some conversation or event related to sex, I assumed I wouldn't have to deal with such discomfort in my own home. My assumption was wrong. At dinner one night when I was sixteen, Amy, Laura, and I were assembled at our round kitchen table. Hanging above the table was something I had never seen in any other home, restaurant, or hotel before: a chandelier made out of the back end of an aircraft engine hanging by macramé lines. The worn metal had a cool, industrial look but I always hated the macramé it hung from; it made the art look like it had been conceived by an overly-proud cat lady whose son worked at NASA. I imagined her tying the macramé knots in her La-Z-Boy chair, the blinds drawn as an episode of *The Price is Right* played on a large console TV. Pictures of her son, who, like her, lived alone, were on top of the TV staring back at her as one of her four cats arched its back and rubbed against her shin.

We were all seated with Mom and Dad beneath the cat-lady-with-NASA-son chandelier eating a beef stew Mom had made. Bits of celery and carrots floated in the broth and, if we were lucky, it was sometimes accented by roasted New Mexico green chilis we had bought in Albuquerque during a visit. Mom heated stacks of tortillas and liberally slathered them in butter and we dipped them into the stew. It was delicious.

For much of the meal, the scene was a picture of Americana – mom, dad, and the kids breaking bread at the end of a school day, chatting about friends and studies. But for reasons that evade explanation, our vignette veered from G-rated drivel to R-rated sexual comedy; at some point, masturbation came up. As Laura asked my parents questions about the taboo subject (in any other family anyway), I put my head down and sipped soup from my spoon as I kept my eyes trained on the floating bits in the broth lest I be pulled into the discussion. It didn't work.

"Pat," Laura said after a few minutes of back-and-forth on issues related to self-pleasure, "how often do you masturbate?"

I looked up, stunned. Dad began laughing. *Not helpful*, I thought.

I wondered how to respond. Of course, my first thought was to deny any activity at all in the chicken-choking department. But I knew this was futile. Nobody would believe it – after all, it wasn't true. Denial would lead to prolonged questioning from my sisters. They had heard Dad make the same scientific pronouncement I had regarding the topic in the past – that 97% of boys do it and the other 3% lie. That didn't leave me much room to maneuver. So, I decided to fess up, but to do so in an absurd, indirect way, hoping it would kill the topic. I put my right hand below the table and between my legs and started moving it up and down, allowing it to pound the bottom of the table rhythmically. I looked up at Laura as I beat the imaginary meat and said, seriously, "I don't jerk off Laura."

Dad erupted in forceful laughter. It was an infectious, high-pitched barking that escaped him as he threw his head back, the front gap between his two front teeth prominently on display. Amy, Laura, and Mom began to laugh too – perhaps more in reaction to Dad's cackle than to my masturbatory mime. Mom, in fact, quickly had tears begin to stream down her face as she tried to swallow a spoonful of dinner. This, in turn made me start to laugh ... laugh hard. Unfortunately, I had taken another puddle of stew off my spoon as the initial bout of laughter had rolled around the table and now it was trapped in my mouth; I was unable to swallow afraid that I would suck the contents from my mouth into my sinuses or lungs by way of an ill-timed laugh. I tried to calm myself so that I could get the food down the hatch. I thought I had succeeded, and between stomach-convulsing laughs I made a go of it. I closed my eyes and tried to force the stew down.

But it didn't work. I inhaled as I swallowed and was immediately thrown into a coughing fit as some bits from the stew were aspirated into my sinus cavity. The fluid and solids now in limbo between my trachea and nasal passages caused a sharp pain reminiscent of that I felt when bile burned my throat upon vomiting. But even that pain was not enough to keep me from laughing. Then, in a half-cough, half-burp spasm, a piece of celery that had been in limbo decided to come up instead of go down. But it didn't make it's escape back into my mouth. Instead, it shot from my nose at near supersonic speeds, landing smack in the middle of the bowl of stew it had occupied just moments before. I swear it splashed when it hit the fluid, its reentry velocity like that of the meteor that killed the dinosaurs.

The scene of celery leaving my nose and diving back into the stew made the table convulse into even more laughter – laughter that bordered on screams.

Amy tried to talk through her laughing, squeezing words out between breaths. "Was-" inhale, exhale, "that food-" inhale quickly, exhale, "that came–" inhale, exhale, "out of your nose?!" The words came with such difficulty, it was hard to understand her. More laughter came at the question.

I was in a coughing fit as my lungs tried to purge the fluid that had been drawn into them. I could only nod "yes" to Amy's question as I tried, unsuccessfully to say, "Celery." I then dipped my spoon back into the stew in front of me and, with the best shit-eating-grin I could muster between coughs, I gently slid the utensil under the floating snot-celery.

"No!" Amy said, horrified, as she watched. "Don't do it!" Her laugh was now part cry. "Pat, don't do it or I'll puke!"

I looked at Laura and her face said *do it*.

Mom was in a humor-filled cry now and Dad's laughing had reached a pitch only dogs could hear. I slowly raised the snot-celery, floating in a spoonful of broth, to my lips as Amy continued to scream at me. I put the contents into my mouth then wrapped my lips around the neck of the spoon and slowly dragged it across my lips as I tipped the handle skyward, pretending to savor its contents. I swallowed it down with a dramatic "gulp."

The table erupted yet again. Laura, Mom, and Dad were laughing. But Amy was, as promised, gagging, her mouth open, lower lip protruding, tongue extended out over her lower lip, and neck wide as if she were going to barf the contents of her stomach back into her bowl. Now I was the one shouting.

"Amy, don't do it!" I yelled at her, genuinely concerned. If she hurled, I was sure I would. After a few dry heaves, she started to cry and all of us, being the supportive family we were, laughed at her.

A dinner that had started with inconsequential discussion under a macramé / engine parts chandelier before it turned to questions about my masturbatory habits had ended with my twin sister trying not to vomit after I had eaten food that had already been inside of me. I wondered if any other family in the history of the world could say they had had a similar experience. I suspected not. We all let the laughter dissipate; the need to simply breathe and give our abdominal muscles a rest forced us to settle ourselves.

As we all exhaled, letting out audible sighs, I scanned the table. Mom was dabbing tears from the corners of her eyes with a napkin. Dad was smiling broadly, unknowingly showing a piece of celery stuck between his teeth. Laura was giggling softly as she dug back into her stew. Amy's frustration with me for having almost induced vomiting in her had melted away and she was now laughing at herself. I knew in that moment I was blessed even as I might have been naïve about how unusual a childhood like mine was. In so many ways I lived inside the world Norman Rockwell painted. It was a world that Rockwell himself didn't know. Married three times and treated for depression throughout his life, Rockwell's psychiatrist was quoted in a 2001 biography as saying that Rockwell painted his happiness, he didn't live it. I lived my happiness. And how much better to live joy than to paint it.

CHAPTER 10: ASTRONAUT

Within two weeks of returning to Houston from Florida after the aborted launch attempt, we learned that STS-41D would survive the reshuffling of the launch manifest. Not only would Dad's mission keep its place in line, it would pick up another payload. In addition to the solar panel experiment, the cargo bay of *Discovery* would now include three communications satellites, not just the two originally planned.

Engineers had discovered that a valve was not working as expected in one of the engines and so the decision was made to replace the motor and launch was slated for late August. We all celebrated the news, knowing that the uncertainty that had been hanging over Dad's head was killing him. But while none of us talked about it, the relief of that decision brought on the worry of knowing that we'd be going through the pre-launch ritual again. While I think my anxiety level was a bit lower than my sisters' and Mom's, I still suffered from an unease that glowed deep inside of me like an ember in a steady breeze. I'd lay in bed in the evening listening to my GE clock radio as the air conditioning kicked on, making it feel as if the home were breathing. As cool air fell over me and my model airplanes twirled on their fishing lines from my bedroom ceiling, I thought of all that changing out an engine on the space shuttle must entail. I had seen photographs of engines on test stands at Marshall Space Flight Center in Alabama, their guts exposed, and images of those photographs came back to me now. How many connections had to be made between the engine and the orbiter? Pipes and fittings and electrical connectors would have to be checked and re-checked. What would happen if somebody missed something? I didn't want to think about it, but it didn't matter what I wanted. The darker elements of my brain were in overdrive and wrested control of my thoughts from the part of me that wanted to believe everything would be okay.

***

We returned to Florida in late August to watch Dad attempt another launch. The atmosphere in and around our condominium complex was decidedly more muted. Much of the family that had made the trip the first time, didn't do it a second. Even if the expense was not a barrier, school in many southern states, including ours in Texas, had already begun. Tourists who might have made the trip to the cape with their children in tow didn't want their little scholars to miss the beginning of classes and so the streets were emptier, the beaches more barren. It didn't matter to me though. Despite my nagging fears, I was eager to go to KSC and step once again through the launch ritual.

On the morning of August 29th, 1984, we were back on the top floor of the LCC. We didn't allow ourselves to get too high, wary about whether the SRBs would ever ignite. Our caution was well founded. For the third time, Dad strapped into *Discovery* and we went through hours of zipping past countdown milestones only to see the launch scrubbed yet again because of a computer problem. Mom, Amy, Laura, and I had moved from weariness to frustration.

The next morning, on the bus ride from the condominium to the LCC, we tried to joke with the other families about the apparent curse on STS-41D, wondering if the crew had set the shuttle record for the number of "strap-ins" before a launch (it had). Conversations were as shallow as the swamps lining the road, from which alligators ominously watched us, their eyes just breaking the surface of the water. The day was clear and bright – unusually clear given the time of year and in stark contrast to the day that the on-pad abort had happened. When we got to the LCC, the launch pad was plainly visible and somehow being able to see the pad more clearly was comforting.

The clock seemed to run downhill as it busted through important milestone after important milestone. When we reached the built-in countdown hold at T-9 minutes, all seemed to be going swimmingly.

Then, the curse was back.

A private aircraft had wandered into a restricted area near the launch pad; *Discovery* would go nowhere until the plane changed course. Mom, Amy, Laura and I just about lost it. "Shoot down the son-of-a-bitch," I said to nobody in particular. Had I used the mild profanity at any other moment – particularly since it had been in the presence of other adults – Mom would have given me a menacing glare and squeeze on the arm. But instead, I got a chorus of "amens" from the other family members and our astronaut escorts. I learned later that Dad and the rest of the crew had the exact same sentiment inside the cabin, except the offender was a "fucker" not a "son-of-a-bitch." I think they got it right. The launch window was going to close shortly and so getting the trespassing aircraft to reverse course as soon as possible was critical. You didn't want to complete a clean countdown only to be thwarted by something not related to weather or a problem with the shuttle itself, the usual causes of delays.

After nearly seven tense minutes, the public affairs announcer's voice cracked through the late summer air confirming some of the background chatter we heard coming from launch control. The aircraft had vacated the area and the countdown was ready to resume.

Moments later we heard the phrase we loved and hated – *The clock will begin again on my mark: three ... two ... one ... mark* – and the countdown resumed its march. We again made our way to the roof of the LCC. Once there, my sisters and I shifted our weight left to right, right to left, trying to bleed off our nervous energy as the minutes slipped away. Mom had her arms folded, her chin in her neck, undoubtedly praying to Saint Jude, the patron saint of hopeless causes, and Saint Christopher, the patron saint of safe travels. She also might have been praying to Saint Joseph of Cupertino, the patron saint of aviators and (believe it or not) astronauts.

"T minus thirty-one seconds; we have a go for auto sequence start. *Discovery's* four computers now have control of critical vehicle functions."

Silence

"T minus twenty seconds and counting."

Silence.

The pregnant quiet between broadcast updates only made my respiration seem louder. Mom, Amy, Laura, and I stood in a line, the intermittent quiet smothering us with a crushing weight.

"T minus fifteen."

Silence – silence on the radios, silence on the roof. I saw the water suppressions system activate as the contents of an entire water tower (300,000 gallons) next to the launch pad was dumped into the flame bucket to protect the pad and the shuttle from damaging acoustic shock waves.

"T minus eleven … ten … we have go for main engine start … six … we have main engine start …"

We saw the tell-tale flash of orange that indicated the main engines were coming to life – a flash we had seen two months before, only to see it die an early death before it morphed into a dangerous fire licking the belly and side of *Discovery*. But this time, the flash grew for a few seconds longer. The water in the flame trench turned to vapor as the hot exhaust of the engines instantly boiled it, creating an ever-expanding cloud of white steam that grew into translucent cauliflower shapes, looking like a time-lapse movie of a building cumulus cloud.

"Go! Go! Go!" I yelled as others did the same, jumping up and down excitedly. The three main engines were coming up to full power and the entropic orange flash that denoted their initial ignition had disappeared to be replaced by nearly invisible exhaust.

"… three … two … one …"

The commentator paused for what seemed an eternity. The rhythm of his countdown was broken. Where was the call for SRB ignition? God let the SRBs light. Please let them light. Then, a flash at the base of the pad on either side of the shuttle.

"… and SRB ignition … and we have liftoff, liftoff of mission 41-D and the first flight of the orbiter *Discovery* and the shuttle has cleared the tower!"

Discovery came into view above the launch gantry giving us our first look at the entire stack free from both the pad and all of the support equipment that kept it alive in the weeks leading to launch. It looked at once majestic and unnatural, a gorgeous apparition that defied the laws of physics. The orange tank from where *Discovery* sucked her fuel gave a stark relief to the shuttle itself and made it seem to gleam more brightly than it had when next to the gray metal of the launch tower. The rocket balanced on top of the white-hot flames of the twin solid rocket boosters. While the liquid engines were bright, they were overwhelmed by the welding torch intensity of the SRBs. That intensity had surprised me the first time I'd seen a launch a few years before. Television cameras couldn't capture it.

"Go, damnit, go!!!" I screamed as tears came to my eyes. My father's launch would be the second of eight shuttle launches I'd witness in my life. And every one of them drew tears from me. It's a very common reaction that I think is related to a maxim stated by Arthur C. Clarke, the famous science fiction writer and futurist: any significantly advanced technology is indistinguishable from magic. The view of *Discovery* pirouetting on thousand-foot flames coming from the SRBs was magic of the highest order – magic that bordered on the mystical, the religious. My tears came from the same place as those shed by pilgrims at Mecca or the Vatican.

"Mission control confirms roll maneuver."

Discovery rotated on its long axis and began to gently tip over to point itself east, tangentially to the surface of the earth. It was beginning its trek across the Atlantic.

Then, the noise hit us. The sound of the main engines got to us first, a smooth whoosh from fifteen seconds ago, then, six seconds after that, the sound of the SRBs washed over us, rolling across the flat, empty land between the LCC and the launch pad. The solid rockets burned with a chest-thumping crackle. The noise drew more tears from me and the rest of the families. Like a symphony in crescendo at the most beautiful part of a film, the noise added to the aesthetics of the visuals: the clear azure sky, the white light of the SRBs, the trail of fire and smoke tracing a graceful arc in the atmosphere. Dad may be getting the ride, but I was getting the view.

"Standing by to throttle down to 65% to pass through the period of maximum aerodynamic pressure."

The space shuttle was already beginning to move too fast for the air to get out of its way. Shock waves began to develop in front of it as it approached the speed of sound. The engines were so powerful, that running them at full power while *Discovery* burst through the sound barrier in a relatively thick part of the atmosphere might tear it apart.

"Forty-five seconds. Altitude three-point-five nautical miles, down range distance two nautical miles, velocity twenty-one-hundred-fifty feet per second." Just forty-five seconds after launch, *Discovery* was at 18,000 feet altitude, traveling one mile every 2.5 seconds.

The next milestone was SRB separation. The solid rocket boosters only burned through the first two minutes of launch and then would separate from the stack, their fuel spent, and parachute into the Atlantic to be retrieved by boats that would tow them back to KSC where they would be refurbished for launch and used again.

Mission control in Houston came through the PA system. "*Discovery*, Houston, go at throttle-up."*

"Houston, *Discovery*, roger, go at throttle-up," came the reply from the cockpit. The engines were now spooling up as the shuttle pierced further into ever-thinning air.

Back on the LCC roof we all had our faces skyward and were beginning to feel some of the tension leave our bodies, carried away as if by the breeze that was blowing the launch plume to the south. Still, there were more than six minutes left before *Discovery's* three main engines would shut down. My guard was not completely down.

"Standing by for SRB separation," came the call from the public affairs officer in Houston.

"Keep watching everybody," commanded Mr. Covey. "You'll be able to see the SRBs separate."

I trained my eyes on the end of the plume which now was arcing to the horizon – *Discovery* was more in front of me than above me now – and waited for separation. I heard the call to Houston from *Discovery* telling mission control that the pressure in the boosters had dropped below fifty pounds-per-square-inch, a signal that the SRBs were out of fuel and separation was imminent.

The announcement from mission control came matter-of-factly: "SRBs separating."

---

* Launch was controlled out of the LCC in Florida until the shuttle was clear of the launch tower. From that point until landing, mission control at JSC was in charge so all calls from the cockpit to the ground began with "Houston." Two of the most famous phrases in the history of aviation began with the name of my hometown: *Houston, the Eagle has landed* and *Houston, we have a problem.*

I saw streaks of smoke flash across the shuttle as the separation rockets of the SRBs pushed them away from the external tank. The still glowing and smoking nozzles at the end of the discarded rockets came in and out of view as the boosters began to tumble, starting a plunge that would be slowed by three massive parachutes closer to the ocean's surface.

We all cheered. I hugged Mom and my sisters. Another big milestone was behind us. If something went wrong with one of the liquid-fueled engines, it could be shut down and the shuttle could limp to an abort site across the Atlantic, make one revolution of the earth and land, or make it to a lower orbit. As long as the SRBs were burning and attached to the rest of the stack, there were no abort options available to Dad and his crewmates; we bid the twin booster good riddance.

The noise of the rocket was now gone and was replaced by clapping and cheering from the viewing areas spread beneath us. The three main engines which were now pointed at us from more than thirty miles away had become a single point of white light, a manmade star visible in the middle of the day but slowly fading. Eventually, *Discovery* disappeared out of view. We were left to listen to the calls out of mission control, keenly tuned to keywords that we prayed we'd never hear: anomaly, abort, alarm. *Discovery* was already at 158,000 feet in altitude and racing east at one mile every second.

"*Discovery*, Houston, single engine press to MECO." The call from mission control meant that even if the shuttle lost two engines, it could still make it to orbit on the remaining one. Another gate passed, one of the most important.

We listened to the rest of the transmissions waiting anxiously for MECO – main engine cutoff – which would happen around eight minutes after launch. At that point, the shuttle would be approaching its final orbital speed of 17,000 miles per hour, or around five miles a second. The potential energy of those millions of pounds of fuel had been turned into kinetic energy, hurling STS-41D – the heaviest shuttle mission to that point – into an orbit just under 200 miles.

Finally, the call came: MECO. We all cheered and hugged each other. Tears were in Mom's eyes. Amy and Laura were emotional as well. We were all ecstatic. Dad would be weightless now, falling with

Discovery over the lip of the earth, only about thirty minutes from seeing his first orbital sunset as they raced toward the terminator – that curtain of fading light that demarcated night from day. On the drive back to the condominiums from KSC, I realized that Dad was passing over us to the south as he completed his first orbit. It had been only ninety minutes since he left pad 39A. How was it possible that he had circled the globe before we had finished watching the launch, gathered our belongings from the LCC office, and made the fifteen-mile drive back to the condos? *Any sufficiently advanced technology is indistinguishable from magic.* It was, indeed, magic. Magic that had – finally – made Dad an official astronaut.

***

We returned to Houston with Mom and Joe Joe. Dad was scheduled to be in orbit for six days. It seemed odd that we would simply carry on with our lives while Dad zipped overhead, circling the globe about sixteen times every day. Amy, Laura, and I went back to school – Amy and I returned to the beginning of our junior year and Laura to the start of eighth grade. While I walked the hallways of Lake between classes, friends asked me what it was like to have my dad in space and I usually answered that it just felt like he was on a week-long business trip. And, in a way, I guess he was.

Clear Lake High School was tied to NASA more than any other school in the country. Just one-and-a-half miles as the crow flies from JSC's Gate 4 (the "back gate"), many of its students were the children of NASA's workers, contractors, and astronauts. In fact, of Clear Lake's 83,000 residents in 1984, it was estimated that one in four of them worked for NASA. Lake was known throughout the Houston area as one of the wealthy "rich kids" schools and I couldn't help but see its culture in the iconic coming-of-age movies of the time. While both George Lucas and Steven Spielberg were speaking to me through their films, so was John Hughes. In a period spanning 1984 through 1986, Hughes directed or produced *Sixteen Candles*, *The Breakfast Club*, *Pretty in Pink*, and *Ferris Bueller's Day Off* (he wrote all of them). The schools in those movies looked like mine: modern, clean, and full of privileged white kids. In fact, Lake in the mid-eighties *was* Hollywood. Several classmates drove Porsches and Mercedes and spent their weekends water-skiing behind their families' boats on Clear Lake or

Taylor Lake. Boys were buff and girls were svelte. The hot weather and proximity to a beach and water sports ensured teens were swim-suit ready.

While by any account the troubles of kids in my neighborhood paled in comparison to those of children in other parts of the world, the pressures of living in a large, well-off bubble where it was difficult to keep up with the Joneses started to show in horrific ways. Between the beginning of August and the end of October in 1984, the same year Dad blasted off in *Discovery*, five students or former students at Clear Lake High School committed suicide as did one other student from our archrival in the same district, Clear Creek High School. Two boys – dropouts from Lake – who knew each other shot themselves, one shortly after the funeral of the other. Another dropout hanged himself from his family home's staircase railing. Then, a sophomore girl shot herself. The fifth suicide was an acquaintance of mine. Gary Shivers was a fellow junior with whom I'd played pick-up soccer in the lumpy fields to the north of our intermediate school a few years before his death. He hanged himself after his parents divorced. Just two days after Gary's death, a fourteen-year-old from Clear Creek High School died of self-inflicted carbon monoxide poisoning.

Rumors of a death pact of some kind started to circulate and while no evidence of such coordination ever surfaced, it was a scary time for both students and parents. In an interview with a *Washington Post* reporter, one mother summed up the feel of my neighborhood: "Everything is too fast, too slick, too quick. It's called immediate gratification." Another woman, the wife of a computer scientists, lamented in the same article the lack of community in Clear Lake, something brought on by the climate.

"This is Texas and you're air-conditioned," she said. "You're all in your own little homes. People run from their cars and go into their houses."

The story had become so big it didn't just appear in the pages of newspapers; it was the lead on *World News Tonight with Peter Jennings* one evening. Reporters crawled around the outside of the school interested in probing a narrative in which well-off teens in wealthy suburbs that abutted the grounds of the Johnson Space Center decided to kill themselves. Two years later, reporters would again be hovering around our school after an equally horrible event that took the lives of five area residents and two others: one a native of New York, the other a teacher from New Hampshire.

***

On the first day of Dad's mission, the first of three satellites was deployed successfully. Then, on the second day, the largest satellite – the first designed specifically for the shuttle's cargo bay – was rolled out of the orbiter. The third day completed the trifecta as the last of the satellites was set free from *Discovery* and then made its way to a higher orbit. Judy Resnik had also deployed her solar array, a precursor to the sort of collapsible structure that would be used on a future space station. The array was about 105 feet long but folded into a box less than a foot deep. The crew took a call from President Reagan while those of us on earth got to have coffee and donuts with Vice President Bush, who made a visit to mission control in Houston on the day before Dad's scheduled return.

Things were going well. Too well, it turned out. On the third day, controllers at JSC reviewing telemetry data from *Discovery* saw unusually low temperature readings around two waste dump nozzles on the orbiter. The nozzles were on the forward left side of the fuselage underneath the left cargo bay door and were not visible from any windows on the shuttle. The purpose of the ports was something Pop Pop could relate to. Like the drainpipe on his motor home that allowed us to dump our sewage into the desert, the nozzles on *Discovery* allowed the crew to dump excess water generated by their fuel cells (which combined oxygen and hydrogen to make electricity) and urine from their toilet into space. Dad described the view of such dumps as spectacularly beautiful since liquid instantly froze in the vacuum of space and turned into glitter-like crystals streaking gracefully into oblivion.

Of course, the freezing temperatures of space that created the ice crystals meant that the nozzles from which the fluid exited the holding tanks on the shuttle had to be kept warm, otherwise the liquid would simply freeze on the side of the vehicle, forming a large urine ice ball. But the indications were that the heaters on each of the nozzles weren't doing their jobs. Using a camera on the end of the robot arm that extended like a cherry-picker from the cargo bay, the crew was able to monitor one of the nozzles during a dump and, sure enough, the beautiful crystal display didn't materialize. Instead, a large ice structure formed in real-time, growing to something that resembled a stalactite. The crew was ordered not to use the on-board toilet anymore out of an abundance of caution; Dad would spend the rest of the mission peeing into plastic bags with socks stuffed into the bottom of them to absorb the urine lest it bounce off the bottom of the bag and glob onto him or, worse yet, become a perfect sphere of translucent yellow floating about the cabin.

While ice on the side of the shuttle might seem innocuous enough, it presented a very real threat to *Discovery*. The mass would come off of the orbiter during reentry and, given its location, could fly back and hit the tail of the spacecraft.* If the thermal protection on the leading edge of the tail were penetrated by the ice, the tail could melt and a shuttle without a tail wasn't going to glide to a landing in the deserts of California. It would tumble out of control, killing the crew in an incendiary show that would have been grotesquely spectacular to view from earth. This scenario was a variation on the chain of events that would lead to the loss of *Columbia* nineteen years later.

Little seemed to work to rid the orbiter of its frozen hitchhiker. By the fifth day, after positioning *Discovery* so that the nozzles faced the sun to warm the area+ and firing control thrusters in an attempt to jar the mass loose, the crew was asked to take steps to prepare for an emergency EVA – a spacewalk. Somebody might have to step outside and knock the piss-sicle off by hand. Dad, one of the two crewmembers trained to do EVAs, might get an unplanned trip outside the orbiter in a real space suit like Neil Armstrong wore.

Mom, Amy, Laura, and I joked about the turn of events when our astronaut escorts filled us in one evening at our home. Dad might be

---

* Concern about this exact scenario had been heightened when NASA officials realized that unexplained damage to tiles in the rear of the orbiter *Challenger* on STS-41B, which had landed seven months earlier, was likely caused by ice breaking free from the same waste nozzle.

+ Ice doesn't melt in space, it sublimates. Sublimation is the process of going straight from a solid to a gas. It's substantially slower than the process of melting.

threatened by his own piss. While space walks had already been performed from the space shuttle (in fact, untethered space walks with jet packs had been performed on STS-41B), nobody was that keen on having crewmembers expose themselves to the danger of such an activity if it wasn't necessary. There was also the question of how exactly Dad or Steve Hawley would get to the globbed-on ice. There were no handholds along the side of the orbiter, no way to "crawl" to the nozzle. They'd be improvising, and NASA hated improvisation. It was certainly not something they'd practiced in the WETF – the Weightless Environment Training Facility – a giant pool where Dad had trained to do spacewalks. Fortunately, there was one other option that was being worked out by the never-daunted engineers at NASA.

A plan was being formulated that would have the crew use the robot arm to knock the ice off of *Discovery*. Some calculations had been done; it could reach the nozzle. But the operation wasn't without risk. The crew wouldn't be able to see the end of the arm while it was maneuvered over the side of *Discovery*. They'd have to rely on programming from the ground and cameras on the arm to ensure they didn't make things worse by damaging the arm while it was deployed or hurting the heat shield with the end of the arm. I secretly hoped that there would be a reason they wouldn't be able to use the robot arm. Dad had expressed his interest in doing a spacewalk – although, admittedly, not an unplanned one. As a mission specialist astronaut, he'd never get the chance to land a space shuttle or be at the controls during launch (not that there was much to do). Hitting a button to release a satellite had its rewards, but any mission specialist worth his or her salt wanted to venture beyond the airlock and conduct work on the outside of the shuttle.

But it was not to be. Early on the sixth day of the mission the robot arm did its job and the ice was unceremoniously nudged from the skin of *Discovery*. It floated away like a small asteroid. Eventually, it would reenter the earth's atmosphere if it didn't sublimate completely before then. The next morning, I read a story from the *New York Times* that a friend had brought to me. "If the mechanical arm had failed to free the ice," it said, "there was an outside chance that the space agency would have authorized Lieut. Col. Richard M. Mullane of the Air Force and Steven A. Hawley to make a spacewalk to take care of the problem.

That would probably have entailed a one-day extension of the mission." I was thrilled to see Dad's name in the *New York Times* but deflated that his mission wouldn't last longer and that he wouldn't have a chance to be the hero that saved *Discovery* from imminent danger by way of a daring EVA.

***

Discovery would be landing at Edwards AFB. Amy, Laura, and I would not be going. NASA would only fly Mom to the landing and while we could have taken commercial airliners to California, all sorts of issues made that impractical. The first was the cost of the flights. The second was the relative remoteness of Edwards. The third was the fact that Mom would be jumping onto a NASA private jet with Dad to return to Ellington Field near our home in Houston shortly after landing. We wouldn't make it back via commercial airliners until a full day after Mom and Dad had returned home. We wanted to be at Ellington to greet Dad and Mom when they landed and thus decided to stay put in Houston.

In landing at Edwards, *Discovery* would be returning Dad to a base where we had lived years before. Edwards was the redwood-gas-cap motor home embarkation point for many a Mullane journey in my early youth. It was where I had almost stepped on the Mojave Green rattlesnake – a snake Dad collected and took by bicycle and coffee can to the base's survival school. It was where Amy and I sat through *Where Did I Come From?* in slack-jawed horror.

It must have been an amazing pseudo-homecoming for Dad. When he had been enrolled at Test Pilot School at Edwards, he thought his dream of flying in space was dead. His poor eyesight had kept him from becoming an Air Force pilot and, to that point in time, only military pilots were eligible to become astronauts. Disappointed but not broken, he opted for the next best thing – serving as a navigator and weapons system officer in two-place aircraft. Then, the shuttle program came along and NASA changed the rules. Engineers, even if they weren't pilots, would be considered for mission specialist roles. Dad used this experience to teach me and my sisters an important lesson: always do your best even when you think it doesn't count because someday it might. Nine years after arriving at Edwards certain he'd never see orbit, he was flying back to the legendary base in the world's first reusable spacecraft, hurling across the Pacific in a plasma-wrapped fireball. He had become the first Air Force navigator to fly in space. It was a small first, but a first nonetheless.

While I would not be at Dad's landing in person, I had seen the very first mission, STS-1, return to earth at Edwards while on the trip where Pop Pop got the motor home stuck in the sand after our sewage dump in the desert. When we arrived at Edwards for *Columbia's* return in 1981, we drove into a geek-ified desert version of Woodstock. Tens of thousands had shown up to see the space shuttle and its astronauts, John Young and Bob Crippen, glide to a landing. Shirtless men sat atop motorhomes that were parked on the hard sand. Women walked around in bikini tops and "Daisy Dukes" (*The Dukes of Hazzard* aired between 1979 and 1985 with actress Catherine Bach popularizing the cut-off jeans look). VW busses painted in psychedelic patterns became hubs where strangers shared drinks and smokes. American flags flew from RV awnings where decidedly buttoned-up engineers cooked hotdogs over Kingsford briquettes for their kids. It was a Fourth of July in Washington D.C. wrapped in a baseball game at Fenway Park sprinkled with Burning Man in Nevada.*

It was, to my mind anyway, the best of America. And not just because of the aerospace flavor of the event. I was struck even as a child by the diverse mix of people the landing had drawn to a dry lakebed sixty miles and a nearly two-hour drive northeast of Los Angles. People of all stripes wanted to be a part of something that was distinctly apolitical and inspiring … something that hadn't been seen since 1969 and Apollo 11's landing on the moon. After centuries of terrestrial exploration, the earth held fewer mysteries than ever before. There were no more mythical continents to seek out. No more rumors of monsters that swallowed ships whole. No lost city of gold to be plundered. Humankind had been left with space travel as the last grand romantic activity that fed our innate desire to explore and conquer … conquer frontiers, conquer physics, conquer death and danger. That

---

* The first Burning Man gathering was still five years away when *Columbia* glided back to earth in 1981. There were between twenty and thirty-five attendees at the event which was held on a San Francisco beach. Thirty years later, Burning Man attracted around 70,000 people to the Black Rock Desert 100 miles northeast of Reno.

desire transcended race, religion, political party, and geography. While *Columbia's* mission hadn't gone to a new planet or made the first alien contact, it had shown that we still had "it" – that we could design machines that had no business doing what they did. We were demigods and the throng of people who had traveled to the Mojave Desert that April day were attending a sort of spiritual celebration of human achievement, a celebration of self. *Columbia* was our idol.

That first return to earth of a space shuttle had as much tension as the first launch. The thermal protection system on the shuttle, a collection of more than 24,000 silica tiles, was unproven. While it was known that an individual tile could withstand the 3,000 degrees of reentry and insulate the underlying aluminum from the heat, there were worries about the reliability of the adhesive used to attach the tiles to the orbiter. Engineers were concerned that the loss of a single tile could lead to a "zipper effect" whereby tile after tile ripped from the belly of *Columbia* after a single breach was exposed. It was a fear that would grip Dad on one of his later missions.

The PA system set up at the *Columbia* landing site viewing areas near Edwards crackled with the narration of a public affairs officer out of JSC. After the shuttle began its reentry, it went into a period of radio "blackout" due to both the lack of an earth-based tracking station in view of *Columbia* and the impenetrable layer of hot plasma wrapping the orbiter and keeping signals from getting to (or leaving from) the spacecraft. We all waited nervously to learn the fate of the crew and their new spacecraft. Pop Pop smoked his pipe in the sun, his baseball cap teetering on his head as usual, his legs crossed in his wheelchair. Grandma stood by his side, wearing sneakers under her flowered, long dress, her face pointed skyward. The crowd had grown quiet. Anticipation and worry rode together, side-by-side on the warming air. Just as a single bright star in a patch of dark sky can make that sky seem darker, so too the scattered, distant noises of a mass of humanity made the silence seem quieter.

Then, as if reading from a script that Steven Spielberg himself had written, the voice of John Young triumphantly echoed over people and their vehicles: "Hello, Houston, *Columbia's* here! We're doing Mach

10.3 at 188." * The crowd roared. They had made it – at least past the hot reentry phase – and were now traveling 10.3 times the speed of sound at an altitude of nearly 188,000 feet, or thirty-six miles. It was hard to believe *Columbia* would slow down enough before its main gear was supposed to touch down on the sand.

Several minutes passed as *Columbia* continued its descent. Radio calls marked lower altitudes, slower speeds.

Boom! Boom!

Two sonic booms punched the air – one formed off the nose of *Columbia*, one off of its massive tail. Another enormous roar came from the crowd, the whistles and hoots not as deep and impactful as the sonic booms, but equally as loud.

More altitude and speed calls came, their frequency accelerating. Eventually the altitudes were low enough that we knew the vehicle would come into view soon. Grandma, Pop Pop and I began scanning the cloudless and vivid sky for *Columbia*. Like a human tidal wave sweeping over the desert, I saw hands begin to go up far off to our left, pointing skyward. As one person pointed out the white form of *Columbia*, he or she turned to a nearby stranger, passing on the information with an outstretched arm and pointed finger. Before the cascading message could reach us though, I spotted it, squinting through my heavy glasses.

"There it is!" I said to Pop Pop, squatting next to him so that his eye could follow my arm.

I wasn't prepared for what we saw. The glideslope of the space shuttle is seven times steeper than that of a commercial jet and its rate of descent is twenty times faster. It all gives a viewer from the ground the impression that the spacecraft is in an uncontrolled fall. Larry Eichel, a reporter from the *Philadelphia Inquirer*, captured what I saw when he explained, "[The shuttle] was dropping so fast that to an eye accustomed to watching the more gradual descent of commercial jets, it seemed inevitable that [it] would crash to the desert floor."

---

* I had already met John Young a couple of times at events with my father and would be around him many more times after that day; that radio call was the only time I ever sensed any sort of emotion from him. He was like Spock from *Star Trek* … if Spock had even less emotion.

Pull up, pull up! I thought to myself as the crowd's cheering softened, probably because of whispers making the rounds about the shuttle's trajectory and whether or not it was "normal."

Then, finally, 2,000 feet above the ground, Young pulled back on the stick to expose more of the underbelly of *Columbia* to the oncoming air and the stubby-winged shuttle seemed to really fly for the first time. The nose continued to rise as the shuttle crept to an inevitable intersection with the ground. *Columbia* had no engines. It was a glider. It had begun its de-orbit rocket burn 5,000 miles ago and now, like one of the gliders the Wright brothers flew at Kitty Hawk, it was sailing quietly to a landing in the sand.

The gear was down and locked. We heard the calls of altitude now measured in hundreds, then tens, of feet until, miles in the distance, we saw the desert sand kicked up by *Columbia's* wheels as it touched down at around 220 miles-per-hour, about fifty to sixty miles-per-hour faster than a Boeing 737. The crowd went crazy. In fact, in one area, it went downright rogue.

In an interview for the NASA Oral History Project, J.O. Creighton (an astronaut in Dad's class of TFNGs) related a story about being in one of several army helicopters that were airborne over Edwards during the landing. He was there in the event that a crash occurred upon *Columbia's* return – he could race to the site in the Huey and then offer expertise to rescue personnel regarding what parts of the *Columbia* wreckage might be dangerous since hazardous propellants were stored throughout the vehicle. Creighton said that after *Columbia* had come to a stop, he and the rest of the helicopter team saw a horde of people in cars and motorcycles break down a barrier and begin racing across the desert toward the shuttle. He described it as something out of the movie *Independence Day* (sounds more like *Mad Max* to me). Since the shuttle purged dangerous gasses even once stopped on the runway – gasses that could kill people standing within a relatively large radius – Creighton and his comrades decided to take action. The helicopter pilots swooped down in front of the speeding vehicles, feigning an attack and kicking up blinding dust as they tried to "heard [the] cars like cattle." They were able to hold off the charging group long enough for security personnel to drive to the area and get the mob to reverse course. I have to admit, it's a tough call for me to decide where I'd have rather been: in one of those speeding cars rushing to the orbiter like a Parisian trying to get to Lindbergh, or in one of those helicopters. In the end I think I'd choose the helicopter. Being in the air is always better than being on the ground.

***

I watched Dad's landing on TV with my sisters, Joe Joe, Grandma, and Pop Pop (Grandma and Pop Pop had arrived a day or two before after driving from Cape Canaveral in their RV). I was disappointed I couldn't be in California but glad that I had gotten to view STS-1's return three years before so that I had a sense of what it was like for Mom and the others watching the landing in person. It was only around 6:30 a.m. at Edwards when *Discovery* touched down and so the shuttle was bathed in the pink glow of a rising sun as it descended over the desert. Commander Hartsfield greased in the landing, the smooth touchdown contrasting distinctly with the menacing trajectory of just moments before. Back in Houston, we all cheered and discussed how surreal the whole experience still seemed. When the launch had finally happened, I assumed that the feeling that it was all a dream would wear off. But it didn't. I watched *Discovery* return to earth not sure if my father was really ensconced in its mid-deck. It made me see how those who were less close to space travel than me might have doubted that men really did walk on the moon.

Later in the afternoon, those of us in Houston drove to Ellington Field, the same airport Dad and I flew out of in our rented Cessna 172s. Local television news vans were parked outside the NASA operations building at Ellington and shoulder-mounted cameras could be seen hovering around the tarmac. There was a gaggle of crew family members and NASA employees there with us as the Gulfstream II aircraft that astronauts used to practice shuttle landings touched down and pulled to a parking area. As the engines were shut down, the door came open and stairs unfolded from within the cabin. Not long after that, Mom and Dad emerged from the airplane, looking so very happy. Amy, Laura, and I were allowed to duck under the makeshift rope barriers that had been erected and we ran to Dad. Joe Joe, Grandma, and Pop Pop followed closely behind us, Grandma pushing her crippled husband in his wheelchair. I waited my turn to give Dad a big hug.

"Patrick!" he said as he embraced me after giving Amy and Laura a squeeze.

"I'm glad you're back Dad," I said, smelling beer on his breath as I squeezed him. The crew had clearly been imbibing on the way home.

"It's good to be back," Dad said through a dimpled smile, although I wasn't sure he meant it. His mission had been relatively short, only six days and one-hour long. Given how busy he had been during the mission with satellite launches, IMAX filming, and various other duties, I'm sure he felt he never had enough time to look out the window or play around in weightlessness. Still, I sensed relief in him that he had survived the ordeal and knew he'd be getting gold astronaut wings to replace the silver ones he had been given when he was an astronaut in name only.

I wanted to ask him a million questions but people from JSC were now talking to him and we were being shooed back toward where the barrier was so that the *Discovery* crew could make some comments at a podium that had been positioned in the blazing sun. As Commander Hartsfield spoke, the rest of the crew stood behind him, flashing alcohol-boosted smiles. Each took a turn at the podium, but they were all clearly anxious to get home and spend time with their loved ones, so any comments were mercifully brief.

After the speeches were done, Dad returned to us with Mom and we all talked as the news reporters we had earlier seen descended on Judy Resnik. The second American woman in space – and fourth woman overall – had more appeal, apparently, than the first Air Force navigator in space.* Pop Pop took pictures of the scene as Grandma stood by him, the pride of a mother evident on her face. Joe Joe scanned the scene with a more subdued pride. Amy, Laura, and I talked excitedly to each other and some of our friends that were in attendance. After several minutes, though, we all began to melt into the NASA operations building, intent on heading home.

---

* As of early 2017, sixty women had made it to orbit. And while the Russians can claim several of the important firsts, including the first woman in space (Valentina Tereshkova) and first woman to do a spacewalk (Svetlana Savitskaya), only four of the sixty women to get to orbit have been Russian.

That evening, we all had dinner together at our house and begged Dad to tell us stories of his voyage. Listening to him, I felt connected to adventurers of the past, imagining Captain Cook, after returning from one of his first two major expeditions (he didn't make it back from his third after pissing off some native Hawaiians), sitting with his family and friends as they peppered him with questions about far off lands and experiences that defied the imagination. Dad talked excitedly about seeing incredible orbital sunrises and sunsets, about the sensation of being weightless, about playing with his food in orbit, about peeing in weightlessness, about seeing lightning from above, and a thousand other things. I absorbed every word. After our meal was finished and the evening descended, Dad was ready to sleep in a real bed with gravity pulling him into the mattress, a mere mortal once again. I hugged him goodnight and went to my own room.

I thought of how fortunate Dad was. His boyhood dream to become an astronaut – a stereotypical and usually unfulfilled dream of kids the world over– had actually come true. Luck certainly played a role. But I knew he had made his own luck. It was a powerful lesson for a boy like me. I resolved in that moment to be bold like my father. I wanted to leave my mark on the world. And I was anxious to do it sooner rather than later. I wasn't sure what form that boldness would take as I tried to fall asleep that evening. But I was convinced that I'd find something.

CHAPTER 11: CHEERLEADER

About eight months after *Discovery's* maiden voyage, I was a seventeen-year-old junior in my spring semester at Lake and found myself standing on the glossy hardwood floor of the school's largest gymnasium. I stood in the center of a line of ten other students, all of us facing the entire freshman, sophomore and junior classes – about 2,500 people. They were a restless throng, alive like a beehive seen from afar. Those of us on the court were all alike: striving for a goal, wishing to be more than we are, wanting to be known in a large public school where anonymity was a social death sentence. Yes, we are all alike save one difference: I was the only one with a penis.

The music started. It was "The Heat is On," by Glenn Frey, a song made popular by the comedy movie classic *Beverly Hills Cop*, which had been released the year before.* I started to dance. The first movement in the choreography was a crisp flexing of the knee with my toe planted on the ground, my kneecap kept time with my bobbing forearm and snapping fingers. I looked like one of the un-intimidating musical gangsters from *West Side Story* preparing to rumble while singing. For a moment, there was silence in the auditorium. Then, like a geyser, an

---

* Glen Frey had a sort of "six degrees of separation" relationship to *Star Wars*. He had co-founded the Eagles with Don Henley after they met while playing together in the band of Linda Ronstadt. Ronstadt dated George Lucas for several years after he divorced his first wife, Marcia. Marcia was one of the Academy Award winning editors of *Star Wars*.

eruption came from the bleachers; it was laughter and it was loud. The cavernous space became an amplifier, each wall and beam catching the noise and throwing it back into the room. The sound was so overwhelming, I wanted to laugh along at the absurdity of it all. It was, after all, outrageous. Boys in Houston, Texas in the early eighties didn't try out for cheerleader. And certainly, the sons of astronauts and West Point graduates didn't try out for cheerleader. Yet there I was, a modern-day gladiator in the Coliseum. Or was I a Christian being fed to the lions? In either case, the masses were amused, and I was getting noticed.

As the routine continued, I was on autopilot. I had rehearsed over and over again in the weeks leading up to the try-out. I *was* the music. The beat took up residence in my spine and commanded my limbs to move. I was killing it. Until, that is, the chorus transitioned to the song's instrumental bridge.

When I had thrown my hat into the ring to join the aspiring young ladies in the tryout, those designing the choreography had not known what to do with me during this part of the song. There were discussions about modifying the dance moves, about having me stand with feet firmly planted, the only movement coming from my arms sharply jerking into crisp angles to the beat of the music, no movement below the shoulders. But in what must have been the purest display of equal opportunity in Houston, Texas in 1985, the idea was abandoned, and it was decreed that I would do what the girls did … exactly what the girls did. And during the instrumental bridge what the girls did was this: they got on their knees, feet under their butts, and leaned back until their shoulder blades came close to touching the floor, their shoulders shimmying the whole way, breasts gyrating to and fro. Needless to say, a shimmy was not in my repertoire and, despite my practice, I looked like a drunk pervert on a cruise out of Jersey trying to limbo beneath a very low bar. It was not a pretty picture. The crowd laughed harder.

My high school had a particularly cruel cheerleader tryout process. Those giving it a go were assessed in three equally weighted categories: academic performance (including teacher recommendations), evaluation by college cheerleaders, and student body vote based on your ability to shake your hoo-has in front of your classmates. I had confidence in my ability to score well in the first two categories. I was a bit of a bookworm, was ranked in the top five percent of my class, and had a number of teachers who would write kind things about me. As for the assessment by the college cheerleaders, I couldn't do any gymnastic tumbling, but I was confident that I was enough of a novelty with just enough talent to get some sympathetic "real" cheerleaders to give me high marks. And, in fact, my turn in front of them made me feel as though I were special, but not necessarily in a good way. Two women and one man sat behind a folding table. The women had cloned faces: bright lipstick atop smiling lips, sympathetic and encouraging eyes peering from deep inside a canyon of mascara, and hair full and parted into feathered wings lacquered into place with ozone-depleting hairspray. When I finished, the affirmative nods were more rigorous than they should have been. "Awww ... isn't he cute?"

And now I was enduring step three: the performance in front of my classmates. I rose from my shimmy and finished out the song, holding my position at the end past the final beat of the music. And then I did the only thing I could do better than my female counterparts: jump very high from a standstill and touch my toes to my fingers on my outstretched arms in mid-air, the creatively named "toe touch." "Go Lake!" I shouted. "Yes Falcons!" I exclaimed. The crowd roared its approval of me, their modern-day Gladiator, as my fellow warriors and I pirouetted on our toes to march in a line out of the gym, making room for the next set of sacrificial victims.

As we walked to the exit, the freshman principal stood near the door and stared at me with a menacing glare. His eyes tracked me; his head unmoving. He had been a football coach at one point in his career and his gaze told me that in his book if boys were doing something athletic it was football, basketball, track, or some other "real" sport. They didn't try out for cheerleader. I stared back realizing a certain pleasure in getting to him. He was a *pendejo*, more insecure than most of the awkward kids he held dominion over and so disrupting his worldview had an interesting appeal for me. I wasn't aware at the time that I was disrupting the world view of a lot of people and his stare was a harbinger of some of the abuse that was yet to come.

In the days after the tryouts I was the talk of the school. I felt like a celebrity walking the hallways, watching clusters of students hold hands to each other's ears as I walked by, whispering as their eyes tracked me. Is that the guy? Is he gay? Why did he do it? The first two questions were easy to answer: yes, I was *that* guy and no, I was not gay. The answer to the third question was simple in some ways, more complicated in others. First the simple: playing basketball had become more of a chore for me. I enjoyed the game itself very much, but the coaches at Lake came out of the Bobby Knight school of motivation – practices were loud, ninety-minute, obscenity-laced affairs.* Despite playing constantly in the years since I tried out for the junior high team when Coach Saxe called me out as an example of how hard work could pay off, the writing was on the wall – I was not varsity quality. The combination of practices that held not even a sliver of joy and the fact that I'd sit the bench during games drove me to re-evaluate how I wanted to spend my final year-and-a-half at Lake and pretty quickly I realized that it wasn't playing basketball. That left me wondering what sort of extracurricular activity might be both fun and résumé-enhancing for college applications. Of course, there were plenty of options available to me in a school so large; not liking basketball and wanting some college application fodder didn't make obvious the choice to try out for cheerleader. I could have played another sport or joined the band, choir, or any number of clubs. So why cheerleading in a school, in a district, and in a state where I had never seen a male cheerleader?

Watching my dad rocket into space and fulfill a lifelong dream in a spectacular way had energized me with a desire to change my own trajectory. It wasn't that that trajectory was bad or destructive. But it was just so … ordinary. I wanted to make a mark in a big way. I wanted to be known. I think it's fair to say I longed for attention. But it wasn't the sort of attention-seeking borne of parents that ignored me or some childhood trauma. And it wasn't influenced by a desire to live up to the accomplishments of my father. I didn't want to be him. Neither he nor my mother pushed me to uphold the Mullane family legacy, to the

---

* Bobby Knight was the legendary coach of the University of Indiana basketball team known for his temper. The same year I tried out for cheerleader, he famously threw a chair onto the basketball court during a game against Purdue when he became angry with a referee.

extent that there was one. I wanted to embody an ideal that was defined by a collision of all the influences in my life: my big screen heroes, my hero the astronaut father, my no-excuses mother, and the belief that the world was divided into the dark and the light and that the light needed more leaders. As strange as it may seem, I tried out for cheerleader because I believed that doing so would help me to approach that ideal.

Then, around the time I was making my decision about quitting basketball and looking for a new path, an eventful trip back to Mom and Dad's hometown shortly after Dad's return from space helped push me to think radically about what I would do next at Clear Lake High School.

***

Dad had been invited back to Albuquerque to be presented with the keys to the city and a participate in "Mike Mullane Day" activities. I don't think Dad was all that keen on the idea of such an event; I sensed he made it a point to attend more for Mom, his parents, and his grandmother than for himself. They had been incredible supporters throughout his life and he unfailingly gave them credit for the sacrifices they had made to put him into space.

The event included a stop at city hall where we all stood in the cool October air and heard short speeches from Mayor Harry Kinney and Dad. If public celebratory events ran a continuum from the tickertape parade given to the Apollo 11 crew in New York City all the way to the ribbon cutting for a new goat rodeo arena in some New Mexico ghost town, the "Mike Mullane Day" celebration was closer to the goats than the moon walkers. Only a gaggle of dignitaries from city hall, a handful of family members, some friends, and a few homeless people were in the audience on the plaza near the center of the city. Dad wore a grey suit with a blue tie ornamented with tiny space shuttles. Mom wore a skirt suit and hairdo that were both reminiscent of the style that Julie McCoy, the fictional cruise hostess on *The Love Boat*, might wear. Her suit was dark and double breasted. A high-collared pink blouse peaked above the coat's lapels. Her hair was short but stylish. I thought she looked more glamorous than she ever had. The speeches were brief and the applause after them even briefer. But we all wore pride-filled smiles nonetheless.

After the visit to city hall, we headed to Saint Pius X Catholic High School, Dad's alma mater. There, the students were called into an assembly in the gymnasium. Mom, Dad, Amy, Laura, Joe Joe, Grandma, Pop Pop, Great Grandma, and I sat in folding chairs arranged in the center of the basketball court as the principal, Father Dennis Andrews, introduced each of us in turn. My great grandmother was presented with a bouquet of flowers and smiled her Cabbage Patch Kid smile as the students gave her a standing ovation. We all loved it more than she did, happy to see her get recognized in such a public way. When my intro came, I stood, trying to be casual and cool as if the attention was old hat.

"Lieutenant Colonel Mullane's son, Pat," Father Dennis announced, turning halfway behind him while motioning in my direction with his arm as he kept his eyes trained on a page in front of him at the podium.

I gave a brief wave to the audience expecting to hear the same casual applause those introduced before me had received. But instead, I was taken aback by something that I at first thought I had imagined: the applause I received was interleaved with more vigorous clapping and the distinctive, high-pitched screams of teenaged girls. I was so confused by the reaction that, for a moment, I thought my fly was open and I was being mocked. As I sat back down while smiling awkwardly, I brought my hand to my crotch as casually as I could to check the position of the pull tab on my zipper. I had visions of my own John Hughes film moment – the geeky, thin, pizza-faced kid standing in front of his peers revealing his tightie whities, ruining (temporarily) his attempt to win the affection of the most beautiful girl in the school. But, thankfully, the tab was in the "up" position. As I settled back into my chair, I replayed the moment, wondering if I had heard what I thought I heard and, if I had, what it meant. In my own school, my pimply face and firm position in the third most important (or, more cynically, second least important) social layer kept female suitors away. I took it to be a universal truth that teenage status traveled with you. Like Hester Prynne's ever-present, red "A" in *The Scarlet Letter*, I believed it was impossible to outrun your high school social classification. But was that true?

As I ruminated, Father Dennis talked glowingly of St. Pius' "famous" son returning to his roots. Dad gave a speech recounting how his interest in space was blossoming during his time at St. Pius and how he owed much to the school and the education it gave him. He didn't tell the story of how in 1962, when he was seventeen, Pop Pop let him stay home to watch John Glenn's launch in *Friendship 7*. It was to be the first time an American was going to orbit the earth, a truly historic happening.[*] The launch went off at 9:47 a.m. on the east coast – 7:47 a.m. in Albuquerque. By the time Glenn and his Mercury-Atlas rocket disappeared out of view of the television cameras and Dad and Pop Pop were sure that he was indeed in orbit, Dad had missed a large portion of morning classes. Pop Pop wrote a note for Dad to take to school saying that he had given permission to his son to miss class. Dad was to deliver the message to the "Dean of Boys," a particularly creepy title belonging to a priest – a title that I'm sure has since gone the way of the Latin Mass given the abuse scandals of the last few decades.

When Dad handed him the note, The Dean of Boys was not amused. He told Dad he would get a "zero" for the subjects he had missed that morning. When Dad got home early in the afternoon (not long after Glenn splashed down in the Atlantic Ocean[+]) and Pop Pop asked how school had been, Dad told him of the penalty he'd been given for being late despite having the note that Pop Pop had scribbled out. Pop Pop became enraged and told Dad to come with him as he

---

[*] The first two Mercury launches – one piloted by Alan Shephard another by Gus Grissom – were "sub-orbital" missions. This meant that the astronauts were simply shot in a high arc that took them into space but only briefly. Like an artillery shell, they arced right back down again without ever fully circling the earth. Their missions lasted just fifteen minutes.

[+] Glenn's mission was only 4 hours and 55 minutes long. According to the New Mexico Museum of Space History, he carried a note in seven languages with him in the event he splashed down in the Pacific near remote islands instead of the Atlantic. It read: "I am a stranger. I come in peace. Take me to your leader and there will be a massive reward for you in eternity." Apparently, NASA budgets didn't allow for the last sentence to end after the word "you."

wheeled furiously to the car parked in his driveway under a large tree. When they arrived at St. Pius, Dad helped an unusually fast-moving Pop Pop back into his wheelchair and, a few minutes later, watched as he rolled into the principal's office with his pipe in his mouth looking like McArthur coming ashore in the Philippines.

"Why did you give my son zeros?" he demanded as he crossed the threshold into the Dean of Boys' office.

Before the priest could formulate a response though, Pop Pop continued, "He gave you a note from me! He stayed home to watch a historic event!"

Pop Pop, on a roll, went on to point out the hypocrisy of the dean's decision to penalize Dad since students were let out of school early on the same day so that they could attend a basketball playoff game. The dean, apparently having a Holy Spirit-induced epiphany, quickly reversed his decision. The zeros were erased.

When Dad finished his talk and presented the principal at St. Pius with a framed picture and small American flag that had been flown on *Discovery*, the assembly broke up and we all mingled on the basketball court as students and teachers flowed out of the bleachers. I stood alone as members of my family broke into little pods of conversation centered on a distant cousin who emerged from the stands or a priest who was a family friend. Then, something miraculous happened – something that made me realize I hadn't imagined the female screams during my introduction. Some St. Pius girls walked up to me sheepishly and asked if I would take a photo with them. They didn't ask for a photo with Dad. They asked for a photo with *me*. I agreed quickly and the four of them flanked me, two on either side. At first, I stood with my arms down straight at my sides, looking like a nutcracker ornament we hung on our tree each Christmas. But when the two girls next to me put their arms around my waist and squeezed in close, I took a deep breath and raised my arms over their heads, letting them come to rest across their backs, my hands gripping their shoulders.

As the flash on the camera popped with a blink-inducing whiteness, I'm sure I looked stunned. As quickly as they had come to me, they dissolved back into the crowed, giggling as they did. But then, another two girls stepped forward and asked for a photo as well. I obliged readily, feeling my own Hester-Prynne-like letter sloughing from me like a skin that was no longer useful. Sure, to some extent the celebrity aspect of my father probably enhanced my looks. But the same factor existed to some small extent back home in Houston and nobody seemed to give me a second thought there. The contrast between my experiences during my short visit to St. Pius and those at Lake reminded me of the sea of obscurity I was drowning in back home and energized me to find a way to break to the surface, to breathe the liberating air of relevance. But to make that escape, I'd have to be bold. I began wondering: what was the boldest thing I could do? My mind was working.

We returned to Grandma and Pop Pop's house at the end of "Mike Mullane Day." Grandma was always cooking and as soon as we entered the house, she put on her apron and returned to casseroles she had begun that morning, busying herself in the kitchen. Great Grandma, her 87-year-old frame spent from a busy day, went to one of the back rooms in the sprawling ranch home to lie down for a nap. The rest of us congregated around my grandparent's console T.V. and watched the local news. We saw ourselves in short snippets, the anchors noting the return of Dad to his hometown after flying into space as they spoke in overly dramatic tones, leaving out the most dramatic development of the day: girls seemed to like me – at least in New Mexico.

When it was time to eat, somebody went to the back of the house to check on Great Grandma to see if she wanted to join us for dinner. But she didn't respond to whispered calls. She had died in her sleep while we watched the news. I cried. The loss of any beloved relative is sad, but I think the tears came mostly from the poignancy embedded in the timing of her passing – it was as if she had planned it. It was so rare we all were together, yet there we were, a few steps down the hallway from where she now lay at peace. Just a few hours earlier, she had stood in front of the applauding St. Pius students holding a bouquet almost as big as her as she radiated pride in a moment that must have seemed surreal to a woman who was born in 1897, who had traveled 1,300 miles by wagon train from Minnesota to Texas, who was six-years-old when the Wright Brothers first flew, and who lived to see her grandson fly into space. She had also endured the Great Depression, two World Wars, Korea, Vietnam, and the terms of seventeen U.S. presidents, beginning with Grover Cleveland. She had lived an epoch life. Given her age and the circumstances of her passing, her death was not the most traumatic of experiences. But the loss of her, the death of several teens from suicides at Lake, the death of colleagues of Dad's in the military, the fear that I had lost Dad after the pad abort of STS-41D – all of it taught me at a very young age that one day does not guarantee the next. I was in a hurry.

My fatigue with basketball, the notice of girls outside the population at my own school, the sense that the future was never guaranteed, and the strong desire to shape history in some small way as my dad had done – these were the things that had put me in front of my fellow students at Lake in an attempt to become a male cheerleader; these were the things that answered the question, "Why did he do it?" The day after the tryouts, the teacher and college cheerleader assessments were reviewed, and the student voting tallied. I made the squad in a landslide. I was the Donald Trump of my high school, scoring a stunning victory because of the votes of the large middle-class of students who felt left behind by the establishment and the top one-percenters. I celebrated with my parents and sisters that night. It's a testament to my parents' unwavering support that they both celebrated my cheerleading success with the same vigor they displayed when I had made the basketball team for the first time four years before. They never once seemed uncomfortable or embarrassed by what I had done. I think that more than anything they admired my chutzpa and the enthusiasm with which I embraced my father's mantra: do well at everything you do, and good things will happen. I felt supported and encourage by my family. But, later in the evening, as the novelty of what had transpired wore off, I began to wonder: what have I gotten myself into? Little did I know.

***

"Faggot!"

The shouted word broadsided me like a flat board smacked against my temple, leaving a ringing in my ears. It was a warm, humid evening at the Clear Creek School District stadium in September of 1985. Our football team was on the field in a losing effort against a district rival early in the season. Whatever prowess Lake had on the basketball court, it lacked on the football field; we were perennial also-rans in the sport. Nonetheless, I was doing my best to stir the crowd into a frenzy in an effort to cheer on the team despite the epithet shouted by a guy I didn't recognize, a guy I'm sure had made his way from the visitors' side of the field to the Lake side. I knew ever since I saw the freshman principal glaring at me as I marched out of the gym during my tryout that I could expect some harassment for having infiltrated the feminine domain of cheerleading – particularly in a place where the early masculinity of boys was defined by two-a-day football practices and weight room high jinks, not a megaphone and choreographed chanting. But I was surprised nonetheless by how overt the hostility could be.

My surprise was to a great extent a function of a relatively peaceful summer. Nobody at Lake had called me a name or beaten me up. Most of my own school was surprisingly supportive of my newfound extracurricular activity. To the extent there were negative rumblings about me, it had mercifully been mostly behind the scenes – the chatter coming exclusively from boys yucking it up at my expense while I was not around. But I heard about it anyway. I came to realize that this hidden, unflattering banter was a form of collective jealousy.

I had gone from obscure nerd to a guy that many of the most popular girls were talking about – although in a resoundingly unromantic way. My name was better known around the Clear Lake community than the starting quarterback or star point guard and that rankled those who thought that the spotlight belonged to them. I let it roll off my back but did feel a pang of frustration and even some guilt. Yes, I had set out to get my own spotlight. But I didn't intend to take it from anybody else. Apparently though, there was only so much light to go around and realizing that made the Catholic ethos of "other people mattered more" gnaw at me. I hated the fact that I'd upset others; but I hated more the fact that it bothered me.

Beyond the popular athlete set, I had also caused great angst among the young women who had made (and not made) the cheerleading squad. The nine girls who I'd cheer with in the coming year had to come to terms not only with the fact that a boy would now be a teammate, but that I had supplanted one of their girlfriends on the varsity squad. While the final ranking of those who tried out was not made public, everybody knew who hadn't made it – who had been ranked eleventh – because of my impetuous act. I had seen number eleven looking dejected in the hallways of school in the days after the tryouts and I felt for her. It was one thing to lose your place on the team. It was another to lose it your senior year and get separated from your friends (many of whom you had cheered with for six years) all because of an upstart who hadn't even thought about cheerleading until a month or two before. In this case too, the fact that I'd inadvertently caused sadness in a girl for whom I had no ill will took some of the shine off of my accomplishment.

Sometime in the months after the tryout, the head cheerleader, Katelyn, planned a slumber party at her house to bring the new squad together. She was a kind person who looked kind and was always so well put-together in all respects. Cheerleading was not her only gig; she excelled at academics and held other leadership positions in the school. Her brown, wavy hair, round face punctuated by dark eyes, and angular nose set atop a perpetually smiling mouth made me feel at ease around her. From the start she treated me as if I'd been part of the Lake cheerleading community for years, not months, and I liked and respected her for that. But when the idea for a slumber party initially had come up, I think there was ambiguity at first about whether I'd be invited.

While at practices with the rest of the team in the weeks before the upcoming get-together, I'd heard some talk about the party, but it always became more muted when I came near and I was never formally invited. Finally, one day, while I stretched a distance away from the girls, I could hear snippets of such conversations again. I got up from the floor and walked toward my teammates, ready to begin practice. As I came closer, there were a few hurried whispers until Katelyn broke from the group and asked if I wanted to attend the overnight party. She asked in a quick breath, as if she might swallow the invite if she didn't get it out.

Her invitation should have been an easy one to accept. I had scored a teenage boy's dream. How could it get any more fantasy-like than to be invited by the head cheerleader to a slumber party at her house with nine young, beautiful women? It was the dream-sequence stuff of the main male lead in any John Hughes film. I had visions of slow-motion pillow fights with feathers floating in the air as the girls – in their bra and panties of course – giggled and invited me to join in. In this fantasy, I'd playfully demur at first. But, after continued begging by the girls,

I'd dive onto the king bed as my fellow cheerleaders, kneeling on the same bed beating each other with their pillows, dove onto me, initiating a playful wrestling match – a match I'd let them win.

It sounded magical. But despite this dream scenario, I hesitated for a heartbeat as Katelyn looked at me. Did they really want me there? Were they just being polite? What would people at the school say?

"Sure, I'll come," I said, surprising myself as I responded in a breathy rush, mirroring Katelyn's delivery of the invitation. If I was going to do this cheerleader thing, I was going to do it large.

I was the last to show up at Katelyn's house. I felt like the proverbial turd in the punchbowl as soon as I walked in – a skinny turd with fading acne and hair parted down the middle walking into a punchbowl of the most popular, pretty girls at school, all wearing t-shirts and shorts. Despite the initial awkwardness (and to their everlasting credit) the girls tried to engage me in conversation, and I did my best to respond to their overtures. At first, the conversations were stilted despite the fact that I was used to stepping into a situation where those around me were already close friends and I was an outsider. My years as a nomadic military brat had trained me well for that. But I was now seventeen years old with hormones raging in the presence of goddesses and so the game had changed substantially. I wasn't a kid at a new elementary school; I was a voyager on another planet. Planet Bonerland.

As the evening wore on and we talked, watched TV, and shared some dinner, things loosened up. They shared with me their feelings about me making the squad which, for the most part, were more positive than I expected. We laughed about my tryout as one of the girls mimicked my dance moves. We discussed the upcoming school year. Time seemed to accelerate as we became more comfortable with each other and before I knew it, it was one-thirty in the morning. Never much of a night owl, I retired to a couch in the family room and closed my eyes as the girls sat cross-legged on the floor and continued to talk. As I was about to fade off into darkness, I heard Gayle, a petite, pretty blonde who was highly sought after by every boy in the school – in no small part because of her large breasts – say, "This bra has to go."

While I didn't open my eyes at first, my mind was instantly shocked awake. Gayle's words shot from synapse to synapse in my brain, urgently trying to find the fastest path possible to the part of every teenaged boys' grey matter where all things boob-related reside. Then, I decided to be daring. I slowly rolled my head to the left in the direction of Gayle and opened just one eye slowly.

I caught Gayle with her hands behind her back and under her shirt just as she unclasped her bra and began to shrug it off her shoulders, letting her breasts free beneath her shirt. As I watched, I was already debating which friend of mine I'd call first to tell the story to. I was in the inner sanctum. In fact, I was like one of the Jewish high priests I'd learned about in CCD at St. Bernadette's.*

Once a year, on Yom Kippur, the Jewish high priest entered the "Holy of the Holies" – the inner, veiled portion of the temple where God was said to dwell – to offer sacrifices to the Almighty. We were taught that the priest wore a rope around his ankle so that if the presence of God struck him dead with wonder, he could be dragged out of the temple.+ I was like that priest inside the "Holy of Holies," where Gayle's free breasts might strike me dead and require my body to be dragged out the front door of Katelyn's house. I imagined my friends Jake and Thomas giving the rope repeated heave-hos from the street in front of Katelyn's. My head would bounce over the threshold as they got me clear of the home and hauled me across the lawn. Once I'd been dragged to the street, a safe distance from the powers of Gayle and her mystical "assets," they'd stand over my body saying things like "He was so young" and "Yeah, but what a way to go." Then, pointing at my crotch, "Look, *rigor mortis* has set in."

As this movie was playing in my head, my brain started to see through the fog of fantasy. I realized my stealthy move hadn't been stealthy at all – they were all looking at me. Nine faces pointed at my ugly mug like sunflowers facing the sun. There was a moment of silence before they burst into laughter. It was as if they were testing me. Maybe they didn't believe I was straight? Maybe they took pleasure in torturing

---

* Like all acronyms related to the Catholic church, CCD represented a string of words that overcomplicated a simple concept. CCD stood for "Confraternity of Christian Doctrine," a.k.a. "Sunday School."

+ Many biblical historians now doubt priests were actually affixed with a rope.

me, knowing that I was a stranger in a strange land? I broke into laughter with them and, now awake, re-joined them for an hour or so more, talking further into the night about the sorts of things teenagers the world over talk about – at least female teenagers.

When it was finally time to sleep, Katelyn gave up her bedroom to a couple of the other girls. The balance of the team was going to sleep in the family room. Katelyn planned to stay with them and offered me her home's spare bedroom which had a queen bed. I was glad for the offer. I was exhausted and didn't think I could sleep well in the same room with all the girls – I had visions of farting in the middle of the night or waking up with an erection. Privacy was welcome. I thanked her and made my way down the hallway as Katelyn took what looked to be a particularly uncomfortable position on the floor, all other furniture having been claimed. Once in the room, I took off my t-shirt and crawled under the covers in my shorts.

I was about to drift off when the door to the room opened and Katelyn entered, walked purposefully to the edge of the bed opposite the side I occupied, pulled back the covers, and crawled into bed with me. I laid as still as a King Tut in his tomb. Was this really happening? I wondered. The night was turning into one of those moments in life that would be remembered even when more important things were forgotten – like my own name or those of my yet-to-be-born children. My heart began an adrenal sprint even as I concentrated to reign it in, sure that Katelyn could sense my nerves and embarrassed at the thought of it. Once under the covers, Katelyn propped up on one elbow and faced me.

"I'm not sleeping on the floor in my own damned house!" she whispered loudly. Then, she added, this time seriously, "But I have a boyfriend, and if you touch me, I will kill you and then he will kill you again."

I was confident in a lot of ways, but not with women. Had I been more daring, I might have thought in response to Katelyn's threat, *Hmmm ... strange foreplay, but I dig it*. Instead, I took it at face value. I didn't say a word as Katelyn rolled over to face away from me as she drifted off. I stayed in my Tut-like entombment pose the entire night, hands at my sides, always on my back, staring at the ceiling, scared to death I'd fall asleep and inadvertently touch her. But she needn't worry;

I was as motionless as a patient strapped to a table while getting a CATSCAN, paralyzed by a cocktail of insecurity, fear, temptation, and fatigue. Sleep did not come.

***

The slur that had been shouted at me early in in the fall of 1985 at a football game was one of many to come. I would most often endure epithets while cheering at "away" games, on the turf or court of a rival school. The brashness of the assaults was notable. Teachers standing plainly within earshot did nothing. Shouting "homo," "fag," or "Nancy" at a male cheerleader didn't rise to a punishable crime in those days. In any case, the name-calling never really bothered me. My parents had instilled in me a confidence that made it easy for me to, if not ignore, then at least deal with the name-calling. Much of that confidence came from how they had supported me when I had decided to try out and when I had ultimately made the team. Dad told me multiple times how proud he was of me – that what I had done showed guts. My feisty mother loved to see me creating some controversy. It was also relatively easy for me to endure the attacks because of what I got to do: hang out with the most beautiful and popular young women in my school. This fact made the offensive and childish slurs more ironic than hurtful.

I had learned how to do some athletic lifts with the girls and would often lift one of them above my head as she sat on my hand. Beautiful girls are sitting on my hand and *I'm* the one who is gay? If I had to be harassed, I was happy to be harassed for being in a position that I knew 95% of guys envied. Still, even within the ranks of my fellow cheerleaders, I had to endure some ribbing. Gayle wrote me a note on Valentine's Day in 1986 that read "Happy Valentines, Fag! Haha! You're a hysterical fag and I love you that way! Love, Gayle." I was just happy to get a card from her.

My twin sister, Amy, had handled my success in the cheerleader tryouts with unbelievable grace. It had to have been hard on her. She had been a cheerleader earlier in our middle and high school careers. While she didn't tryout with me going into our senior year, she often had people say to her things like, "Wow, must be hard to have a brother who is a cheerleader when you are not. That's like you making the football team and him getting cut." Many people said this to her (and me) in a light-hearted but clueless way, not realizing that it cut her and made me feel a surge of guilt, inadvertently placing responsibility on me for Amy's cheerleader-less status. It implied that high school life was a zero-sum game: I made it, so she couldn't.

Amy and I didn't have any mysterious twin powers – I didn't feel her pain or joy as if we were each a part of the same whole. But I had enough sensitivity to know that she was burying some insecurities my success in the cheerleading realm had stoked. I think she was self-aware enough to know that those insecurities were not because of who I was or what I had accomplished; she didn't blame me. But that didn't make them any less difficult to manage. In the end, she channeled any frustration she had into defending me. If she was going to have to put up with the bullshit of other's enjoying the irony of a household with high-school-aged twins where the boy was the cheerleader and the girl was not, then, by God, she was going to make sure nobody gave her brother crap.

Her commitment to defend me was made clear during a basketball game at Pearland High School in the late fall of 1985. Between quarters of the game, while the teams were huddled around coaches at their respective benches, our cheering team took position in the center of the court, faced Lake fans on one side of the gym, and began a choreographed cheer. Our backs were to the fans of the other team, which outnumbered the Lake contingent since the game was on their home court. While we executed our cheer, I was openly jeered by guys (it was always guys) in the stands behind me.

"Homo!"

"Queer!"

"Fag!"

The words came in quick volleys like bullets shot from a Gatling gun. Again, no teacher, coach, or administrator in attendance did anything. But I didn't need them to. I just ignored the taunting. I had become so accustomed to the slurs and ambivalence of adult staff that I knew how to kick into autopilot and simply do my duty on the court.

We finished the cheer as fans from Lake cheered loudly, clearly trying to drown out further homo-phobic put downs that now came even more enthusiastically as we made our way to the sideline. The students and parents from Lake had begun to embrace me and while some would still resent or feel threatened by what I had done, there was nothing like students from another school ridiculing me to rally the home fans to my defense. "He may be a homo," the thinking went from those who didn't particularly like me as a male cheerleader, "but he's our homo!"

As the clapping faded and the taunts from across the court did as well, and with the teams still huddled at their benches, I saw Amy rise from her seat in the stands next to Mom and Dad and clang down the metal bleachers. She was wearing a wooden heel and the sound of her footfalls on the steel stands hinted at a walk with purpose. She was on a mission. She stepped onto the hardwood and, rather than walking parallel to the sideline to go to the concessions or restroom, she walked straight ahead to the center of the court.

Clip-clop, clip-clop, clip-clop.

The sound of her heel on the floor drew attention to her. Even some of the players looked up from their huddles.

What the hell is she doing? I thought. The gym had now gone eerily quiet as attendees started to wonder the same thing I was. Then, she began to speak...loudly.

"That's my twin brother out there …."

Oh God, no, I thought.

"…and I don't appreciate you making fun of him!" Her voice became even louder as she finished the sentence. It was as if her words were storming a heavily fortified hill. It got worse.

"So, just FUCK OFF!"

Then, as if the words weren't enough, she raised her right hand and gave the Pearland fans a one-finger salute they'll never forget.

Holy shit! I thought. I was too stunned to talk, to move, to breath. Everybody else in the gym likewise stood in shocked silence. Did what I think just happened really happen?

Amy spun on her heel and clip-clopped her way back to the stands matter-of-factly, as if she had just announced that somebody had left their lights on in the parking lot. Before she could make it back to the bleachers though, I heard one more comment rise like a puff of smoke above the students on the Pearland side.

"The homo's sister is protecting him!" came the soft retort, as if spoken from behind a cupped hand. Giggling snickers came in unison from across the hardwood.

I was mortified.

On the drive home that evening with Mom and Dad, I laid into Amy. The only thing worse that being called names by boys from another school was having your twin sister defend you. She shot right back at me, unclear as to how "helping" her brother could be taken by me as anything other than the loving gesture of somebody who shared my blood and with whom I also shared the same womb. With the help of Dad ("Amy, Pat doesn't need you to defend him") and Mom ("Pat, Amy was just trying to help") we eventually reached a tension-filled détente and sat silently in the back of our Chevy Citation looking out the windows as we drove home in the dark. While her actions at the time were incredibly embarrassing for me, they did come from love and from having been put in a strange position by my role as a Lake cheerleader. As the years progressed, I came to understand that better. But in that moment, I felt like my testicles had been cut off.

CHAPTER 12: COLLEGE BOUND

Not too long before I tried out for cheerleader, I was back in full space nerd mode as Dad came home to announce that he had been chosen for a second space shuttle mission, also on *Discovery*. We were all surprised and thrilled at how fast a second assignment had come. Dad's first mission ended just six months before he learned of being added to a new crew. While he would have been thrilled at the prospect of being assigned to any vehicle that was going to be leaving the planet, he was over-the-top with enthusiasm for his next adventure.

Dad would be flying on the first space shuttle to be launched out of Vandenberg AFB on a mission designated as STS-62A. Vandenberg sat along the coast of California on real estate that has to be the most expensive military property in the world. Just fifty-five miles north of Santa Barbara and thirty-five miles south of San Luis Obispo, the base would have made a spectacular resort. Rolling hills came to truncated ends as dramatic cliffs that disappeared into the ocean, their lofty heights ideal perches for boutique hotels nestled among wineries, all accessed by the famed Pacific Coast Highway that ran north to San Francisco and south to Los Angeles. It was possible to watch a launch in Vandenberg after lunch and drive to dinner at Pebble Beach Golf Club that same evening.

The launch complexes nestled into small valleys that seemed too tight to accommodate them made for dramatic views – the sort of views that looked like they came from a James Bond film showing the secret lair of a villain who planned to launch some sort of space weapon on his way to world domination. A launch from Vandenberg was the stuff of science fiction and I was thrilled Dad would get to experience something even more fantastic than a blastoff from Florida.

More thrilling than the novelty of a west coast liftoff, though, was what a launch from California meant for the orbit of the shuttle. From Vandenberg, *Discovery* could be launched south across the Pacific entering an orbit that would take it over the north and south poles. Known as a polar orbit, this track was one that could not safely be achieved from Florida. Because the coast of California crept east the further south you went (as did the rest of North and South America), a rocket launched from Vandenberg on a southerly heading wouldn't cross over land until it was in orbit over the coast of Antarctica, 7,500 miles distant. This was not true of an identical launch from KSC; the shuttle would (at relatively low altitudes) cross over the length of Florida to the south meaning its solid rocket boosters might fall on West Palm Beach, leaving a lot of wealthy people pretty pissed off. It wasn't safe to head for the south pole (or north pole for that matter) from the Sunshine State.

But that begs the question: why launch in a way that sends a shuttle over the poles at all? Because doing so meant that the shuttle and, more importantly, any payload it might release from its cargo bay, would eventually cross over the entire planet; as the spacecraft traveled from pole to pole, the earth would be spinning beneath it. This was not true for a launch out of Florida which confined the shuttle to passing over a swath of the earth around the equator that got no further north or south than 57°. While this meant the shuttle could pass over almost all land masses south of the equator (the southern tip of South America is at about 55° south latitude), it meant much of the northern hemisphere would not be over-flown, including almost all of the Russian land mass. In fact, Moscow, a "southern" city by Russian standards, was at nearly 56° north latitude, approaching the limits of the northern most track the shuttle could traverse.*

All of this meant that polar orbits were particularly interesting to the military. Low-earth-orbiting spy satellites are almost always in polar

---

* About 68% of all the Earth's land is north of the equator. While oceans dominate the world, they *really* do in the southern hemisphere.

orbits for this reason – they see the entire globe. And while the United States had been sending spy satellites into polar orbits for decades (the first satellite put into polar orbit launched from Vandenberg in 1959), no humans had ever been to polar orbit. Dad and his crewmates would be the first and as such would see things no humans had. They would fly *through* the northern and southern lights, look directly down on the fjords of northern Scandinavia, see the mountains of Antarctica, and get a view of South Georgia Island and Elephant Island, important landmarks in the story of a voyager Dad loved to talk about when sharing tales of adventure with me: Ernest Shackleton.

Dad's mission on STS-62A? No surprise – it was classified. The mission would be a Department of Defense (DoD) mission. The views of the entire earth that Dad would get to see were apparently views the payload of *Discovery* was interested in seeing as well. We would be kept in the dark about what Dad would be doing on his polar orbit voyage. While in some ways this disappointed me, it added to the science fiction-like traits of the mission and I relished telling people at school when they asked me what Dad would be doing on his next trip to orbit, "Can't talk about it; it's classified," as if I were in the know.

***

My stint as a cheerleader at Lake raised my profile so much that I was elected senior class president at the beginning of my final year of high school. I had ascended the social status ladder faster than a space shuttle on its way to orbit, my confidence growing along the way like the plume I saw when *Discovery's* engines came to life. The class presidency, varsity cheerleader role, decent grades (I was ranked 42nd in a class of around 750), and better than average SAT scores made me think I might make a competitive college applicant to some of the better schools in the country. I began filling out applications and writing essays after settling on a hodgepodge of institutions to apply to. Stanford, the University of Texas (UT), all three of the major service academies, and the University of Notre Dame made up the list of schools where I'd try to gain admission.

The only institution I had ever visited when I began applying was the University of Texas. And the only other school I planned to visit before I had to make a decision on where to go was the United States Military Academy at West Point (USMA). There was no expectation in an age before cheap airline tickets and crazily competitive college admissions that I would do multiple visits to prospective colleges. At least not in my family.

I could explain each of the college choices save one: Notre Dame. Despite being raised Catholic, I had no connection to the school, I didn't follow college sports, and knew nothing of its academic programs. It was far away, cold, and hard to get to. The other options had more logical underpinnings. Stanford, I figured, would be warm and I was interested in engineering, which it was well known for. The University of Texas was close to home and was familiar to me because of other students' connections to the school through parents, brothers, or sisters. The service academies were cultures I understood having listened to my father's tales from his days at West Point and hanging out with astronauts who had attended the Air Force Academy and Naval Academy.

In the end, I suppose Notre Dame was thrown into the mix for a number of reasons: despite my interest in UT, I was pretty sure I wanted to get out of Texas; I wasn't sure I wanted to endure the stress of life at an academy; and Notre Dame was well respected enough academically. Besides, even in 1986, Stanford had an acceptance rate of only around 18%, so a non-academy, out-of-state backup was desirable (Notre Dame's acceptance rate at the time was above 40%).

In addition to working on my applications for the schools, I was also filling out the paperwork to compete for a Reserve Officer Training Corps (ROTC) scholarship. I knew that Mom and Dad had limited means and understood that a degree from private Stanford or Notre Dame would not be possible without some help.* The most generous ROTC scholarship would pay for all tuition, books, and fees and even included a monthly stipend – in return, I'd give four years to the military as an officer upon graduation. If I won a scholarship, all that Mom and Dad would have to pay for was room and board. That's not to say that I sought the scholarship just for the money. I had always

---

* Tuition, room, and board at Notre Dame in 1986 came in at around $12,355 – the equivalent of nearly $28,000 in 2018 dollars. While expensive, it's a bargain compared to the actual full cost in 2018: nearly $69,000 per year.

known I'd go into the military. It had been a family tradition at least four generations old and had been the only life I'd ever known as a child. It was the natural progression for a kid who thought a lot about duty, current events, adventure, and leadership.

In the fall of 1985, Dad and Mom took a trip back to West Point and I decided to tag along since I was seeking admission there. Dad had taken his West Point battalion's flag into orbit and would be returning the banner to his alma mater. I planned to spend some time with him and Mom, but I would also do what a lot of high school students did when considering West Point: I'd spend a day with a cadet to see what life on the shores of the Hudson was really like. The three of us flew to New York City together where we were picked up by a van sent from West Point. The driver of the van was not what I had expected when imagining a government employee from the nation's 183-year-old minter of army officers. I had visions of being greeted by a drill sergeant in a flat-brimmed hat who talked in short bursts. Instead, we got a woman in her mid-sixties whose sentences came like a languid river – long and slow. I wondered if she was a decoy of some sort, meant to lull prospective cadets and new plebes into a sense of complacency before their arrival at West Point, thus making the shock of their first days at the academy even more stark.

***

West Point is a gorgeous place and has a history almost as old as the country. The spit of land it occupies (the "point" in "West Point") juts into the Hudson in much the same way the horn of Africa thrusts into the Arabian Sea. The installation, with its broad, green parade ground, called "The Plain," surrounded by heights ornamented with majestic granite buildings, was described well by Charles Dickens in his travel memoir *American Notes for General Circulation* after a visit to the school in 1842:

In this beautiful place, the fairest among the fair and lovely Highlands of the North River : shut in by deep green heights and ruined forts, and looking down upon the distant town of Newburgh, along with a glittering path of sunlit water...hemmed in, besides, all round with memories of Washington, and events of the revolutionary war : is the Military School of America. It could not stand on more appropriate ground, and any ground more beautiful can hardly be.

Inhabited by American military units since 1778, West Point has the distinction of being the longest continually occupied army post in the United States. The location was at one point during the revolutionary war called "Camp Arnold" in honor of its commander, Benedict Arnold, the same man who would later, in 1779, try to give up West Point to the British. A list of influential graduates of the academy reads like the index of a U.S. history book. Jefferson Davis, Robert E. Lee, William Techumseh Sherman, Ulysses S. Grant, "Stonewall" Jackson, George A. Custer, Douglas McArthur, George S. Patton, and Dwight D. Eisenhower all graduated from West Point. So too did two of the crewmembers of Apollo 11: "Buzz" Aldrin, the second man to walk on the moon and Michael Collins, the Command Module pilot.

In some circles the most famous cadet from West Point might be an orphan and former student at the University of Virginia who served with distinction in the army as an enlisted man before finding himself on the banks of the Hudson. Edgar Allan Poe never graduated from West Point, though. He was dismissed after being court-martialed for refusing to attend classes and chapel. He didn't care – in fact, he set out to get himself expelled in order to pursue a passion to write poetry.

During our first morning at West Point, Mom, Dad, and I walked the grounds. As we strolled around The Plain on a brilliant September day and looked out over the Hudson, I couldn't help but think of how amazing it would be to sit in a chair that Patton might have occupied or sleep in a room that Eisenhower slept in. In the mid-morning, the grounds were relatively empty and quiet, and I imagined contemplative strolls in a smart uniform and a wheel cap, pausing every now and again to take in the views and smell the sweat of history seeping from the walls and walkways. Birds chirped, red-tailed hawks glided, breezes blew – this place was a resort. Dad was clearly glad to be back among the granite stone and flying flags and told funny stories of food fights in the mess hall and defiling a statue of George Washington and his horse by painting the equine's balls a vibrant color. I started to imagine what chicanery I'd involve myself in as a plebe on The Plain.

My sense of belonging grew as Dad, Mom, and I were greeted by school officials who were welcoming and engaging. They were kind people who loved the mission of the school and seemed to care about those connected to it in some way, from the astronaut graduate to his greenhorn son. I received enthusiastic handshakes and encouraging smiles when the staffers learned of my interest in becoming a part of the class of 1990. I began to think that I could be a West Point man. After some chit-chat, it was time for me to leave my parents to meet the cadet I would spend a portion of the day with to get a sense of what life at the military academy might be like. I hugged Mom and Dad goodbye and made my way, with a spring in my step, to the meet-up point.

In fairly short order, I realized that the sights of the morning and the history of the place had struck me mentally impaired. While Dad on that day had waxed sentimental upon returning to his alma mater and told funny stories of collegiate pranks and bonding with classmates from around the country, he did not repeat stories he had told earlier in my youth of how brutal West Point was – of how, when he graduated, he threw his academy uniforms into a dumpster and told my mother (whom he'd marry a week later) that he never wanted to see the place again. In *American Notes*, Dicken's understood what my father understood and what I had forgotten about West Point when he wrote that "the course of education is severe, but well devised and manly." Dickens then noted that this severity made it a very difficult program to get through: "Whether it be from the rigid nature of the discipline, or the national impatience of restraint, or both causes combined, not more than half the number who begin their studies here, ever remain to finish them." Translation: West Point was hard.

I met the cadet I'd spend the next few hours with outside one of the dormitories. He was in a short-sleeved, white shirt with grey epaulets, grey pants with a black stripe running the length of the leg, and a white service cap, its black brim brought so low over his forehead and the bridge of his nose that it made it hard for him to look me in the eye without tilting his head back. He shook my hand vigorously and quickly, as if he were a politician short on time going down a very long receiving line. He did everything else in the same urgent manner. He spoke fast, walked fast, blinked fast. After some quick pleasantries, where each of us asked the other the same questions (Where are you from? Did you always want to come to West Point?), we began our

THE FATHER, SON, AND HOLY SHUTTLE

tour by entering the dormitory – called a "barracks" by the academy – so that I could see the living quarters of a cadet.

While still relatively quiet outside, stepping into the barracks was like stepping into a sort of busy, neat prison, where echoing shouts bounced off of ubiquitous hard surfaces. Plebes were walking the hallways but not in the lazy, wandering way typical college students do.* Rather, they were walking quickly with their heads slightly down and right shoulders touching the wall as if they were mechanically pulled along by a cable hidden inside the façade – they moved like human cable cars. I learned that plebes were not allowed to walk the hallway without having their right shoulder on the wall. This meant that crossing a corridor required them to go to one end of it and walk back the other side, their shoulder touching the opposite wall.

While walking the hallways in such a manner was maddening, it was better to be walking than standing still. If a plebe wasn't in motion, it was because his back was to the wall, chest puffed out, and chin pulled in as he was grilled by an upper classman who was usually testing the plebe's knowledge of minutia all were required to know: the meals being served in the mess hall that day, the score of yesterday's Yankees game, the name of the first Commandant of Cadets at the academy. My escort moved through this chaos like a bubble bouncing along white-water rapids, seemingly oblivious to all that was happening around him. He showed me a plebe's room and talked to me a bit about a cadet's day before we walked (he told me that, actually, nobody walks, they all "marched") briskly to another building where I would sit in on a history class.

The instructor in the class was not what I expected. He wasn't a military man. In fact, he was about the furthest thing from an army officer I could have imagined. He seemed very young, his boyish face making him look closer in age to the students in the room than to some tweed-jacket-wearing, middle-aged stereotype. A civilian instructor was still relatively rare at the academy in the mid 1980s when no more than

---

* *Plebes* is the term for a "freshman" at West Point. It's not surprising that the word the Romans used to describe commoners with no status or standing is used to describe newbies at West Point. In fact, a Roman *pleb* might have been treated better by those of higher status than his namesake at West Point.

5% of faculty were non-military. By 2018, around 25% of instructors at West Point were civilian academics owing to a law signed in 1992 that drove an increase in the use of civilian faculty in an effort to save money. As class began, the professor quizzed his pupils on readings from the night before and then began to move into a lecture.

Not long after the interactive back-and-forth with the students had ended, the head of the cadet next to me began to loll forward in a slow creep until his chin hit his chest as he was lulled to sleep by a combination of the white-noise voice of the professor and a very warm room. After the cadet had endured several head-snapping shocks back to coherence, the instructor noticed him.

"Mr. Baker," the professor said, "Why don't you stand."

It was an order said like a suggestion. Mr. Baker dutifully rose, taking his text in hand as he did and opened it to the page being discussed. He stayed in that position for most of the rest of the class shifting the weight of the heavy book from arm to arm. Making cadets stand, I learned, was a favored way to force them to stay awake, and stress them further. Everything at West Point was seen as an opportunity to use stress to steel the soul. How could you handle being shot at by communists (the Soviet Union was still four years away from its fall from the superpower ranks) if you couldn't stay awake in class? How could you shit in a frigid forest with artillery falling around you if you were bothered by standing during a fascinating lecture in a climate-controlled room? As I pondered these questions myself, I was beginning to wonder if I really wanted to shit in a forest while being shot at.

After the class, it was time to go to the mess hall for lunch. To call West Point's dining facility a "mess hall" is like calling the White House a yurt. Washington Hall is large enough to feed at one time the more than 4,000 young men and women who make up the entire corps of cadets in a setting that is more evocative of a sixteenth-century church in the countryside of England than a food service structure owned by the U.S. Government. Arched stained glass windows adorned with wrought iron threw light onto colorful battle flags that hung from beneath wood beams that crossed the ceiling at regular intervals like yard markers on a football field. A large (30 x 70 feet) mural depicted William the Conqueror at the Battle of Hastings, Napoleon and

Wellington at Waterloo, and Meade at Gettysburg; it was an homage to the professional military soldier and a reminder of the history that officers and armies shape. The wood, iron, glass, and stone that comprised the beefy edifice along with the frenzied activity of fit, disciplined cadets within it, gave me the sense that America was indomitable. The scene was a physical manifestation of what free people could do and the lengths to which they would go to remain free. It embodied all that my heroes – real and imagined – did. It oozed the West Point motto: duty, honor, country.

Washington Hall has several wings that came together like spokes intersecting at the center of a wheel. Where the hub of the wheel would have been, there was a dais – called the poop deck – that allowed a speaker to address all of the cadets at once. Dad was going to be standing on that platform right before lunch to present the flag he had taken into space to the Commandant of Cadets. As much as I enjoyed being at the academy with Mom and Dad, I was self-conscious about making a "potential cadet" visit while Dad was making his prodigal son appearance back on the post. I worried that I'd be a marked man in a way – viewed as the punk kid who might only get into West Point because he was a legacy. My escort had said to me when we'd met, "Your dad is the astronaut, right?" When I told him "yes" he mentioned that he and a number of cadets in his class were looking forward to seeing him in Washington Hall. But his words fell flat. I didn't get the impression that he and his friends were really looking forward to anything. They had seen kids like me – the sons of astronauts, politicians, and general officers – come through before and were probably praying I'd be declined an appointment to the academy. Or maybe not. As I watched the hazing of the plebes in the mess hall, I began to think that if they really want to teach a punk legacy a lesson, the best way to do so was to hope he was admitted and then have your way with him for his entire plebe year.

When we got to the table where we'd eat, I took my seat when my nine tablemates did. The upper classmen were hazing the plebes for infractions that I didn't know could be infractions. How a plebe stood, sat, poured a drink, or acknowledged his fellow cadets was possible fodder for a strapping-down by an upper classman. It made being a guest at the table immensely uncomfortable. Since there was no way to engage with those around the table – what was I going to do, strike up a conversation with a plebe or interrupt an upper classman in the middle of hazing somebody? – I was left to sit dumbstruck as if I were an explorer who'd been invited to an island chief's ceremonial meal where the customs were completely unfamiliar.

The appearance of the Commandant of Cadets and my father on the poop deck yanked me out of my paralyzed state as the room came to attention. More than 4,000 cadets shot upright, their chairs noisily shooting back along the floor behind them as the backs of their knees locked. As Dad presented the flag, I noticed my host whispering to another upper classman across from us at the table as he nodded his head toward me. "That's his dad," I could see him say as he leaned at the waist to shorten the distance between them. The young man across the table nodded and then swept his eyes toward me. We made eye contact as I smiled awkwardly (*yeah, that's my pop!*). He had a hint of derision in his eyes. I was certain that I was the asshole legacy in this cadet's mind.

When the brief ceremony was over, the uncomfortableness returned.* The plebes set about serving the upper classmen after announcing each dish as it arrived.

"Sir, the green beans with bacon are on the table!"

"Sir, the meatloaf is on the table!"

Everything arrived "family style" – boats of food with a lone spoon or fork. The plebes served the rest of the table as if they were nervous waiters at a strange, swanky restaurant where every patron was pissed off.

They served the rest of the table, that is, except for me.

It's not that I expected to be served. But I did expect to eat. I was, however, completely in the dark as to the etiquette as a guest. It certainly didn't seem right that the plebes would serve me. But it also didn't seem appropriate me to lift myself partially from my chair, bend at the waist, and lean across the breadth of the table to pull the baked beans toward me.

---

   * The ceremony had to be brief. Cadets only had twenty minutes to eat. The efficiency with which so many mouths were fed in such a short time was something to behold.

As I sat flummoxed, the cadet across the table from me who had given me the uncomfortable stare earlier rose from his seat and held out his hand across the table. *Finally*, I thought. I grabbed the plate in front of me and held it out to him, happy that I'd finally be served.

Uh-oh.

He wasn't offering to serve me; he was introducing himself.

The guy who had given me the you're-a-fucking-legacy-punk-who-probably-doesn't-deserve-a-spot-at-this-revered-institution stare had stood to introduce himself to me by offering his hand and I had offered, in return, my plate, confirming that I indeed was a fucking-legacy-punk-who-probably-doesn't-deserve-a-spot-at-this-revered-institution. My face flushed with the heat of embarrassment. I had just confirmed every stereotype this future officer likely held. I was the entitled son of the colonel and astronaut. I'd whistle into West Point based on the credentials of my dad – not my own merits – and expect to be treated with kid gloves.

When I realized my mistake, I put the plate down quickly, and acted as if I wasn't ever really going to hand it to him in the first place. I stood and shook his hand. His grip was crushing. I looked into his eyes but had to look away quickly. There was a fire in them that told me exactly what was going through his brain. He was praying I would be at West Point the following year. He would make it his personal mission to seek me out and make my life miserable. He would put me through all manner of hazing as he pulled his classmates into the fun.

"Hey, Schroeder. Come here," he'd say to his buddy. "Look at this asshole." He'd point at me as I hung from a pull-up bar on my thirty-first of one hundred punitive pull ups.

"This is Mr. Mullane. He thinks that because his dad is a ring knocker and astronaut that his shit don't stink. How's your shit smell now Cadet Mullane? Where's your daddy now?"

Schroeder would then, unhelpfully, join in.

"Oh, I've heard about you Cadet Mullane. Weren't you the cheerleader who asked my friend here to serve you some meatloaf?"

It was true. I was an asshole. "No excuse sir," would likely be the only response I could provide and the only one that would be accepted.

I ultimately served myself sheepishly, but only took a very small portion of the main course, afraid that reaching for additional food would only make me look more entitled, as if I – a high school student who would walk out of that dining hall a free man, returning to my carefree senior year – had equal claim on the calories meant for young men and women who would return to months more of a harsh and demanding life. In resisting the urge to serve myself more food lest I incur the wrath of the cadet across from me, I had learned a lesson that plebes did in their first hours at the academy: doing things – any manner of things – was an opportunity for an upperclassman to find fault, to pick at a scab, to tear you a new one. So, it was best not to give them those opportunities. I was happy to go hungry.

The rest of the meal, while only twenty minutes long, seemed interminable. The cadet who had offered me his hand was so preoccupied by my incomprehensible disrespect, that he didn't even harass the plebes at the table as he had when we'd first arrived at Washington Hall. I was the red cape; he was the bull. And the plebes were glad for it. He sat seething as he ate, glancing to me periodically, memorizing my face and all its features. I'm convinced that if I passed that cadet on the streets of Manhattan today, he'd grab me by my collar and pin me to a nearby wall before beating me into a bloody pulp. He would not forget me.

Soon, dessert arrived, and I was glad for what it meant: the meal would shortly be done.

"Sir, the cherry pie is on the table!" a plebe announced with gusto.

At the arrival of the pie, the plebe retrieved his wheel cap and pulled from within in it a round template with lines radiating from its center at various angles. It looked like some sort of maritime navigation aid. But its purpose was more pedestrian. It provided precise markings that allowed the plebe to accurately cut the pie into pieces of exactly equal sizes, mitigating the risk of more hazing for a pie-cutting infraction.

The plebe placed the template above the pie and used a knife to mark along the edges the locations where a cut was to be made. I noticed that cutting a cherry pie was a challenge even with a template given the syrupy nature of the dessert's interior. Seeing this reminded me of a story Dad had once shared with me. At a West Point meal many years before, lore had it, a plebe made the usual announcement when the same desert was served at his meal. "Sir, the cherry pie is on the table!" he exclaimed before taking a knife in hand to cut the pastry with his pie-cutting guide. But upon piercing the crust and slicing lines across the center, the pie, predictably, began to disintegrate into a gooey mess. Anticipating a tongue lashing from the upperclassmen he was serving, the plebe dropped the knife and picked up a spoon. He then vigorously stirred the pie until the crust and the fruit made a homogenous mix.

"Sir, the cherry cobbler is on the table!" he announced, amending his earlier proclamation. Now that's a guy I'd follow into battle.

***

The trip to West Point left me doubting that I wanted to go to any academy. But I kept my mind open as I waited to see what would happen with my other choices and whether I'd receive an ROTC scholarship. I applied through the early admissions processes of those schools that had them. I heard back quickly from Stanford – it was a "no." I probably shouldn't have been surprised. As part of my application, I had written and essay about how the cartoon cat Garfield would make a great presidential candidate, thinking that the creativity and off-the-wall nature of the piece would make up for SAT scores that were not quite Stanford-like and would also appeal to the quirky nature of the Left Coast. It clearly didn't work. In retrospect, writing about a fictional character that was not part of a literary classic probably did more to remind the admissions committee of my weak SAT scores than assuage them of any concerns the standardized test might have raised. I did, however, get into Texas. As far as large state schools went it was a nice option and I was glad to have at least one place that wanted me.

Not soon after hearing from Texas and Stanford, I was notified by West Point that I had received an appointment to the academy and was told by a local Naval Academy representative that an appointment there would be forthcoming as well. I was proud even as I was unsure of whether I'd accept admissions to either place. Mom and Dad were congratulatory, but they remained surprisingly silent on the entire college application process. They expected my sisters and I to go to a university, but they did little in the way of actively encouraging us to think big about what our options might be. Applying to competitive schools outside of my home state was all my doing. Some of this may have come from Mom and Dad's own experiences; Mom never graduated from college and Dad practically fell into West Point, his parents having filled out most of his application for him. So, while Mom and Dad expected that, come the fall of 1986, we should be on a campus somewhere, they were ambivalent about the details of how we'd end up on that campus.

In December of 1985, I was notified by Notre Dame that I had been accepted there. It was also looking likely that I'd receive the ROTC scholarship. As I weighed my options, my father finally chimed in with some advice. And what he said was liberating.

"Pat," he said, "don't go to West Point because I went there. Lots of guys need that structure and discipline, but you are much more mature than I was at your age. So, go if you want to, but go because *you* want to go."

I am sure he didn't know how much those words meant to me. It was clear in that moment that he was conscious of his own success and the burden that could put on me, his only son. After all, how many people had a father who was a bona fide astronaut? It wasn't a normal profession. It was a vocation that children of seven or eight dreamed of when they weren't dreaming of becoming the President of the United States or a professional athlete. It was a career so rare that it seemed impossible to really exist and is why those same dreaming children eventually moved on to other things, assuming that others did as well.

But Dad didn't.

Not only did he stick with his dream, but he harbored it when nobody had yet done what he dreamt of doing. Astronauts didn't even exist. It was four years between the launch of Sputnik – when Dad's aspirations to fly in space began – and the first time a human made it to orbit (Yuri Gagarin of the U.S.S.R. in 1961). That was rare and special, and he knew it. He didn't want me trying to live up to some standard of success he never meant to set. He didn't want me chasing ghosts.

Not long after he told me to choose based on where I thought I'd best fit, I learned I had won a four-year ROTC scholarship from the U.S. Air Force. I could go to Notre Dame and have my tuition, books, and fees paid for. I could graduate and be commissioned as a second lieutenant. I could live a "normal" college life and have the same rank as the plebe who would have to go through a lot more shit to get his "butter bars" (the gold second lieutenant bars designating the rank). I decided that I wanted a more normal college life and so I let Notre Dame know I'd be attending in the fall of 1986. I also let the Air Force know I'd be taking the scholarship.

I would be shipping off to a place I'd never been to before in an age when it wasn't even possible to do a virtual tour on the internet. I'd be going in blind. But I was excited. I had always known that going to college at a school with a large number of Clear Lake High School graduates would saddle me with the baggage of who I'd been from the time I arrived in Houston in 1978 – a nerdy, awkward, and strait-laced kid. At Notre Dame, far from anybody who knew me as that boy, I could be a different version of me. I could remake myself.

Going into the Christmas of 1985, I felt as though things in my life were falling into place beautifully. Having my college decision out of the way before the winter holiday of my senior year, knowing I'd be going into the Air Force and that a scholarship would pay for my degree, and looking forward to Dad's historic launch from Vandenberg within the next twelve months had me buoyant. Life was good. And then, January 28, 1986.

CHAPTER 13: COLD DAY

"Pat – you need to go to Mr. Neil's office."

Ms. Trahan, my economics teacher, had just taken a note from Angela, a girl who lived down the street from me in the Brook Forest subdivision. Angela, like me, worked in the office one period a day – a cushy "class" for seniors who had enough credits to take it easy their last five months at Lake. She had cracked the door open a few moments earlier and handed a small slip of paper to Ms. Trahan, who had nonchalantly told me that I needed to report to the principal's office.

I rose from my desk, leaving my books, perplexed at why I was being summoned. It was a Tuesday morning in late January and I was enjoying my last semester at Lake after getting my immediate future squared away – in fact, I was wearing a light Notre Dame sweatshirt I'd found at a nearby sports apparel store so that the world would know where I'd be in the fall. The weather that day had buoyed my spirits too. While Houston's summer months were brutal, the winter months could be quite pleasant. A cold front had passed through the day before on its march eastward and it had been a chilly by Houston standards, 52°, about ten degrees cooler than normal. But on that Tuesday, the temperature had recovered nicely, and the day was approaching 70° with clear, blue skies and low humidity. I had an Ocean Pacific tee on underneath my Notre Dame sweatshirt so that I could shed the long sleeves later when the temperature rose.

While I was confused as to why I was being asked to go to the office, I was initially unconcerned. I wasn't the kind of kid who got into trouble, so I knew the summons was not related to having some tough discussion about an infraction earlier in the day. But when I got to the classroom door and stepped into the hallway, my anxiety ratcheted up a notch; I noticed that Angela looked horribly distraught. Her eyes were puffy. She had clearly been crying.

"What's wrong Angela?" I asked as we began walking down the long hallway lined with lockers.

"Nothing," she said, and then added, awkwardly, "It's okay." *What's okay?* I thought. If "nothing" was wrong, why say "it's okay?" She was lying and I knew it.

Then, it hit me. *Oh God.*

Dad was out west – I couldn't remember where – with the rest of his STS-62A crew. They were doing some training together for their upcoming launch. As was customary, particularly for a crew getting close to a mission, they hadn't flown on commercial flights to their meetings. They had taken their NASA T-38 jets.

Dad had been in an accident. I was sure of it.

He told tales frequently of flying in those jets and about how trips in them with other astronauts often wasn't a typical "take off and climb to your cruising altitude" endeavor. They would fly low level over the deserts of the west, pulling up to get over power lines. They would "dog-fight" each other over the waters of the Gulf of Mexico, like teens recklessly racing cars. They'd dart in and out of valleys and canyons, giving themselves little time to recover if an engine flamed out or ingested a bird. They'd do all the things you'd expect hot-shot fighter jocks to do, letting testosterone and adrenaline fuel risk-taking in pursuit of a drugless rush.

"Angela," I said, pleading, "please tell me what's wrong." She didn't answer.

I was living a horrifying déjà vu. I was on the roof of the LCC again, knowing Dad had died but having no confirmation of it, the hint of ambiguity gnawing at me relentlessly, a drip-drip of nightmarish horror. Where was Mom? Was Amy being called out of class too? Laura had stayed home from school that morning, she was sick. Did she already know? I fought tears and anger as I trailed Angela. Her head was down. The hallway seemed to stretch as we walked, our destination and clarity around what was going on seeming no closer with every step.

The central office at Lake had a glass wall that faced out into one of the main arteries through the center of the school. As Angela and I finally came to the end of the hallway where my class was, we entered the area in front of the office and I could see a group of people huddled around a television on a cart. The back of the T.V. was facing the hallway though so I couldn't tell what they were watching. And, in fact, I had no reason to believe that what they were watching had any relevance to my removal from class. I noted their gathering in passing, frustrated that they seemed more concerned with what was being broadcast than the anguish I was feeling.

"Pat," the senior principal, Mr. Neil, said to me as I entered the office, "something happened to *Challenger*."

I was confused. *Challenger*? The space shuttle? Then I remembered, there was a launch planned for that morning. I had seen the news while getting ready for school and recalled that blastoff had been delayed that morning because of a faulty fire detector near the launch pad that had to be replaced. The reporter mentioned in a verbal footnote that NASA had also sent an ice inspection team to the launch pad overnight; it was unusually cold in Florida. They were getting the brunt of the cold front that had made Houston chilly the day before and into that morning. But besides noting a delay and the cold weather marching eastward, I hadn't given the launch much thought.

It's a strange irony that the mission that would launch a teacher into space was of relatively little consequence in our school district. In a town where launches were the life's work of so many and astronauts showed up at parent-teacher conferences, sporting events, and school plays, the launch of *Challenger* with Christa McAuliffe didn't elevate the mission to a level deserving of special attention. Our town had already lived through twenty-four launches that put the lives of our neighbors, parents, and friends at risk. The presence of a woman from New Hampshire who was a temporary visitor in our world didn't reach the threshold of uniqueness that would make the launch a must-see event.

"What do you mean–"

I started to respond to Mr. Neil, but my words got caught in my throat as I turned to face the television. There, I saw the replay of the launch and the subsequent disintegration of *Challenger*. I let out an audible gasp and immediately felt tears come to my eyes.

"I wanted to be sure the astronaut kids knew," Mr. Neil said quickly and with a hint of apology, explaining why I had been dragged from class.

In the instant after he said this, I felt a range of emotions that were virtually impossible to reconcile. Dad was alive, then? I couldn't help but be relieved. But the moment I felt the relief that came with that realization, I was awash in a smothering guilt. Sure, Dad was safe. But, despite talk on the television about rescue crews being dispatched to search the Atlantic for *Challenger* survivors, I knew with certainty that Dad's colleagues were dead. It was a crew I knew well. Four of *Challenger's* astronauts were TFNGs, chosen in the same astronaut class with Dad: Commander Dick Scobee, Mission Specialist Ellison Onizuka, Mission Specialist Ronald McNair, and Mission Specialist Judy Resnik. Pilot Mike Smith, Payload Specialist Greg Jarvis and teacher Christa McAuliffe rounded out the seven-person crew.

The loss of Judy hit me hardest. She and Dad had shared a rookie flight on *Discovery*. Single and far from a family she was partially estranged from, she had spent a good deal of time at our home. In an age when women were relatively absent from the world of military aviation, she seemed exotic to me. She was petite with long, black hair that curled into tight coils around an olive-skinned face. To a teenaged boy who was noticing not only girls my own age but attractive older women, she seemed more like a star in a movie about female astronauts than an actual female astronaut. Of course, today this rings of sexism – because it was. But I was a child of an aviation community of the late seventies and early eighties that was dominated by a fraternity of men – only men. While I never recall Dad saying anything disparaging about women and their ability to do (or not do) something, the ethos of the network he lived in – and that I associated with by extension – was hyper-masculine. Women didn't have to be disparaged because they were completely excluded; it's easy to be ambivalent about people who don't occupy your own club.

I watched and re-watched the conflagration that ended *Challenger's* ascent, each viewing bringing more pain. The room had become crowded. Amy arrived and we hugged each other, bringing more tears from me and from her. With the addition of each student, teacher, and administrator to the office, the anguish in the space accumulated like rain filling a cistern. While the rest of the country began to mourn in the way people mourn for a celebrity they loved but never really knew, my Clear Lake community began a lamentation in the old-world, biblical sense. It was the sort of all-consuming sadness that a town might experience when seven firefighters from the same station were killed in a single fire. Except it was worse in so many ways; the residents of the community the firefighters were from were not collectively responsible for the fire. But even in the moments after I first saw what would become the iconic image of the *Challenger* loss — a ball of liquid oxygen and hydrogen vaporizing and igniting as the two solid rocket boosters twisted into the sky in an unguided, meandering walk — I knew that the cause of the disintegration would ultimately be laid at the feet of the very people who now shed tears in Clear Lake.

Again, the lessons from a life as the son of an aviator came home to roost in a disturbing way. The causes of crashes in the aviation world were almost always pilot error.* Even when a mechanical failure occurred, it was most often the reaction of the pilot to the anomaly and not the failure itself that resulted in a crash. But it was virtually impossible for pilot error to have been the cause of what was playing on an endless loop in the main office. The pilot and commander of a space shuttle were not in control of the vehicle during launch. Computers were. *Challenger's* crew was along for the ride. So, if the incident was not caused by those on *Challenger* it was almost certainly caused by some latent design flaw that had always existed — a design flaw that men and women in the homes around the Johnson Space Center and throughout the network of NASA contractors were collectively responsible for. It was a design flaw that had undoubtedly been lurking when *Discovery* rocketed skyward with Dad on it sixteen months earlier. I knew that in addition to the crushing sadness in those

---

* It is estimated that approximately 80% of aviation crashes are the result of pilot error.

homes around Clear Lake that evening, there would be a lot of soul searching, a lot of "what did I miss?" questions.

School came to an end that day shortly after *Challenger* was torn to pieces. Classes weren't officially canceled but nobody could pretend that things were normal. The phones in the office, which were silent in the moments after I got there, began to ring with an urgent persistence. Parents were calling in, wondering what the plan for the rest of the day was, many asking to come and get their children. The administrators knew that it was prudent to let people go home given the distraction of the heartrending loss and, besides, there were concerns about the press descending on the school and the circus atmosphere that might create. On that day, three of my fellow students at Clear Lake High School lost a parent – Janelle Onizuka and Scott and Allison Smith. Their affiliation with Lake would quickly be discovered and the administrators knew that in short order news vans would be parked out front with their antennae telescoped skyward, beaming sorrow through the ether, just as they had done during the suicide "epidemic" a year-and-a-half before.

Mom arrived at the school not long after I had made it to the office. She had been crying and started to again as she hugged Amy and me. I asked her: "Mom, where is Dad?" I knew he was alright, but I still need to hear it from her.

"He's in New Mexico, at Los Alamos. But he's on his way home with the rest of the crew. I talked to him," she added. I let out a breath and some of the tension nesting deep within me released, leaving my body like a demon succumbing to an exorcism.

Mom knew many of the administrators at Lake and spent some time in the office talking to them with the quiet reverence that always accompanies a discussion of deaths that came early and unexpectedly. An announcement was made over the intercom and at the next bell students went to payphones to contact their parents, some crying as they did. Mom, Amy, and I left the office to head home. The *Challenger* loss had happened at around 10:40 a.m. central time, about two hours past its scheduled launch. Nearly an hour had passed by the time we were leaving the school. The cafeteria was near the main entrance to Lake and we passed by students who were eating in stunned silence or apathetically picking through their plates. A pall had descended upon us, a pall no less traumatic than if the cloud of fuel and debris from *Challenger* fell onto our school from above.

Once home, I turned on the news and watched the wall-to-wall coverage of the disaster. Steve Bell, an anchor on ABC, was narrating recorded footage that showed a parachute descending with an indistinguishable form beneath it, noting that there was hope that it was the shuttle's "escape capsule." It was maddening for me to watch.

There was no escape capsule.

I didn't know what the parachute was, but I knew that it wasn't saving the life of anybody on *Challenger*. He went on to explain that there was no information available yet from NASA. How could there be? They knew what everybody watching television that day knew – that the shuttle appeared to explode right after the "go at throttle up" call. But beyond that, there was a vacuum of information.

Bell then said, "Now we'll go to Larry Speakes at the White House who apparently has an announcement coming up ...."

Speakes, the Deputy Press Secretary for President Reagan, said that the President had been in the Oval Office with some senior staff preparing for a lunch with the press to talk about the budget and State of the Union address.* The Vice President and several others came into the Oval Office and informed President Reagan of what had happened, then all of them then did exactly what I had done – they turned on the T.V. to see what was being reported. When Speakes was done with his announcement, the images transitioned to the ABC studios in Washington again. Peter Jennings had joined Bell in the studio. The man I watched every night with my father was now reporting on the deaths of Dad's friends.

As I watched, I wondered where the families of the crewmembers were. The wives, husbands, and children would have been where I was two years before during the launch of *Discovery* – on the roof of the LCC. But the extended family members – including Christa McAuliffe's parents – were in a more accessible viewing area and the images on television of their faces transitioning from elation to confusion to grief were some of the hardest to watch that day. I remembered my own experiences on the roof when I thought Dad had

---

* The State of the Union address was to have happened that evening but was subsequently delayed owing to the loss of *Challenger*.

been killed and experienced for just a moment the special anguish that comes from thinking your loved one had perished violently and in full view of the entire world. Of course, I had gotten to experience a joyful relief when I realized Dad was going to be fine. But my high school classmates – Janelle, Allison, and Scott – and McAuliffe's parents wouldn't get that blessed absolution.

We stayed glued to the television all day and couldn't help but wonder out loud what the loss of *Challenger* would mean for the entire shuttle program. It was a bit selfish, but Mom, Amy, Laura, and I began to realize that a cancellation of the shuttle program would leave us in a state of limbo. If there was no shuttle, there would be no need for astronauts which meant there would be no need for Dad to stay in Houston. Would he go back to the military? Or join a defense contractor? I couldn't imagine Dad doing the latter. It would be like asking Indiana Jones to work with snakes. Dad would have hated a "normal" job.

But any fears we had initially melted away bit-by-bit as we watched more coverage of the launch and loss of STS 51-L. The country was mourning in a way that we found surprising. Shuttle launches had become routine enough that it was hard to know if the population cared while things were going well. But the reaction to the accident that morning had shown that America did care.* For every comment by a pundit or citizen about how tragic the day had been, there was one proclaiming that the loss of *Challenger* was a price that the country expected to pay in the interest of advancing the goals of exploration and scientific discovery, that we must press on. The survival of the program would depend a lot on what was discovered as the cause of the accident, but it seemed clearer to me as the day wore on that the sentiment of the country would not kill the shuttle.

---

* Contrary to popular belief, the launch of STS-51L was viewed live by very few people. Those networks that did cover the launch cutaway right after liftoff, too impatient to get back to regular programming. CNN carried the launch from liftoff through the loss, but it was a new, six-year-old network without the reach it has today. The few students watching in their classrooms were viewing a satellite feed NASA had set up because of Christa McAuliffe's position on the crew, not a live network feed.

In the afternoon, Mom drove to Ellington Field to pick up Dad as he returned in a three-aircraft formation with the rest of the STS-62A crew from Los Alamos. Amy, Laura, and I stayed home.

Ellington had become for me a location dripping with meaning. It was where I had gone excitedly with Dad to hop into Cessnas and fly together through the milky skies of southeast Texas. It was where we had gone to greet Dad upon his return from his first mission to space. And now, it was where he'd return full of grief and uncertainty after the tragic loss of friends and the possible loss of his opportunity to return to space again. It would not be the first time that Dad would be apart from Mom for significant events in both their lives. Dad got engaged to Mom via the U.S. Mail, there was no dinner at a nice restaurant, a velvet box, and a bent knee. He was living alone in Florida when he was almost killed before bailing out of a crashing airplane. He was out of town when he was selected as an astronaut. And now, he was a thousand miles away when *Challenger* was lost.

While Mom was gone to get Dad, I heard the phone ring in the kitchen. I didn't rise to get it though; I was too immersed in the television news. But Amy or Laura must have answered, because the ringing stopped fairly quickly. I thought nothing of it.

When Dad and Mom returned home, we all came together in a small pod of tear-laden hugs. Dad looked worn. Even now he didn't cry, but he didn't have too. He was hurting. His features, usually firm and radiating optimism and good humor, now appeared drawn and more elastic, as if the accumulated joy in his life was melting from his face. It was the first time I ever saw him looking so forlorn and it bothered me. But the look didn't last long as his sadness turned to anger in short order when Laura mentioned to him that a reporter had called while he was gone.

"A reporter?" Dad asked.

"Yes, he asked if you were home and I said no," Laura answered proudly, knowing she had said the right thing. "Then he asked me how you felt when *Challenger* blew up."

Dad's features now became hard with anger. He started to say something then stopped himself and took a deep breath. Then, calmly, he said to all of us, "Nobody answers the phone. Let the answering machine get it. You understand? For the rest of the day, we won't answer any calls." We all nodded.

I was old enough to understand the anger he had. It was at best inappropriate for a reporter to call an astronaut at home hours after his friends had died and ask him how he felt – but at least Dad knew what he had signed up for. Interviewing the fourteen-year-old daughter of an astronaut in the hours after such a tragedy, though, was downright slimy.

That evening, Dad drank a Coors Light and ate some pecans while we tuned into *ABC World News Tonight with Peter Jennings*. The broadcast didn't start with the usual theme music, trumpets lofting high in pitch and then falling as drums compelled them onward again. It started with the video that began at the "Go at throttle up" call and the subsequent disintegration. Peter Jennings explained that the entire newscast would be devoted to the loss of *Challenger*. Dad sat silently but his anger of earlier had dissipated and he transitioned into an analytic mode. An ABC correspondent showed slow motion video of the apparent explosion and she was pointing out what others were already noting: there appeared to be a flame growing at the lower right side SRB in the moments before "go at throttle up." Was this the "smoking gun?"

As the newscast continued, Dad seemed to relax, to the extent that was possible on such a traumatic day. When Peter Jennings was done with his broadcast, we flipped channels to another station and heard the speech President Reagan had given from the Oval Office that day. "Sometimes painful things like this happen," Reagan said, "it's all part of the process of exploration and discovery; it's all part of taking a chance and expanding man's horizons. The future doesn't belong to the faint-hearted, it belongs to the brave."

"I can't believe the reaction to it," Dad said as he swallowed some beer. "I thought for sure people would be saying it was time to cancel the program."

If I had told him at that time that the shuttle program would go on to fly an additional 109 missions and would even survive the loss of another shuttle (*Columbia* in 2003), he'd have had me committed. The increasing confidence we had that public sentiment – at least in the hours after the loss – was on the side of NASA, seemed to let some of the earlier apprehension out of our house. Maybe we could stay in Houston. Maybe Dad would still get a chance to fly out of Vandenberg.

***

The next several months were a blur. I was finishing up my senior year right around the time that the Rogers Commission – an investigative body put together to determine the cause of the *Challenger* disaster – delivered its final report to President Reagan. Dad was shocked at how quickly the cause of the deadly accident had been determined and even more shocked at how quickly the report was completed – five months. The cause of the loss of *Challenger* was determined to be a failure of two O-rings at the bottom of the right SRB.

When I first heard the term "O-ring" I thought of the small rubbery rings I had seen Dad use during a plumbing project at home; I envisioned tiny gaskets going into a leaky faucet. Indeed, before the ubiquitous use of the term in relation to the loss of *Challenger*, O-rings brought to mind for most Americans what they did for me: nothing more than a glorified rubber band. But the O-rings referred to in the *Rogers Commission Report* were enormous. They were the same diameter as the SRB itself, about twelve feet across, and served a very important purpose.

SRBs needed O-rings because of a fundamental attribute of their manufacture and assembly: they were not made as one piece given their size but were manufactured in segments that were stacked and bolted together at KSC. Inside each of those segments was the solid fuel, a mixture of chemicals that was the consistency of a hardened paste.* But the fuel didn't fill the entire inside of each segment. Rather, there was a hole down the center of the fuel so that when all the segments were stacked, the SRB was like a pencil with the lead removed. This was because the fuel didn't burn from the top down or bottom up. Rather, it burned from the inside to the outside. At T minus zero, the

---

* A NASA website describes the fuel as having the consistency of a "hard rubber typewriter eraser." The description is a bit perplexing as it exists on a website that was created sometime around 2005. By that time, many younger readers had never used a typewriter, much less a "hard rubber typewriter eraser." Leave it to NASA to use an indecipherable anachronism to describe an exotic rocket fuel.

SRB was ignited by a small solid rocket inside and at the top of the booster which shot a flame down the length of the SRB's hollowed-out center, igniting the inside walls of the fuel "tunnel." The flame consumed the interior circumference of the fuel as the booster burned, making the diameter of the donut hole in the middle of the fuel grow as the shuttle ascended.

Unfortunately, this design had a weakness. At the point where two segments came together, there was a natural path for fire to burn between the fuel in two joined segments. If flame found that path and made its way all the way to the outer skin of the booster, the results could be catastrophic. To guard against this happening, there was a set of redundant O-rings that ran the full circumference of the booster that were supposed to seal the segments and prevent hot gasses from finding a path to the metal body of the rocket containing the combustion.

Challenger was lost because both O-rings succumbed to hot gasses leaking between two segments, allowing flame to pierce the skin of the booster and burn away at both the external fuel tank and the mount that connected the booster to that tank. At almost the same instant, the hydrogen storage portion of the external tank ruptured as the flame from the booster carved an incision in it and the mount joining the SRB to the external tank failed, forcing the top of the right SRB into the top of the external tank. *Challenger* was no longer a sleek, aerodynamic assembly that could be controlled. It was like an airplane that had lost a wing in flight while traveling at supersonic speeds. The atmosphere ripped *Challenger* apart. The fuel in the external tank blossomed into a half-ignited, white and marmalade-colored ball of vapor as the SRBs, liberated from the external tank, diverged from each other, writing a "Y" in the sky with their plumes. In the final analysis, *Challenger*, didn't explode; it tore apart.

Much was made of the cold weather that morning in Florida contributing to the failure of the O-rings. While the low temperatures did reduce the flexibility of the seals and increase the likelihood of hot gasses escaping, the sobering fact was that *Challenger* could have happened on a warm day. And in fact, since the SRBs were parachuted back to earth for reuse, data had been gathered that showed that on seven missions prior to the loss of STS-51L, there had been O-ring damage of varying degrees. More troublesome was that many of these incidents occurred on days when the temperature was quite warm; sensors measured the joint temperatures in those seven instances and they ranged from a low of around 53° to a high of around 75°, all significantly warmer than the freezing temperatures on the morning of January 28th, 1986.

The first mission that saw complete blow-by of one of the primary O-rings was halfway between the first launch of the shuttle and the destruction of *Challenger*. It was Dad's first mission, STS-41D. During his maiden flight and unbeknownst to him, the only thing standing between his successful trip into orbit and certain death was a secondary O-ring which had provided just enough of a seal to keep the flames at bay. When I learned this, my skin went cold. He survived a pad abort and fire only to be within seconds of dying off the coast of Florida, sharing the fate of the *Challenger* crew. Fortunately, the boosters on STS-41D had run out of fuel and been jettisoned before he met the same fate as his seven friends on that eventful day in early 1986. Dad's nine lives were going fast.

While the rapid progress in the investigation of the *Challenger* accident and the national sentiment to continue funding the program kept our spirits as high as they could be during this dark period, Dad was still down. He had no idea when he'd have a chance to fly in space again … or if he'd have a chance at all given the turmoil in the shuttle manifest the flight stoppage had caused. One thing was for sure, though: if he did get a chance to go into orbit a second time, it wasn't going to be in a shuttle launched from Vandenberg.

NASA scrapped the idea of launching from the west coast because doing so meant the use of a newly designed SRB. This new type of rocket was necessary because launching south out of Vandenberg meant that the shuttle wouldn't benefit from the earth's eastward rotational "boost" that a launch out of KSC offered. A polar orbit launch was like taking off from the deck of an aircraft carrier without a catapult; the same rocket couldn't carry the same amount of payload into a polar orbit that it could into an equatorial orbit. One way to counter this performance deficit was to make the shuttle stack lighter. Every pound taken out of the weight of the stack was a pound more payload the shuttle could loft into space. NASA had planned to make the system lighter by using new "filament wound" solid rocket boosters rather than the steel cases the program had used for east-coast launches. But the risk of using a whole new SRB design was considered too great and so missions from Vandenberg were scrapped. If Dad flew again, it would be out of KSC. He mourned the loss of his chance to see polar orbit.

CHAPTER 14: MOVING ON

I graduated from Clear Lake High School on June 1st, 1986, just four months after *Challenger* and eight days before the *Rogers Commission Report* was delivered to President Reagan. I baked in the nearly 90°, humid air outside of Hofheinz Pavilion, an arena on the campus of the University of Houston, before filing in with the rest of my classmates to *Pomp and Circumstance*. I sat on the stage with administrators and honored guests, rising early in the ceremony to take the podium and give my graduation address as President of the senior class. I said a few forgettable words shaped significantly by my belief that the completion of high school was not some pinnacle but a brief stop on the way to real greatness. I finished by reading a poem called "Desiderata." The spiritually infused prose seemed fitting given the moment and I read the last portion of the poem with pride, my voice rising as I articulated each word with an overemphasized clarity that I hoped gave them rhetorical punch:

And whether or not it is clear to you, no doubt the universe is unfolding as it should. Therefore, be at peace with God, whatever you conceive Him to be. And whatever your labors and aspirations, in the noisy confusion of life, keep peace in your soul. With all its sham, drudgery and broken dreams, it is still a beautiful world. Be cheerful. Strive to be happy.

As I reflected that day on my high school career, I think it was fair to say that I had done a good job of striving to be happy even if my time at Lake had in some ways been less eventful than that of many of my classmates. I hadn't had a beer. I hadn't smoked a joint. I hadn't been all the way with a girl. Sure, I had a girlfriend or two, one of them a fellow cheerleader for a while until she dumped me on a school ski trip to Colorado. But despite being well known at the school, I was not the boy that every girl wanted. I wasn't particularly handsome and any charisma I had around adults seemed to leave me like an army abandoning its general when I had to talk to a pretty girl. Short notes written on the back of senior pictures from female friends showed how they viewed me. One of the most beautiful girls in our class wrote, "Pat, you're really a super person with a great personality." No, not "great personality!" The two words were like a scalpel to the balls. Argh. She continued: "You're really involved in alot [sic] of activities at school & I am very envious!" Stating facts I knew to be true – that I was involved in a lot of activities – made it read like a book report, not the love note I hoped it would be. "Good luck in college and in the future!" she finished, signing it, "Love ya!"

I know it wasn't fair for me to be critical. What else was she going to write? She wasn't my girlfriend and didn't have any interest in me no matter how much I wished it otherwise. I guess I was just hoping for a little more creativity, a short couple of sentences that said that she wanted to kiss me even as the words told me to stay away from her or she'd get a restraining order.

Any frustration I had though was offset by the optimism in the poem I read at graduation. I had confidence the universe was unfolding as it should. I was going away to college at a place where nobody would know me. At Notre Dame, I could reinvent myself, be a cooler version of Pat Mullane.

The summer months before heading to college raced by. I spent a lot of time mowing lawns and working at a drug store. Shortly before I graduated, in May, the movie *Top Gun* was released. The film told the story of pilots at the Navy's Fighter Weapon's School. The school was in some ways like the Air Force's Test Pilot School at Edwards, a school my father had attended.

I used much of the money I made in my two jobs to go to the theater as often as I could. I watched the film a good six or seven times that summer. I had dreams of flying in the Air Force and the movie stoked those dreams like bellows firing a wood burning stove. It didn't matter to me that it was a movie about the Navy and I was going into the Air Force. The Top Gun culture I saw on the screen was the culture I had known as a child and had been a part of as the kid of an astronaut. I was thrilled to see that culture shared with and embraced by the general population.

While I didn't know it at the time, the movie would help me immensely in the year to come. The film had raised the profile of military aviators in a way that recruitment ads played during the halftime of NFL games never could. And unlike an ad run during a sporting event, *Top Gun* had elevated the status of military men – and aviators in particular – among a different population altogether: young women. The handsome Hollywood stars in flight suits and formal uniforms caused swooning across the country.

Notre Dame had a particularly large ROTC presence, most of us easily identifiable by our closely shorn hair. Early in my freshman year while at a party crammed into a small dorm room, a young woman asked me if I was in ROTC. When I replied proudly, "Yes, in the Air Force," she responded eagerly (longingly) with, "Just like in *Top Gun*?"

There was a gleam in her eyes and I knew her mind was wandering to the volleyball scene in the movie and she pictured me as one of the buff, shirtless aviators diving into the sand to dig a ball from the dirt before taking to the skies to save humanity once again.* I was too clueless to press the advantage she had given me.

"Well, *Top Gun*, was about the Navy. I'm in the Air Force," I said as if I were a docent at the Air and Space Museum correcting a petulant child during a Q&A session.

"But *Top Gun* was about airplanes," she said, giving me another opportunity to make myself interesting.

"Yes, but the Navy has airplanes too," I said, unwittingly finding a way to kill that opportunity.

"But you are in the Air Force, right? The Air Force flies planes."

---

* In fairness, I *did* have a six-pack like some of those shirtless actors in *Top Gun*. But mine was due to my scrawny-ness, not chiseled muscles. With virtually no body fat, I looked more like a prisoner of war after two years of captivity than an athletic fighter pilot/actor.

Eventually I gave up. By the end of September, I had learned my lesson and when asked if Air Force ROTC was just like *Top Gun*, I answered with an assured, steely-eyed confidence, "Yes, exactly."

***

When not working or at the movies, my hobby of flying remote controlled planes occupied much of my time. I knew that I wouldn't be able to continue flying at college and thought that I might as well get in as many flights as possible. I also was more daring, knowing that if I crashed, I probably wouldn't go through the time and expense to rebuild the plane since I couldn't take it with me to Notre Dame anyway. I'd drive to an open field near our home – one of the few left in the rapidly growing Clear Lake area – and spend hours flying my RC glider, searching for thermals to stay aloft, often racing back to the car when a building storm began to rumble with thunder.

RC plane flyers are frequently struck by lightning; standing in an empty field with a box attached to a metal antenna was practically inviting a strike. When I did see dark clouds on the horizon, I'd race to gather my gear and then sprint across the field, often getting to the car as heavy drops hammered me in the moments before the sky fully opened up. Mom would chastise me when I came in through the back door, my wet t-shirt giving away how close I'd come to being caught in the full onslaught. She would tell me that I was going to kill myself, but she never stopped me from going out again. I think years of similar warnings to Dad had worn her down. They were reflexive in nature, but she had no expectation that we'd listen.

In addition to my glider, I also had a motorized remote-control plane. Dad and I would take turns flying it on Johnson Space Center property, using a patch of asphalt designated by a local flying club as the runway. I loved to go out there with him. As with our flights in real airplanes out of Ellington Field, we'd be up as the sun was rising to get my plane in the air before the atmosphere got hot and windy. The asphalt we used as a runway was no more than a few hundred yards away from an enormous static display of a Saturn V rocket laid on its side like an old man permanently reclined in retirement. I'd hold the radio transmitter in my hands, the weight of it borne by a strap around my neck, and, with my left thumb on the throttle and the fingers of my right hand on the control stick, I'd command the plane into the air and fly it toward the Saturn V before entering a rectangular pattern, flying "touch and go" landings over and over again, adding in some acrobatics in between.

Once, while between flights, I was refueling my plane. At the end of the fueling process, I had to reconnect a small, rubbery hose to a metal fuel inlet port on the side of the engine's carburetor. The tube was wet with fuel and slippery. I was having trouble slipping it back over the protruding inlet port. Dad was watching over my shoulder and turned my trouble sliding the metal protrusion into the hole of the tube into a crude sexual joke. I responded in a way that most children do when their parents say something off-color, letting out an exasperated, "DAD!" But I wasn't really that upset. While the joke itself might have been juvenile, his use of it in front of me signaled that he was starting to view me as an equal, as a man. And I was starting to feel like one. College was only a few short months from starting and I had no trepidation about leaving home to make my own way. I had explored the boundaries of my own comfort in so many ways in my eighteen years that leaving my parents, sisters, and home seemed not only easy, but necessary. I would miss them, but I would miss more the lost opportunities if I played it safe and stayed in southeast Texas.

***

While Dad was helping launch me into manhood, I sensed Mom was coming to the realization that her own life was about to change significantly. The loss of both Amy and me to college at the same time was going to be a blow to her. She'd only known being a mother and wife. She had never lived alone, instead sharing the home she'd grown up in with her parents until she left to marry a man she barely knew and who would ship off to Vietnam less than two years later. Amy, Laura, and I had been her constant companions while Dad was training, flying, fighting, crashing, and launching. We were her touchstones in an uncertain world, a world defined by a man who bounced around the globe with her in tow, a man who might die violently at any moment.

As my time to leave home approached, I thought a lot about Mom and how she had raised us. Over the years, I had become more confused about how she could seem distant at times. She loved us but she did so in a mostly stoic and sometimes tough way. Part of this was undoubtedly a function of who her own parents had been. If grandparents are always more loving toward their grandchildren than they are to their own children, then my own experiences with Joe Joe hinted at how tough he must have been on Mom. Dad and his profession, I came to believe, also played a part in how she raised and loved us. The threat of loss was perpetual. It was hard for her to give of herself fully when so much energy had to be diverted to protection from pain that may – or may not – come. But as the summer progressed, she softened as if she realized that two of the only constants in her life, her twins, might leave her without knowing that her core was a wellspring of love, that another part of her existed.

One day Mom and I were out running some errands, my departure for Notre Dame not more than a month off. We had gone to a local mall and when lunch rolled around, she asked if I wanted to grab a bite at a nearby restaurant. I agreed and several minutes later we were sitting down to eat. She seemed distracted. After several moments of banter that seemed forced, she sighed and looked out the window on one side of our booth, the light coming through the blinds painting stripes across her face. A moment of silence hung between us.

"Pat, there's something I've been wanting to share with you," she said.

Before I could respond, she continued as if she needed to maintain some sort of conversational momentum. "When I was seventeen, I got pregnant by a boyfriend from high school – not your dad. I had the baby and I gave him up for adoption." Her voice warbled and accelerated as she finished the sentence. Tears began to drip from her bottom lids, and she reached for a napkin.

Her statement came with such abruptness and so out of context that I was unable to respond. My mind was racing. And the first thought racing through it was: Did Dad know about this?

"Your father knew before we were married," Mom added as if clairvoyant. She sniffled.

"Oh," I said, still unable to formulate a complete sentence.

"You said 'him' – you had a son?" I asked.

"Yes, a boy."

"Do you know where he is?"

"No." She answered quickly as if she had anticipated every question I would have. It occurred to me that she probably had – how many times had she rehearsed this conversation? How many times had she been on the verge of telling me and lost her nerve, retreating to the comfort of a secret from long ago that had little chance of being unveiled?

"Do Amy and Laura know?"

"Amy, yes. Laura, no. But I'm going to tell her soon."

I was still reeling. I had no idea what to say next. We sat silently for a few heartbeats.

"Well, thanks for telling me," I said. I was ashamed as soon as the words left my mouth. Mom had never opened up to me about anything. And now she was, and it wasn't about how she had once smoked a joint when she was younger or had cheated on a chemistry exam in high school. She had just told me, her "only" son, that she had another son, a son she had given birth to under what had to be scandalous circumstances given the era in which it happened and the values of the family she grew up in. That deserved a response more empathetic than "thanks for telling me." I hated myself.

"I went to a Catholic home for unwed mothers," Mom said, thankfully taking charge of the conversation. "Nonnie and Joe Joe were not happy," she added, smiling a little as she did.

I smiled back and felt a surge of empathy and love that was completely absent just moments before, a flashflood of emotion rushing down a bone-dry desert arroyo.

"Oh my God, Joe Joe must have had an aneurysm," I said laughing a little as I felt my muscles start to loosen, releasing a tension I hadn't known I was holding.

"You could say that," she said, laughing along with me as she did. I loved Joe Joe, but he had been hard on me as a kid and knowing that Mom had caused him angst brought forth just a little *schadenfreude* in me.

Mom went on to tell me of the scandal it caused in her family, about how relatives were told she had gone off to college when, in fact, she was in another city working in a facility for the aged run by the Sisters of Charity as she awaited the arrival of her baby, her work emptying bedpans and cleaning sheets paying for her room and board.

While she didn't go into too many details as we sat in that restaurant, she shared enough with me to make it obvious that the reaction of her own parents and her treatment by nuns during her indentured servitude was nothing short of cruel. All concerned let her know that she had stained herself in an irrecoverable way, that her sin was mortal. She found herself utterly alone, abandoned by her family, her God, and her church. This revelation confused me. Mom had, during my eighteen years, been a devout Catholic. How could she embrace an institution that had caused her so much pain? In contemplating this question, it came to me how strong she was. Despite rejection by those she loved, by a church that had been an ever-present companion to her in her childhood, and by God himself (if she believed the nuns at the home where she worked), she was the one who had stayed faithful. She had been the one to forgive, to find mercy in her heart for those who had rejected her. It indicated to me a capacity for love and compassion that I hadn't known was there. I wanted to hug her.

"Have you ever tried to find him?" I asked after she had given an overview of that eventful time.

"No," she said, "Your dad and I have talked about it, but we figure if he hasn't reached out to find me, then we should leave well enough alone." As she said this, there was anguish in the spaces between her words. She knew it was the right answer, but it wasn't the answer her heart wanted to give.

Only then did I contemplate that I had a half-brother somewhere in the world. It felt surreal to me. He would have been twenty-three-years old, five years older than me – if he was still alive. I couldn't help but wonder where he was, what he was doing. I had never considered what it would be like to have a brother. Truth be told, I'm not sure I would have wanted one. Sharing the attention of my father with another boy seemed difficult to consider. I would have hated giving up the front seat of the Cessna when Dad and I flew or sharing time flying my remote-controlled planes. It was a selfish thought, but it was a real one. Now that I was going off to college though, the idea of having a brother seemed romantic in a way. I imagined, of course, all of the good outcomes. Maybe he had graduated from college recently and was also an aviation buff? Maybe he was famous, a star in one of the movies I loved? Maybe he was a doctor living down the road? A professional athlete? While these fantasies were wonderful to imagine, I knew that Mom and Dad were right – whatever he had decided to do with his life, he hadn't decided to share it with Mom. I wondered if, for Mom, it felt like another rejection in a litany of them related to a pregnancy from so many years before.

"Thank you, Mom, for telling me," I said again, but this time more authentically, not as verbal filler.

"I'm glad I got a chance to," she said. The tears were drying now. The relief in having shared her secret with me was obvious. Her shoulders had relaxed; they were no longer pulled up toward her ears. Her face, while still recovering from the tears of moments before, was beginning to soften, the puffiness evaporating from her eyes.

Mom paid the check and when we got to the car, I gave her a big hug and told her I loved her. I probably meant it more than I ever had. As we drove home, I couldn't help but consider whether her long-held secret had something to do with the distance that had existed between her and me. Did the sight of her second son remind her of her first? Did she look at me and add five years to my face and frame, trying to imagine what the boy she had given up for adoption might look like, if his mannerisms were like mine? If so, did it cause a hurt deep within her that made it harder for her to be close to me, as if I weren't real but an apparition from the past, the ghost of somebody else? It also became apparent to me in that moment where her connection to Amy came from, where her apparent desire to live through her daughter originated. Mom had not experienced her teens in the way that many girls did. Nonnie and Joe Joe were, by all accounts, wardens in a prison home that allowed her little freedom. In one of the few moments where she was free, she had become pregnant and any ability to chart her own course, to live her own life, had been stolen from her. Was it any surprise that she saw in Amy a life that she never had and a desire to be a part of that life?

Many years after Mom first told me her secret, she would share with me that a few days after her first son's birth, she had gone to the nursery a floor below where she lived with the other unwed mothers and asked if she could hold her baby. This was in defiance of an order from Nonnie who had told Mom before the birth, "Don't you dare hold that baby, I don't want you getting attached to it." When the nurse brought Mom her son, Mom unswaddled him and checked his fingers, toes, and limbs, completing that ancient ritual all mothers undertake, confirming perfection. She held him close for a while, his tiny hand around her pinky. After several minutes it was time to return him to the nursery. In the waning moments of what would be their only time together after his birth, she kissed him and told him to be good for his new parents. Then, she told him that she loved him before she handed him back to a nurse and turned to leave, knowing she would likely never see her son again. How did she endure the anguish of that moment? It was yet another question in an endless list of questions I would never be able to fully answer. But in a strange way, there was comfort in the questions even if there were no answers, because along with those questions came a thinning in a shell around Mom, a thinning that had shrunk the distance between us, a thinning caused indirectly by somebody I'd never met: my half-brother, wherever he was.

***

Houston had been the place I laid my head for eight years by the time the summer of 1986 rolled around. It had been the closest thing to a hometown that I'd ever known, my time there doubling the longest span I'd ever spent anywhere else. But I knew that even it – like so many places before – was simply a stop on the way to somewhere else, not just because I would be leaving to go to school, but because I knew that Mom and Dad wouldn't stay when Dad's time at NASA was done. And, in fact, four years later, Mom and Dad would relocate back to their hometown of Albuquerque, New Mexico after Dad flew in space two more times shortly after launches resumed two-and-a-half years following the loss of *Challenger*.

I went back to Clear Lake in 2006 for my twenty-year high school reunion. Walking into a hotel ballroom containing my classmates was the most nervous I'd been walking into a room since I shuffled into the Clear Lake High School gym to try out for cheerleader. Most of the attendees had stayed in Texas, many of them forming bonds with others in ways I didn't expect. The reunion revelers were no longer confined to the social strata they occupied as teens – at least not the same ones they had been assigned to twenty years earlier. Two sworn enemies from high school had both gone to the University of Texas and ended up becoming good friends. Partiers and pot heads were now successful real estate developers and bankers. Kids who had never set foot in a church, water skiing instead on Taylor Lake while I was going to Holy Week services at St. Bernadette's, were now born-again Christians. Coming "home" wasn't nearly as grounding as I expected it to be. It was, in fact, a reminder of just how ungrounded my life had been.

In some ways I envied my classmates and their comfort with each other and with the place they called home. I sometimes wished I had that sense of permanence. But then my thoughts would inevitably turn to what I likely would have had to give up – driving the open roads of the west that fell over the horizon, floating on mountain streams that turned to raging white rivers, living in the hometown of Wilbur and Orville Wright, watching rockets streak skyward at Cape Canaveral. Adventure was my foundation. My family the bricks stacked upon it. I found my own sort of permanence in those things.

While in town for the reunion, I took a drive past our home on Laurelfield Drive in the Brook Forest subdivision and got out to take some pictures. The pine tree that had been planted as a sapling in the front yard when the house was built no longer relied on guywires to brace it against the wind. It was enormous, casting a shadow on the yard and house, as if it were keeping guard for me while I was gone. I recalled how, in that yard one year, I had tested a balsawood cylinder that Dad had helped me build for a science fair project that investigated Bernoulli's Principle, a fluid dynamics equation related to fluid speed and pressure. Dad or I would climb on a ladder and spin the cylinder with a drill and let it go, watching it "fly" across the yard, its spin giving it lift and causing it to move forward rather than fall. The principle our experiment demonstrated was one baseball pitchers used every day in an effort to get a pitch to "move" one direction or another, confusing a batter. We had outfitted the cylinder with reflective tape and Dad set up his camera and took time exposures of it in the late evening when the sun had mercifully set. I wondered what had happened to those pictures as I thought of more moments like that one. I was surprised at how much the gray brick spoke to me, wanting to share more stories with me. I decided to knock on the door.

An elderly man answered. He turned out to be the person who had bought the home from my parents more than twenty years before. I told him that I had lived in the house back in the mid-eighties.

"You're the kid of the astronaut?" he said.

"Yep," I replied.

"Would you like to see the house? C'mon in." He stood back and motioned to me. I protested weakly, feeling bad now about interrupting him. But he was warmly insistent, and I couldn't resist the pull.

As with the home in Ohio that I had visited many years after living there, the Houston house seemed smaller than I had remembered. But it was familiar, an old coat that fit. It felt so familiar in fact, I couldn't help sharing my musings with the owner as we walked slowly through the home. As I stepped into the entry I looked to the right and saw the built-in shelves that used to hold our television. That was the place were Dad and I watched the news each evening, me jumping up every now and then to turn the VHF or UHF knob at his direction. Moving to the high-ceilinged family room, I recalled a picture that had been taken there during a party for the STS-41D crew. They had had t-shirts made with their "Zoo Crew" personas painted on the front with an airbrush. They laughed about the caricatures, pointing to each other's renditions and laughing like school kids at a carnival. They were so happy to be part of the same team. I felt a pang of sadness remembering Judy Resnik in that photo as she stood in our family room; she would die on *Challenger* less than two years after the t-shirt party in our home.

Through the back windows I saw our kidney-shaped pool and the pergola attached to the house. Sally Ride had sat there several times with the Zoo Crew, having a beer and trading stories with her colleagues. When I told the owner of the home this, his eyes widened and mouth gaped and I could tell he was filing the tale away to one day tell all of his friends of the history that once sat in his backyard. His reaction made me realize how little I had appreciated that history while I was living it. To the left was the kitchen and the breakfast nook where I had shot celery through my nose into a bowl of soup after pretending to masturbate under a macramé/aircraft engine chandelier (I felt it best to leave out the fake masturbation part of the story for the sake of the owner – generally self-pleasure is not a "first time you meet somebody" topic).

After about thirty minutes walking through the rooms, our tour ended. We walked back to the front door, he opened it for me, and I stepped back into the Houston heat, thanking him.

"Any time," he said, then added, "you had one heck of a childhood."

I smiled. "Yes, I guess I did."

***

As I prepared that summer to head to South Bend, I was sorting through things in my room as I packed for college when I found two letters written to me, one from Mom and one from Dad. They had been written when both attended a couples retreat at our church in April of 1985. Those in attendance had been asked to write letters to their children. Mom had written a separate note for each of us in her beautiful longhand on light green stationary paper.

"The day you and Amy came into this world was the happiest day in my life next to marrying your father," she wrote, the angled fluidity of her penmanship making the words seem even more meaningful. She told me how happy she was to have had two healthy children – a boy and a girl – at once.

"Many years have gone by," she continued, "and I want you to know that the joy you brought me the day of your birth has carried through 'til now. There have been sad days but only to be followed by joy." I wondered what sad days she was referring to. When she wrote the note, she hadn't yet told me of my half-brother and the anguish her pregnancy had caused for her and her family. Now, I couldn't help wondering if she was referring to those days. I couldn't know. She finished by saying that I would always have her support and love and that I should never forget how much she loved me and how proud she was of me. Reading the note again so shortly after she had told me about her other son gave me a warmth I hadn't felt the first time I read it more than a year before.

Dad's note was hammered out in the harsh fonts of a dot-matrix printer and was one letter to all three of us children. It may have been less aesthetically pleasing than Mom's, but the words were no less emotionally exposing. He noted that his work had become consuming, that he was gone a lot and worried that he might have, without intent, become one of "those" fathers who was a father in name only, so, he wrote, "this letter is a good idea." He followed with a paragraph for each of his children. Mine went thus:

Where do I begin to say "I love you"? I guess with my first born – Pat. You have become such a son as would make any father proud. You are a loving, caring, sensitive person who will certainly bring immeasurable happiness to all the lives you touch. You certainly have brought abundant happiness to your mother and me. I'm proud that, as you have matured, you have become the leader instead of the follower. And the goals you have set for yourself are high and admirable ones. I'm also proud that you have recognized, to a far greater degree than most teenagers, the ultimate source of help and love in this universe – our God and creator. Always retain those characteristics. The world is so full of selfish people. But you can and will make a difference by your passing. Nothing gives me greater pleasure than to realize that single fact – when I am gone, I will have left a seed of love in the world – you.

I put the letters away in an envelope with a clasp, folded down the metal wings to seal it, and smoothed it with my hand, letting my palm rest on the yellow paper. I put the envelope back into my desk drawer, knowing that Mom would file them away for posterity when she found them several years later while packing to move once Dad left the astronaut corps. I took a deep breath and let it out slowly, taking one last look around my room. The air conditioning kicked on and my models hanging from the ceiling moved in the artificial breeze coming from the air vent in the ceiling. I watched the tiny aircraft for several moments, each one eliciting a memory. Many of those memories involved Dad. He was at my side helping me make the model. Or he was buying it for me. Or he was admiring my work as I proudly showed him the end result of my construction efforts. Dad and aviation. My two fathers.

My packing for Notre Dame done, I stood and walked from my room, beginning yet another journey to a place I'd never been before.

ABOUT THE AUTHOR

Patrick Mullane graduated from the University of Notre Dame in 1990 with a degree in Mathematics and was commissioned a second lieutenant in the U.S. Air Force. He spent nearly five years in the Air Force, working in an organization that operated intelligence-gathering satellites. Later, he attended Harvard Business School where he received his M.B.A. in 1999. Patrick currently manages an online education group and lives in the Boston area with his wife, Mary. Between the two of them, Mary and Patrick have three grown children - Sarah, Sean, and Katie - and two furry friends, Tucker and Emma.

ACKNOWLEDGEMENTS

There are many who helped me get this manuscript over the finish line. Thanks to my family – Mom, Dad, Amy, Laura, and Mary for your sage advice and suggested edits.

Thanks also to the community on Facebook known as "Space Hipsters." Several members of the group read all or portions of my story and helped make that story better. Rebecca Siegel lent a particularly helpful hand. If you are a space enthusiast, I encourage you to become a member of the community; just search for the group "Space Hipsters" on Facebook.

CONTACT ME

PATRICK@PJMULLANE.COM

Printed in Great Britain
by Amazon